Heroic Horses tells the tale of a number of military horses and their contributions in a range of wars and conflicts across the globe from the Napoleonic era to the Korean War. The book recounts the stories and exploits of some famous war horses and some far less well-known, along with those of their riders, and in so doing describes the history of those wars and campaigns.

The theme is the heroic nature of the horses' service and how different breeds have made varying contributions, based upon the breed characteristics and the individual nature of the mounts concerned. The breeds of horses which feature include; Thoroughbreds, Arabians, Basuto Ponies, Mustangs, Australian Walers, South African Boerpeerds, Hunters, Appaloosas, and even a Mongolian Pony, along with mentions of numerous others.

The objective is to tell the war story from the horse's perspective and hence understand the campaigns from an equine perspective. This is the first book that will tell the stories of many equine heroes, rather than of a particular horse, and the first to base the history not only around the war concerned but also around the breed.

Captain Duncan Forer joined the Royal Navy in 1988 having completed his degree in Maths and Anthropology at Durham University and a PGCE at St Catharine's College, Cambridge. After Dartmouth he had a range of instructional and sea going appointments, during which time he became Portsmouth Command Light Heavy Weight Champion. His last job as a Lieutenant was taking young officers to sea in HMS *Brave*, visiting South America, the Falklands and South Georgia. Promoted to Lieutenant Commander in 1997, he took charge of the Training Support department at HMS *Sultan*, after which he studied for a Masters in Education at Brunel University. Following a period in the MOD in London, during which time he organised a mountaineering expedition to Iceland, he was promoted to Commander and undertook various staff and training appointments which culminated in being the Commander in charge of Recruit Training at HMS *Raleigh*. On promotion to Captain he again worked in the MoD before joining the Defence Academy's Technology School as the Assistant Head in February 2017. Duncan is married to Fleur and they live with their son Alfred, in Devon. Marriage came with horses as part of the package, requiring Cricket, Rugby, Running, Mountaineering and Boxing to take a back seat to grooming and mucking out duties. This has the benefit that he is allowed to ride his Appaloosa, *Sylvaner*, across Dartmoor in the company of Alfred on his pony *Patchy*.

HEROIC HORSES

Tales of Equine Courage from Waterloo to Korea

Duncan Forer

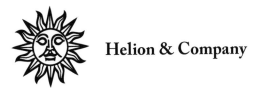

Helion & Company

Helion & Company Limited
Unit 8 Amherst Business Centre
Budbrooke Road
Warwick
CV34 5WE
England
Tel. 01926 499 619
Fax 0121 711 4075
Email: info@helion.co.uk
Website: www.helion.co.uk
Twitter: @helionbooks
Visit our blog http://blog.helion.co.uk/

Published by Helion & Company 2019
Designed and typeset by Mach 3 Solutions (www.mach3solutions.co.uk)
Cover designed by Paul Hewitt, Battlefield Design (www.battlefield-design.co.uk)
Printed by Hobbs the Printers, Totton, Hampshire

Text © Duncan Forer 2018
Images © as individually credited
Cover illustration: An incident during the Battle of Balaclava, 25 October 1854

ISBN 978-1-911628-80-4

British Library Cataloguing-in-Publication Data.
A catalogue record for this book is available from the British Library.

For details of other military history titles published by Helion & Company Limited contact
the above address or visit our website: http://www.helion.co.uk.

We always welcome receiving book proposals from prospective authors.

Contents

List of Illustrations   iv
Introduction   v

1   Copenhagen: The Aristocrat   7
2   Ronald: The Leader   28
3   Tartar, Old Baldy, Dandy and Other Battlers: Equine Heroes of the American Civil War and the West   48
4   Comanche: The Survivor   66
5   Appaloosas: The Heroic Breed   84
6   Warrior: The Jumper   105
7   Arabs of Empire: Vonolel, Maidan, and Maharajah   124
8   Monty: The Film Star   150
9   Sandor and Sergeant Reckless: The Last Equine Heroes?   173

Bibliography   194
Index   201

List of Illustrations

All images Open Source unless otherwise noted.

Wellington on Copenhagen, painted by Thomas Lawrence.   i
Artist's impression of Wellington and staff at Waterloo.   i
Lord Cardigan leads the Light Brigade on Ronald, Balaclava, 25 October 1854.   ii
Old Baldy.   ii
Comanche as pictured in a contemporary postcard.   iii
Author on his Appaloosa 'Sylvanner'.   iii
Two Basuto ponies on trek in South Africa.   iv
Lord Roberts on Vonolel.   iv
9th Lancers charge during the Second Afghan War of 1878-80.   v
Desert Arabian.   v
Bolton astride favourite mount 'Monty'. (Family collection)   vi
Australian mounted infantry, Palestine 1917.   vi
'Warrior' in 1934 by Sir Alfred Munnings.   vii
Brigadier-General Jack Seely and staff, c. 1917.   vii
Amedeo riding Sandor photographed with his Spahy orderly photographed
    on 26 December 1935, the day after the cavalry actions at Selaclaca.
    (The dedication of the photograph is to his Uncle Rodolfo, the father
    of his future wife Beatrice. Oddly, the original photograph was mistakenly
    reversed when it was printed, making it appear that his right hand was
    wounded.)   viii
Reckless and her combat trainer, Sgt. Joseph Latham and after the
    Korean conflict.   viii

Introduction

There is for very good reason the expression, "old war horse". The martial virtues of honorable, loyal, brave and enduring service are often exemplified and embodied within the equine species. It is those virtues which this book intends to honour. The nobility and loyalty of the trusty stead is familiar to all horse lovers and riders, and even those whose contact with the species is vicarious, via a bet or awestruck admiration, can appreciate that this is not just any other species. This book does not attempt to provide great strategic or tactical insight. It merely seeks to celebrate a species which for the vast majority of human history has been fundamental to that most significant and abhorrent aspect of human culture, warfare. Whilst the focus is, for reasons of the quality of the historical record, confined to the nineteenth and twentieth century, the sentiments of the book are equally applicable to preceding centuries, even if the names and records of the equine participants are now lost. There is no sense in which this book is a protagonist of horses in war. Indeed it is great relief to the species that the internal combustion engine has removed their unrequested and enforced participation in the greatest moral and sociological fault in the human condition. Nevertheless, it is intended to tell the tales of their virtues of loyalty, trust and bravery, along with their physical qualities of speed, strength, endurance and durability which have made them the indispensible, blameless facilitators of so much human and equine misery. Whilst the author would never place the moral worth of a horse above that of any human being, he and no sane student of ethics, could ever place any moral blame against any equine participant in any human war. Hence, they are without moral fault in the history of warfare and deserve our respect, honour and admiration, regardless of which human side they happened to be fighting on. They are the blameless heroes of many wars and conflicts and this book merely seeks to tell their honorable story.

What is known of horse psychology suggests that the prime motivator for equine behaviour is safety. Heaven for a horse is to be in the safety of a herd where they know someone is looking out for danger, usually in the form of predators, whilst they can get on with the important job of eating. It is for this reason that they hate being on their own and hate being placed in confined spaces. It is amazing that man has so often thought, and still thinks, he is doing his horse a favour by placing him in a warm cosy stable on his own. In fact this is a stressful situation for a horse, especially if they cannot see another horse. They seek company first, then food, water and shelter; shelter is best entered once it is known to be safe and the exit from the shelter has been established. Hence, horses look for a leader in the herd whom they can trust and once they have found their leader, and leadership structure within the hierarchy of the herd has been established, they can relax into a sense of security. If any horse raises the alarm, which can take the form of suddenly standing tall and lifting their diaphragm, the whole herd are sensitive to this slight movement and can accelerate to a gallop in a fraction of a second. This stampede to safety is their primary escape mechanism. It doesn't take a horse whisperer to see how the human has often been able to establish a position of leader within a herd and with a particular horse, and how this trust can then be used, or misused, to get the horse to perform. Within the military, this bond of trust has been exploited for centuries and it is this trust and honesty which is most valued by cavaliers of all eras. These same cavaliers have often exploited the flight to safety mechanism of the horse to deliver a controlled stampede in the form of a charge. That the cavalry charge exploits the horse's fear and yet the horse still performs for his trusted rider is perhaps the ultimate exemplar of military virtue, in the form of courage, displayed by the horse. Man has also exploited the physical speed and endurance of the horse to its utmost, sometimes to the extent that the horse has literally been ridden to death.

In war, the human, even if he is conscripted, usually has a degree of comprehension about why he is being asked to be disciplined and undertake dangerous tasks. The human sometimes has the option to participate or not, or, when this option does not exist, to take his chances with desertion. The horse has no such comprehension or choice and is instead placing blind trust in his rider. Within the Royal Navy, with which I am most familiar, the espoused military virtues are Courage, Commitment, Discipline, Respect, Integrity and Loyalty. The other Armed Services of the United Kingdom, and indeed of other countries around the world, all have similar espoused values or recognise these as important virtues within a soldier, sailor or airman. I hope that this book will show how the horses described in the chapters ahead have displayed these virtues, and in particular, through the integrity of just being a horse without endless introspection, have given respect and loyalty to their riders. Their deeds are often outrageously courageous, their feats of endurance make human notions of commitment look second division, and their unquestioning discipline in the face of the horrors of war is exemplary. This book is a celebration of the horse as a paragon of military virtue. We in the military still have a great deal to learn from them, even if the horse has been passed over for technological reasons as a means of delivering military capability and now is only associated with military ceremonial.

I hope the true stories in this book will inspire military people to achieve more and that for horse lovers, it will give new insight into the noble, honest and remarkable species that places such trust in its human owners.

Duncan Forer

1

Copenhagen: The Aristocrat

Sir Arthur Wellesley, to be known later as the Duke of Wellington,[1] was in Ireland in May 1807 when he heard of the British expedition to Denmark to seize the combined Danish and Norwegian fleets and keep them out of French hands. He was appointed to command an infantry brigade in the Second Battle of Copenhagen[2] during which the men under his command took many prisoners, preventing the relief of the city and leading to its subsequent surrender. Another of the brigade commanders, Thomas Grosvenor,[3] had taken his favourite mare, Lady Catherine, with him on the campaign, unaware that she was with foal at the time.[4] She was sired by the registered thorough-bred stallion, John Bull, who won the 1792 Epsom Derby, out of an unregistered "hunting mare" by the Duke of Rutland's Arabian.[5] Lady Catherine had raced under General (then Colonel) Grosvenor's name as a five-year-old in 1801 and the foal's sire was the thoroughbred racehorse, Meteor, who had been bred by Lord Grosvenor. Meteor had won the Prince of Wale's Stakes, the King's Plate, the Jockey Club Plate, the Oxford Gold Cup, and was second in the Derby of 1786.[6] Meteor, was retired in 1791 to the Earl of Grosvenor's stud and by the time the foal was born, Meteor was 25 years old. When he died in 1811, the colt, who was to be named Copenhagen[7] in

---

1   Field Marshal Arthur Wellesley, 1st Duke of Wellington, KG, GCB, GCH, PC, FRS (1 May 1769–14 September 1852)

2   16 August–5 September 1807

3   30 May 1764–20 January 1851

4   Kathryn Kane, *From Denmark to Belgium: Copenhagen: Wellington's Great Warhorse* (Posted on 14 January 2011). See <https://regencyredingote.wordpress.com/2011/01/14/from-denmark-to-belgium-copenhagen-wellingtons-great-warhorse/> (Accessed on 2 January 2018).

5   In honour of Copenhagen's notable military service, Lady Catherine is believed to be the only half-bred mare ever entered into the *General Stud Book* of England. She is noted in the stud-book to have been "sent to Ireland."

6   Kane, *From Denmark to Belgium*

7   1808–12 February 1836

honour of the battle, was three years old. Through his sire, Copenhagen, was also a grandson of the great and even more famous racehorse Eclipse.[8]

Eclipse was the outstanding, undefeated 18th century British Thoroughbred race-horse. He was foaled during and named after the solar eclipse of 1 April 1764, at the Cranbourne Lodge Stud of his breeder, Prince William Augustus, Duke of Cumberland[9]. It was at this stud that his sire, the Jockey Club Plate winner, Marske stood, his dam, Spiletta (foaled 1749) who was by Regulus,[10] who was in turn by the Godolphin Arabian.[11] After the death of Prince William in 1765, Eclipse was sold for 75 guineas to a sheep dealer from Smithfield, called William Wildman who started racing him at the age of five on 3 May 1769 in Epsom. After his second victory in May 1769 the Irish adventurer Colonel Dennis O'Kelly[12] purchased Eclipse in two parts.[13] Supposedly, it was at this time that O'Kelly used the famous phrase "Eclipse first and the rest nowhere," before making his bets for this race. At that time, a horse that was more than 240 yards behind the lead was said to be nowhere and Eclipse is still remembered in this way, often without recognition of the origin of the phrase to refer to any dominating victory. His jockey was John Oakley, supposedly the only jockey who could handle Eclipse's temperamental manner and running style of holding his nose very close to the ground. Eclipse won 18 races out of 18 starts (plus seven heats), including 11 King's Plates, supposedly without ever being fully extended, winning a total of 2,149 guineas and proving far superior to all competition. He was so superior that he never needed to be whipped or spurred and eight of his victories were walko-vers.[14] During this time he raced over 63 miles and walked 1,400 miles to race meet-ings across England. He is commemorated and celebrated each year with the renewal of the Eclipse Stakes at Sandown Park, a Group 1 flat race, for three-year-olds and older, run over a distance of 1¼ miles and 7 yards.

By 1771 nobody was betting on rival horses and Eclipse was retired to stud due to lack of competition after a racing career of about 17 months. He stood at O'Kelly's Clay Hill Stud, near Epsom,[15] and was to sire 335 winners,[16] and although he was never the leading sire in Great Britain and Ireland, he finished in second place 11 times, usually

8   1 April 1764–26 February 1789
9   26 April 1721–31 October 1765
10   Regulus was an undefeated Thoroughbred racehorse stallion foaled in 1739
11   The Godolphin Arabian (c.1724–1753), also known as the Godolphin Barb, was an
     Arabian horse and was one of three stallions that founded the modern Thoroughbred race
     horse bloodstock (the others were the Darley Arabian and the Byerley Turk).
12   1725–87
13   50 percent in June 1769 for 650 guineas, 50 percent in April 1770 for 1,100 guineas.
14   A. Whetstone & C. Welch, *The Little Book of Horseracing* (: Green Umbrella Publishing,
     2008), p.37.
15   During 1788 he was relocated to Cannons Stud, Edgware (Middlesex).
16   Whetstone & Welch. *The Little Book of Horse Racing*, p. 37. Although the number varies
     with different reports, ranging from 325 to 400.

behind Herod.[17] He died due to an attack of colic on 27 February 1789, at the age of 35.[18] His skeleton is now housed at the Royal Veterinary College, Hertfordshire, although it cannot be said for certain whether all the bones displayed are really from Eclipse. His hooves were made into inkstands, although the fact that there are at least five Eclipse-hoof inkstands means that there is some doubt on the authenticity of at least one. A necropsy on Eclipse found that he had an abnormally large heart, a trait which has been seen occasionally in his descendants, including Secretariat[19] and Phar Lap.[20] In 1970, the Royal Veterinary College estimated that nearly 80 percent of Thoroughbred racehorses had Eclipse in their pedigree,[21] a percentage that has naturally increased with time and the inevitable inbreeding in the Thoroughbred population. Eclipse's daughters produced many famous racehorses and, importantly for our story, these included John Bull, the Derby Winner, who was Lady Catharine's sire.

So if ever there was a horse born for a General to ride it was Copenhagen. Through both his sire and his dam lines he was descended from two of the thoroughbred foundation sires, both the Godolphin Arabian and the Darley Arabian. Lady Catherine was sent home as soon as it was discovered she was in foal and in 1808 gave birth[22] to a strong, sturdy colt, which was, of course, registered in the *General Stud Book*, and heading for a career on the racecourse. Eclipse's genes were evident in his appearance and temperament since he was chestnut in colour, like his grandsire, with the exception that Eclipse had one long white stocking on his right hind, while Copenhagen had shorter white socks on both hind legs.[23] Copenhagen also had a narrow white strip, known as a blaze, running down nearly the full length of his face, from between his ears to his muzzle. He also inherited a lot of Eclipse's nature, being a handful from a young age. Whilst Meteor had stood at a small 14 hands, Copenhagen was 15.1

---

17 Herod (originally King Herod; April 1758–12 May 1780) was one of the three foundation sires of the modern Thoroughbred racehorse, along with Matchem and Eclipse.

18 Whetstone & Welch. *The Little Book of Horse Racing*, p.37.

19 Secretariat (30 March 1970–4 October 1989) was an American Thoroughbred racehorse that, in 1973, became the first U.S. Triple Crown winner in 25 years. He set race records in all three events in the series – the Kentucky Derby (1:59⅖), the Preakness Stakes (1:53), and the Belmont Stakes (2:24) – records that still stand today.

20 Phar Lap (4 October 1926–5 April 1932) was a champion thoroughbred racehorse whose achievements captured the public's imagination during the early years of the Great Depression. Foaled in New Zealand, he dominated Australian racing, winning a Melbourne Cup, two Cox Plates, an AJC Derby, and 19 other weight for age races. He then won the Agua Caliente Handicap in Tijuana, Mexico, in track-record time in his final race. At the time of his death he was the third highest stakes-winner in the world.

21 Whetstone & Welch. *The Little Book of Horse Racing*, p. 37., asserts 98%.

22 Copenhagen was either foaled after the battle in Copenhagen and named in honour of the British victory or Lady Catherine was returned to England before his birth and Copenhagen was foaled at Eaton Hall in 1808. The *General Stud Book* entry for his dam does not support the notion that he was foaled outside of the United Kingdom.

23 Kane, *From Denmark to Belgium*

hands high with a muscular physique on a small compact frame, but the colt did not share his grandsire's nor his sire's key attribute of speed.

Over the course of the next two years Lord Grosvenor entered him into twelve races. His first start in his three-year-old season was at the Craven Meeting in April 1811, where he was third in a 100-guinea sweepstakes race, and soon after that won a 50-guinea match race at the Newmarket Spring Meeting. At Huntingdon on 6 August, Copenhagen won a sweepstakes race, and the next day was third in a Gold Cup race. At Northampton, Copenhagen was third in a County Purse race after finishing second in all of the heats, and was third in the Oatlands Stakes at the Tarporley-Hunt meeting on 7 November. Copenhagen started three times in 1812 as a four-year-old. At Chester on 4 May, he was third in a £50 Maiden Plate run in three heats, finishing 5th in the first heat and second in the remaining heats. A few days later at the same meeting, Copenhagen finished third in a £70 Cup race run over three heats, finishing fourth in the first heat and second in the remaining heats, and was fourth in a Handicap Sweepstakes in the final start of his career. Horses no longer run in heats but the stamina and durability required to run repeat races would stand him well in the future on campaigns. Copenhagen was retired from racing at the end of the season. In addition to his two wins he had also placed at least third in nine races out of his twelve career starts.

After his last race, in May 1812, at the age of four he should have gone hurdling and then chasing, but Lord Grosvenor made the decision to end the colt's racing career. He was sold to Sir Charles Stewart,[24] the adjutant-general of the army in Spain and Portugal for the considerable sum of £300.[25] Copenhagen was sent to Lisbon in 1813 with a contingent of other horses but that same year Sir Charles was assigned to Prussia and being short of funds decided to sell his stable. So Wellington, purchased two of the horses, one of them being Copenhagen.[26] The chestnut Thoroughbred may have been only a moderately successful racehorse, but he was to become the superb battle horse and preferred mount of the Duke of Wellington.

Wellington was born in Dublin into a wealthy Anglo-Irish aristocratic family and was known then as the Honourable Arthur Wesley, with a pedigree as distinguished as Copenhagen's. He was the third of five surviving sons (fourth otherwise) to The 1st Earl of Mornington[27] and his wife Anne, the eldest daughter of the 1st Viscount Dungannon.[28] He spent most of his childhood at his family's two homes in Dublin and Dangan Castle, in County Meath and went to school in Dublin and London

---

24   Charles William Vane, 3rd Marquess of Londonderry KG, GCB, GCH, PC (18 May 1778 – 6 March 1854), named Charles William Stewart until 1822 and known by his courtesy title as The Lord Stewart from 1814 to 1822.
25   Kane, *From Denmark to Belgium*
26   Kane, *From Denmark to Belgium*
27   19 July 1735–22 May 1781.
28   c. 1694–30 January 1771.

before Eton,[29] which he hated.[30] In 1785, a lack of academic success combined with a shortage of family funds, forced the young Wellesley and his mother to move to Brussels. He continued to show little sign of distinction but enrolled in the French Royal Academy of Equitation in Angers, where he became a good horseman and learned French, both skills which were later to prove to be very useful.

Wellesley was commissioned into the British Army in 1787,[31] serving in Ireland as aide-de-camp and seeing action in the Netherlands and in India, where his elder brother Richard,[32] now known as Lord Mornington,[33] had been appointed as the new Governor-General of India. He fought in the 4th Anglo-Mysore War[34] at the Battle of Seringapatam[35] and was appointed governor of Seringapatam and Mysore in 1799. As a newly appointed major-general he won a decisive victory over the Maratha Confederacy at the Battle of Assaye in 1803, but in June 1804 he applied for permission to return home. When his brother's term as Governor-General of India ended in March 1805, the brothers travelled together back to England. He was raised to the rank of lieutenant general and in June 1808 he accepted the command of an expedition to attack Spanish colonies South America but whilst preparing to sail his force was instead ordered to sail for Portugal, to take part in the Peninsular Campaign.

Wellesley defeated the French at the Battle of Roliça[36] and the Battle of Vimeiro[37] in 1808 but was superseded in command immediately after the latter battle. Napoleon himself entered Spain with his veteran troops to put down the revolt and the new commander of the British forces in the Peninsula, Sir John Moore,[38] died during the Battle of Corunna in January 1809. The terrain in Spain was very tough and horses lasted only 15 days rather than the normal 25 before they needed re-shoeing resulting in the 7th Hussars loss of 560 horses due to lameness during the Corunna campaign.[39] The general state of horsemanship was not good and there was a constant tension between speed and good order in the charge where British cavalry were eager to gallop into combat.[40] The average weight of a horse was about 1000lbs and it could carry a

---

29 From 1781-84.
30 Since it had no playing fields at the time, it is highly unlikely that he ever said, "The Battle of Waterloo was won on the playing fields of Eton".
31 C. Hibbert, *Wellington, A Personal History* (London: Harper Collins, 1997), p.9.
32 Richard Colley Wesley, 1st Marquess Wellesley, KG, PC, PC (Ire) (20 June 1760–26 September 1842), styled Viscount Wellesley from birth until 1781 and known as The Earl of Mornington from 1781 until 1799.
33 In 1798, he changed the spelling of his surname to "Wellesley"; up to this time he was still known as Wesley, which his oldest brother considered the ancient and proper spelling.
34 1798–1799
35 5 April–4 May 1799
36 17 August 1808
37 21 August 1808
38 13 November 1761–16 January 1809
39 Louis, A. DiMarco, *War Horse: A History of the Military Horse and Rider* (Yardley Pennsylvania: Westholme Publishing, 2008), p.213.
40 DiMarco, *War Horse*, p.214.

quarter of its own weight or 250lbs but the average weight of a British Light Dragoon with his kit in 1776 was 316lbs. It is little wonder that Wellington described Spain as "the grave of horses.[41] Nevertheless, the Peninsula was the only theatre where the British, with the Portuguese, had provided strong resistance against France and the Cabinet appointed Wellesley to head all British forces in Portugal.

Wellington arrived in Lisbon on 22 April 1809 and took to the offensive, crossing the Douro river and routing Marshal Soult's[42] French troops at the Second Battle of Porto.[43] With Portugal secured, he advanced into Spain where on 27 July 1809, at the Battle of Talavera[44] the French advanced in three columns and were repulsed several times throughout the day at a heavy cost to the British. In the aftermath Marshal Soult's army advanced south, threatening to cut Wellesley off from Portugal. The lack of supplies, coupled with the threat of French reinforcement in the spring, led to the British deciding to retreat into Portugal. In 1810, a newly enlarged French army invaded but Wellington prevented them from taking the Lisbon Peninsula by constructing, in complete secrecy, massive earthworks called the Lines of Torres Vedras. The thwarted and starving French invasion forces retreated after six months, but Wellington's pursuit was frustrated by a series of rear guard actions by Marshal Ney.[45]

In 1811, the French returned toward Portugal and Wellington narrowly checked them at the Battle of Fuentes de Onoro.[46] His army fought Soult's 'Army of the South' to a mutual bloody standstill at the Battle of Albuera in May, but the French retreated to the twin Spanish fortresses of Ciudad Rodrigo and Badajoz, the 'Keys' guarding the roads through the mountain passes into Portugal. In 1812, Wellington finally stormed Ciudad Rodrigo, and then moved south to besiege Badajoz for a month before capturing it in bloody night assault. Now campaigning in Spain, he routed the French at the Battle of Salamanca,[47] and liberated Madrid on 12 August 1812. Next he attempted to take the key fortress of Burgos, which linked Madrid to France, but failure, due to a lack of siege guns, forced him into a headlong retreat. The French now abandoned Andalusia, and combined the troops of Soult and Marmont, to outnumber Wellington who withdrew. By 31 October 1812 he had abandoned Madrid too, and retreated first to Salamanca then to Ciudad Rodrigo, to avoid encirclement by French armies from the north-east and south-east. Wellington spent the winter reorganising

41 DiMarco, *War Horse*, p.216.
42 Marshal General Jean-de-Dieu Soult, 1st Duke of Dalmatia (29 March 1769–26 November 1851).
43 12 May 1809
44 27–28 July 1809
45 Michel Ney 1st Duc d'Elchingen, 1st Prince de la Moskowa (10 January 1769–7 December 1815).
46 J. Laffin, *Brassey's Battles: 3,500 Years of Conflict, Campaigns and War A-Z* (London: Brassey, 1986), p.175.
47 Laffin; *Brassey's Battles* p.374.

and strengthening his forces, whilst Napoleon withdrew many soldiers to rebuild his main army after his disastrous retreat from Moscow.

On 20 May 1813 Wellington led a new offensive, this time striking through the hills north of Burgos, and switched his supply line from Portugal to Santander on Spain's north coast. This led to the French abandoning Madrid and Burgos. It was at this point in 1813 that Stewart sent Copenhagen to Lisbon, travelling for three weeks in the ship's hold, away from the light and air. Horses could not be kept on deck, since many had difficulty maintaining their footing and could easily be swept overboard. Most of the horses were placed in body slings below decks and kept on short rations, unable to move around naturally. These horses were often weakened and had some difficulty walking steadily when they reached their destination, having to be given time to recover and return to a normal diet before they could safely travel beyond the port of arrival.[48]

Copenhagen was "rising five," the preferred age for a new cavalry horse and was a strong, sturdy horse, whose Thoroughbred pedigree made him highly desirable. His Arabian blood gave him exceptional stamina and endurance, and his exposure to crowds and noise at the race courses of England had done much to prepare him to remain calm amidst the din of a battlefield. Wellington caught up with the French army at the Battle of Vitoria on 21 June and launched his attack in four columns. Wellington personally led a column on Copenhagen against the French centre, while other columns looped around the French right and left. Thus, Copenhagen quickly proved himself a superior battle mount. After hard fighting, Thomas Picton's[49] 3rd Division broke the enemy's centre and soon the French defence crumbled. Joseph Bonaparte,[50] who had been appointed King of Spain by his brother, narrowly escaped although the battle led to the collapse of Napoleonic rule in Spain.

Armies primarily used mares and geldings since stallions often became difficult to manage and vocal around mares who were in season, creating unwanted noise which could be dangerous during any military action which required stealth. However, many generals and cavalry officers rode stallions, appreciating their strength and stamina and Copenhagen managed to avoid being gelded. If a stallion was skilfully trained and treated kindly, they were remarkably loyal and obedient, and their aggression could be put to good use by an experienced horseman who could control of his mount. Wellington was well able to handle Copenhagen and knew he needed regular hard exercise to keep him physically fit and mentally stimulated. He kept a pack of hounds in the Peninsula and hunted whenever he could, both for the sport and to exercise his challenging mount. He also kept a couple of hunters, as his other seven war horses were not appropriate for hunting, but those long days in the hunting field strengthened

48   Kane, *From Denmark to Belgium.*
49   Lieutenant General Sir Thomas Picton GCB (24 August 1758–18 June 1815).
50   Joseph-Napoléon Bonaparte (7 January 1768–28 July 1844) elder brother of Emperor Napoleon Bonaparte.

and toughened the chestnut horse, building Copenhagen's stamina and the trust and loyalty between Wellington and his partner.[51]

When not in a battle situation Copenhagen was tetchy and difficult, often kicking out at stable hands who came too close but he was unflinching amidst gunfire and repeatedly exhibited great stamina. More concerning to Wellington's grooms was that he preferred to eat lying down, which is often a sign of serious illness or injury. However, after thoroughly examining him, it was clear he was perfectly sound and comfortable lying down when he dined which was an indication that he was by nature a very confident horse.[52] A general, particularly when commanding in action, needed a courageous, calm and steady mount so that he could observe and direct the progress of the battle from his saddle. Copenhagen was such a horse, brave and unflinching despite the noise, smoke and fury swirling about him. Later the Duke said of him: "There may have been many faster horses, no doubt many handsomer, but for bottom and endurance I never saw his fellow."[53]

Wellington and Copenhagen's next engagement was at the fierce and gruelling Battle of Sorauren,[54] part of a series of engagements in late July 1813 called the Battle of the Pyrenees in which a combined British and Portuguese force held off Marshal Soult's French forces attempting to relieve Pamplona.[55] The Anglo-Portuguese forces were busy assaulting San Sebastián but were frustrated by the obstinate French garrison, suffering heavy casualties in a failed assault at the end of July. Marshal Soult launched a counterattack and although the French initially enjoyed local superiority, the tough terrain combined with stubborn British and Portuguese resistance slowed the French advance to a crawl. On 27 July 1813 the main French column marched to attack Sorauren where the heavily outnumbered British forces were drawn up on the Oricain ridge. Wellesley made a dramatic ride on Copenhagen along the ridge in front of the cheering British and Portuguese troops and Soult postponed the attack until the next day, by which time Allied reinforcements had arrived. The fighting at the top of the ridge was bitter and bloody, but the defenders held the French until midday, when Wellington sent his reinforcements to assault the French right flank. More fresh units reached the field and Soult soon ordered a withdrawal. On 30 July 1813 the retreat from Sorauren cost the French many casualties, and with his momentum lost, Soult withdrew into France to prepare his defence against the imminent Allied offensive. The Soult offensive is often compared to the Ardennes offensive in 1944, both being a last desperate attempt to ward off the enemy and both consuming the last military resources of a tyrant.

51   Kane, *From Denmark to Belgium*.
52   Kane, *From Denmark to Belgium*.
53   Kathryn, Kane, *Bloody Sunday: Copenhagen and the Waterloo Campaign* (Posted on 21 January 2011). See <https://regencyredingote.wordpress.com/2011/01/21/bloody-sunday-copenhagen-and-the-waterloo-campaign/ > (accessed 2 January 2018).
54   28 July-1 August 1813
55   25 July-2 August 1813

Wellington pursued the war into southern France in the spring of 1814, where Imperial forces were greatly demoralised by fighting in their own country, and were further shaken by news of repeated Coalition victories in northern and eastern France. Allied campaigning in Spain and the endless guerrilla war had resulted in 100s of 1,000s of French casualties between 1808 and late 1813. Napoleon also diverted many southern forces to bolster his armies in northern and eastern France after allied victory at Leipzig in October, 1813. After Soult's defeat by Wellington at the Battle of Orthez on 27 February 1814,[56] the French Marshal retreated north behind the Adour River to Saint-Sever. Soult was on the horns of a dilemma. He could defend Bordeaux to the north-west or Toulouse to the east, but he could not protect both. The French army would have difficulty obtaining food near Bordeaux and it would place the Garonne River in their rear, so Soult decided to defend Toulouse.

With Soult moving east, Wellington seized Bordeaux, the third-largest city of France on 12 March 1814. A ten day lull followed, during which time Wellington's reinforcements began to arrive. He hoped to ensnare Soult's army but the French avoided the British flanking columns to reach Toulouse where Soult placed his 30,000 soldiers behind the city's walls and fortifications.[57] On 4 April 1814, Wellington's engineers threw a pontoon bridge across the flooding Garonne north of the French city. After the Anglo-Allies crossed, the bridge gave way, trapping the men for three days. But Soult failed to take advantage of his opportunity to defeat Wellington's army in detail. Meanwhile, at midnight on 7 April 1814, the official couriers left Paris with news that Napoleon had abdicated and that the war was over. Wellington began his attack on Easter Sunday, 10 April 1814 and Copenhagen carried Wellington throughout the battle. This was Wellington's and Copenhagen's final battle against their rival Soult and the Allied divisions were badly mauled storming the French redoubts, with Allied losses exceeding French casualties. As Wellington pulled back to reorganize his shattered units, Soult escaped from the town with his entire army by the Carcassonne road. Wellington and Copenhagen entered on the morning of 12 April 1814 and that afternoon, the official word via Bordeaux of Napoleon's abdication and the end of the war reached them. A few hours later, this was confirmed when the official couriers arrived from Paris and on 17 April 1814, Soult finally agreed to an armistice.

Wellington and Copenhagen both remained in Toulouse for a couple of weeks as Napoleon was exiled to the small island of Elba. Wellington was hailed as the conquering hero by the British, and created "Duke of Wellington", a title still held by his descendants. He became the British ambassador to France in Paris and often hunted with the royal family on Copenhagen, though he also often rode his favourite hunter, Elmore, who was rather better behaved in public.[58] Most of the women of Paris

---

56   Laffin, *Brassey's Battles* p.317.
57   Laffin, *Brassey's Battles* p.429.
58   Kane, *From Denmark to Belgium*

were fans of the great *Monsieur Villianton*, and many requested a ride on Copenhagen, but he would not allow them aboard unless he was present. Such requests continued, even after the Duchess arrived in October of 1814.[59] Wellington remained in Paris until 15 January 1815 when he left for the Congress of Vienna,[60] and it seems likely that Copenhagen travelled to Austria with the Duke.[61]

On 7 March 1815, news reached the Duke of Wellington, as he was waiting for his horse to be brought around for a hunt in the park at the Shönbrunn Palace, that Bonaparte had escaped from Elba on 26 February 1815, landed in Italy and was marching north. He sent the horse, perhaps Copenhagen, back to the stable and went to inform the other Congress delegates.[62] They all laughed, thinking the Duke was having them on, until there was corroboration of the Duke's announcement. Louis XVIII fled to Belgium whilst Napoleon, who had regained control of the country by May, faced a renewed alliance of Allied forces. Wellington travelled north by carriage, with Copenhagen in company, arriving in Brussels on 4 April 1815 as Commander-in-Chief of the British-German army and their allied Dutch-Belgians, all stationed alongside the Prussian forces of Field Marshall Gebhard Leberecht von Blücher.[63] Napoleon's strategy was to isolate the Allied and Prussian armies, and annihilate each one separately before the Austrians and Russians arrived. On the evening of 15 June 1815, while he was dressing for the Duchess of Richmond's ball, Wellington received a dispatch about Bonaparte's troop movements. With implacable British composure, he attended the ball, to avoid any impression of flap or panic, though he gave marching orders to many of his officers. He returned to his hotel bed at about 3:00 a.m. for a few hours of sleep, but was up again at 5:30 a.m. to give more orders. At 8:00 a.m. on 16 June 1815, Wellington was mounted on Copenhagen and, after a two-hour ride south, arrived at the cross-roads of Quatre Bras just after 10:00 a.m.[64] He spent until about 1:00 p.m. examining the situation with his staff officers which gave Copenhagen a rest after the two hour ride from Brussels.[65] The Duke and a few aides then rode the hazardous six miles over to the headquarters of Blücher at Wavre. Once again, Copenhagen had a brief rest while the two commanders climbed a nearby windmill to survey the area with their telescopes. Both saw Napoleon looking back through his own telescope in a similar manner.

Wellington rode Copenhagen back to the cross-roads at Quatre Bras and as they neared, they heard French cannon signalling the advance on the Prussians at Ligny. With the situation at Quatre Bras deteriorating Wellington galloped Copenhagen to

59   Kane, *From Denmark to Belgium*
60   September 1814 to June 1815
61   Kane, *From Denmark to Belgium*
62   Kane, *From Denmark to Belgium*
63   Gebhard Leberecht von Blücher, Fürst von Wahlstatt 16 December 1742–12 September 1819.
64   Kane, *Bloody Sunday*.
65   Kane, *Bloody Sunday*.

the battlefield. Wellington was everywhere on Copenhagen, ordering and encouraging his troops, and by a series of rapid counter-strokes he was able to deflect the French attack and eventually drive them off. Under a fierce assault from the French Chasseurs, the Brunswickers and the Netherlanders broke and fled leaving Wellington and his aide, Lord Fitzroy Somerset,[66] caught in the open with a group of French cavalry heading straight for them. They galloped for their lives to the square of the 92nd Gordon Highlanders, under the command of Sir Thomas Picton. The infantry square provided safety against cavalry because no horse would charge at multiple rows of bayonets, regardless of how hard their rider pushed them on. Nevertheless, Wellington spurred Copenhagen on and the brave, trusting stallion galloped straight towards the wall of the bristling Scottish square. Wellington bellowed, "Ninety-Second, lie down!" and jumped Copenhagen over the lowered heads, and retracted bayonets of his own troops, with Somerset close behind.[67] The square quickly reformed with the Duke inside, calmly ordering volley after volley as the French attack was beaten off. Had Wellington been riding another horse or been a less capable rider the course of history might have been changed. We will hear more in the next chapter about Lord Somerset when, by then known as Lord Raglan, he was the commander of British forces in the Crimean War.

By 9:00 p.m. Quatre Bras had become a tactical draw with Ney's forces unable to attack Blücher, and Wellington unable to send troops to relieve the Prussians who retreated toward the small town of Wavre. Wellington rode Copenhagen the three miles to Genappe, stopping at the *Auberge Roi d'espagne* (The King of Spain Inn), where he was informed that the Prussians had been severely mauled. He was in bed by midnight but up again by 3:00 a.m., when he called for Copenhagen and rode at speed back to Quatre Bras.[68] There he dispatched Colonel Gordon to Ligny to get the full facts.

At 6:00 am on Saturday, 17 June 1815, Wellington rode out on Copenhagen to await Gordon's report. He paused with the 92nd Highlanders who lit a fire for him in a small hut in which he consulted his staff officers, until Gordon arrived at 7:30 a.m. on his lathered horse, confirming the Prussians were in retreat at Wavre. After discussing the situation with several of his senior officers, he left the hut to pace out his thoughts for nearly an hour, while Copenhagen stood nearby, grazing and dozing. Shortly before 9:00 a.m., a courier came with a personal message from General Blücher, reporting his defeat but stating that he and his army were in great heart. The defeat of the Prussians at Ligny, and the indecisive battle at Quatre Bras, now compelled Wellington to retreat north to a ridge on the Brussels road, just south of

---

66   Field Marshal FitzRoy James Henry Somerset, 1st Baron Raglan, GCB, PC (30
     September 1788 – 29 June 1855), known before 1852 as Lord FitzRoy Somerset.
67   Kane, *Bloody Sunday.*
68   Kane, *Bloody Sunday.*

the small town of Waterloo, and by 10:00 a.m. he ordered his army to fall back level with the Prussians.

Wellington mounted Copenhagen and rode forward to survey the retreat. Occasionally relaxing on the grass, he read a London newspaper and laughed at the society gossip in its pages, at one point rolling himself in his cloak and dozing for a short time with the pages of the newspaper shading his face, while Copenhagen grazed nearby. Then he was back in the saddle, looking calm and collected, giving his anxious officers the confidence that everything was according to plan. From Copenhagen's back, Wellington raised his telescope to see a single horseman silhouetted against the distant hills to the south. Napoleon must have been astonished to discover his prey had flown Quatre Bras, denying him the opportunity to dispatch Wellington's army before mopping up the Prussians.

We must assume that Napoleon was on his famous iron grey Arabian stallion, Marengo[69] and many readers will wonder why I have not included him as one of the top heroic horses in history. This is because I believe that Marengo was an unwitting fraud, playing his unrequested part in the artifice of the Napoleonic legend. He was only one of many horses used by Napoleon during his career, a notion that was explored in-depth in Jill Hamilton's book *Marengo: the Myth of Napoleon's Horse.*[70] Born in Egypt in 1794, Marengo was a small light grey Barb (an African breed), standing only 14.1hh, but was allegedly incredibly reliable, steady, and courageous. Captured by Napoleon's troops during the Battle of Abouki in 1799, he was imported to France as a six year old and added to the General's stable, with the imperial crown and N motif branded on his left thigh, signifying him as one of Napoleon's personal mounts. Napoleon was said to prefer the small Arabian to a tall and high spirited thoroughbred since, thoroughbreds represented the upper elite's horses. A more credible reason was that Napoleon was a poor rider. His toes pointed downwards, and he slouched and slipped back and forth and laterally in the saddle, wearing holes in his breeches! Due to his erratic riding style, his personal mounts had to undergo extreme training to make them steady, good-tempered, gentle gallopers, and easy amblers, who could cope with dogs and pigs running through their legs, drums and trumpets suddenly sounding, flags waving, swords and bayonets slashing around them, and shots winging by their heads.

The horse was re-named Marengo after the French victory at the battle in 1800 during which he allegedly carried his rider to safety. This started Marengo's 15 years of service which included the Battles of Austerlitz in 1805, Jena in 1806, at Wagram in 1809. It is alleged that not only did he carry the graceless Napoleon in warfare from the Mediterranean to Paris, Italy, Germany and Austria, but also, at age 19, on the 3,000 mile arduous trek to Moscow and back in 1812, through winter snows,

---

69   Marengo is generally thought to be the horse pictured in Jacques-Louis David's dashing painting, *Napoleon Crossing the Alps.*

70   Jill, Hamilton, *Marengo: The Myth of Napoleon's Horse.* (London: Fourth Estate, 2000).

near starvation, treacherous going, poor shelter and often minimal care. However, Napoleon kept meticulous stable records which show that many of his horses were renamed and it is probable that Marengo was in fact a number of different horses.[71] Part of the Marengo myth is that for the entire day of 18 June 1815 Napoleon partnered his grey stallion but in actual fact, Napoleon, suffering ill health, spent most of the Waterloo campaign travelling in a coach.

At Quatre Bras, within moments of seeing Napoleon, a long line of French lancers were seen coming along the road towards the retreating British troops. Then, with a thunderclap, the heavens opened in a torrential downpour as the British rear-guard made a swift retreat before the rain made the roads impassable. Wellington, on Copenhagen, rode at a leisurely pace to Waterloo where he stayed in the small inn in the centre of the village requisitioned for his headquarters. Fortunately it had a stable, so Copenhagen had a roof over his head against the pouring rain.

Wellington was up at 3:00 a.m. on Sunday, 18 June 1815, and had finished breakfast by 6:00 a.m. when he again mounted Copenhagen and rode a mile and a half south of Waterloo to inspect the ridges where his forces were already taking up their positions. He had 60,000 troops,[72] of which 14,000 were cavalry. Of these 5,000 were British in two Heavy Cavalry Brigades.[73] General Lord Edward Somerset commanded the Guards Cavalry Brigade consisting of the 1st and 2nd Life Guards, The Royal Horse Guards (the Blues) and the King's Dragoon Guards, a total of 1,090 men and horses. General Sir William Ponsonby led the Union Brigade of 1st Royal Dragoons, 2nd Scots Grey Dragoons and 6th Inniskilling Dragoons, 1,181 men and horses.[74] Wellington created three strong points, the farmhouse of Hougoumont on his right flank to the west, the farm house of La Haye Saint in his centre and the village of Papelotte to the east. The main Brussels road ran through the centre of his line to the east of La Haye Saint and a hedge lined road ran along the top of the ridge. He placed some of his artillery forward of the road but most behind the slope with his Heavy Cavalry Brigades in the centre to the rear.

Wellington halted his chestnut stallion under a great elm at Mont Saint-Jean, at the intersection of the Ohain and Brussels roads, on one of the highest points of the ridge, near the centre of his line. From here, he could keep an eye on the farmhouse at Hougoumont, his weaker, more exposed flank, but it also meant he himself was a target. He paused here to take tea with some riflemen, and then went on a tour of his lines, riding Copenhagen over most of the battle field, very muddy after the heavy rain

---

71   Horses owned by Napoleon included a tall, pure-white Norman parade horse, Intendant (affectionately nicknamed Coco by the Imperial Guard) and Mon Cousin who was name changed to Austerlitz after the famous victory. Cirus and Ingenu both became Wagram and Ali was called Marengo. Conversely Moscou became Tcherkes following the Russian campaign.
72   Of which 20,000 were British.
73   DiMarco, *War Horse*, p.220.
74   DiMarco, *War Horse*, p.220.

of the night before. This mud delayed Bonaparte, who had to defeat Wellington before the Prussians arrived, from bringing his forces into position. Therefore, Wellington could afford to fight a defensive battle. Taking the fortified flanks would consume time and therefore Napoleon decided to attack the centre and the Battle of Waterloo commenced with what was only a diversionary attack on Hougoumont at 10:00 a.m. At 11:00 a.m., Wellington decided to call up companies of the Coldstream and Scots Guards to strengthen the farmhouse. Just before 11:30 a.m., the French cannon opened up, with the British artillery immediately responding. Wellington calmly rode Copenhagen back under the elm, and for the next hour and a half, despite the stray bullets which occasionally whizzed past, Wellington kept an eye on the critical engagement at Hougoumont, sending in additional reinforcements as needed.

At 1:30 p.m. 18,000 French infantry attacked through the Allied centre,[75] resulting in Allied troops in front of the ridge retreating in disorder through the main position. The French stormed the most fortified Allied position, La Haye Sainte, but failed to take the farmhouse. An Allied division under Thomas Picton met the French head on, engaging in an infantry duel in which Picton fell. At this critical point Lord Uxbridge[76] launched two of his cavalry brigades at the enemy, with Wellington personally leading up the Life Guards, saying "Now, gentlemen, for the honour of the Household troops". The Guards Brigade charged in two lines and broke the French Cavalry scattering cuirassiers before them, before carrying on and smashing into the left flank of the French infantry. At the same time the Union Brigade charged from the east. The Scots were to be in a second line but, eager to charge, all three attacked together, catching the French infantry off guard, destroying the columns and driving them to the bottom of the slope. They captured two French Imperial Eagles, including that of the 45th French Regiment,[77] taken by 6ft 4in Sergeant Charles Ewart of the Scots. The Union Brigades 1,181 horsemen forced 10,000 infantry from the ridge,[78] securing the allied front despite fierce fighting and heavy casualties, and inspiring Lady Butler's[79] equally famous picture and the most memorable scene in the great film, *Waterloo*.[80] Between them the two brigades had routed 18,000 infantry, captured 3,000 prisoners

75   DiMarco, *War Horse*, p.221.
76   Field Marshal Henry William Paget, 1st Marquess of Anglesey, Bt, KG, GCB, GCH, PC (17 May 1768–29 April 1854), styled Lord Paget between 1784 and 1812 and known as The Earl of Uxbridge between 1812 and 1815
77   DiMarco, *War Horse*, p.222.
78   DiMarco, *War Horse*, p.223.
79   Elizabeth Southerden Thompson, Lady Butler (3 November 1846–2 October 1933); a famous British painter of historical and military battle scenes.
80   *Waterloo* was a lavish 1970 Soviet-Italian feature film directed by Sergei Bondarchuk and produced by Dino De Laurentiis, famous for its lavish battle scenes. It stars Rod Steiger as Napoleon Bonaparte and Christopher Plummer as the Duke of Wellington with a cameo by Orson Welles as Louis XVIII of France. Other stars include Jack Hawkins as General Thomas Picton, Virginia McKenna as the Duchess of Richmond and Dan O'Herlihy as Marshal Ney.

and taken back La Haye Saint.[81]. Now out of control, the charge, ignoring the bugle's recalls, carried on 300 yards south towards the French artillery, putting 40 guns out of action. However, they found that their route back was blocked by French lancers. Only 200 Royal Horse Guards were left in reserve to engage the French but much of the Heavy Brigade managed to escape. However, the Union Brigade had over-reached itself, and were crushed by the fresh French horsemen hurled at them by Napoleon, with three out of seven regimental Commanding Officers being killed, along with Ponsonby himself. The Scots Greys had eight out of 23 officers killed or wounded. The Guards Brigade suffered 553 casualties and the Union Brigade 525, a 44 percent casualty rate.[82] Nevertheless Napoleon was now left with few options and the Prussians were approaching.

With his centre now secure, Wellington returned on Copenhagen to his command post under the centre of the ridge where a little before 4:00 p.m., Marshal Ney mistook the movement of casualties to the rear for the start of a retreat, and tried to exploit it by breaking Wellington's centre with an unaccompanied cavalry charge. He sent forward the cavalry across the muddy field, strewn with human and equine casualties and already churned up by the British heavies. This slowed the French cavalry who were hit by the British artillery whose gunners then dashed for the safety of the British infantry squares on the reverse of the slope. The charging French cavalry attacked the squares again and again, each at heavy cost but with few British casualties. The squares stood fast for over two hours and each charge repeated the carnage as by now many horses could barely walk. Counter charges by the British Light Cavalry did further damage and Ney himself was displaced from his horse four times. The Duke galloped Copenhagen along his front, strengthening his line as required and encouraging his men as he moved constantly among his squares, ignoring the incoming shells. Eventually it became obvious, even to Ney, that cavalry alone were achieving little and the failure of 10,000 French horsemen contrasted with the 2,000 British earlier in the day.[83] The success of the British Heavy Brigades shows that, as with a horse race, many factors determine success of a charge such as, topography, going, speed, surprise, aggressiveness, psychology and mud. Belatedly, at about 4:30 p.m. Ney organised a combined-arms attack, directed along much the same route as the previous heavy cavalry attacks.

However, at this time the first Prussians arrived to link up with Wellington's left flank, so Napoleon, now seriously pressed, dispatched troops towards this new threat. He knew he must smash Wellington's forces quickly, so he ordered Ney to take La Haye Saint and clear the way for his main force to attack. The farmhouse fell soon after 6:00 p.m. and the French moved horse artillery up towards Wellington's centre and began to destroy the infantry squares at short-range with canister. Wellington's

81   DiMarco, *War Horse*, p.224.
82   DiMarco, *War Horse*, p.225.
83   DiMarco, *War Horse*, p.229.

centre was now on the verge of collapse but the Prussian Army were at hand and the Charleroi road was swept by their round shot, which permitted the two fresh cavalry brigades on Wellington's extreme left to be moved and posted behind the depleted centre.

By 6:30 p.m., Wellington was worried that it would not be long before Napoleon would send his Imperial Guard against him but Copenhagen, despite the tension, remained as calm and steady as his rider, who ordered up all his remaining reserves to reinforce his thinning centre. His fresh battalions of untried Brunswickers and Nassauers broke and ran almost immediately, but Wellington urged Copenhagen into their midst to rally them and stop their flight, turning them to fill the gap in the line.

With the French army now fiercely attacking all along the line, Napoleon sent forward the Imperial Guard. Marching through a hail of canister and skirmisher fire and severely outnumbered, the 3,000 Guardsmen advanced to the west of La Haye Sainte and proceeded to separate into three distinct attack forces. One, consisting of two battalions of Grenadiers, defeated the Coalition's first line and marched on. A relatively fresh Dutch division was sent against them and Allied artillery fired into the victorious Grenadiers' flank. This still could not stop the Guard's advance, so the Dutch brigade charged the outnumbered French, who faltered and broke.

Further to the west, just to the right of his centre, were Maitland's[84] 1,500 1st Foot Guards who, on the Duke's orders, were lying down to protect themselves from the French artillery on the back side of the ridge, out of sight of the French. Wellington wheeled Copenhagen and galloped to where the 1st Foot Guards were still lying below the ridge and shouted, "Now, Maitland, now's your time!" as the Imperial Guard came closer. He then commanded, "Stand up, Guards!" Maitland's guardsmen instantly rose to their feet to deliver a punishing volley which brought down the first ranks of the Imperial Guard and halted them. The Chasseurs deployed to counter-attack, but began to waver and a bayonet charge by the Foot Guards then broke them. Under this onslaught they too broke and the 1st Foot saw the unprecedented sight of the blue-coated backs of the Imperial Guard in retreat. Wellington ordered in the 95th Rifles, who began to cheer when he appeared. "No cheering, my lads, but forward and complete your victory!"[85]

The Duke gathered Copenhagen's reins and galloped with Uxbridge back to his elm at Mont Saint-Jean. Wellington swept the eastern hills with his telescope and saw that the enemy's right was under fire from the Prussians who had finally arrived. Uxbridge urged caution, but Wellington's military judgement demanded otherwise and he cried, "Oh, damn it! In for a penny, in for a pound."[86] With the Imperial Guard in headlong retreat a ripple of panic passed through the French lines as the astounding

84   General Sir Peregrine Maitland, GCB (6 July 1777–30 May 1854). He also was a first-class cricketer from 1798 to 1808.
85   Kane, *Bloody Sunday*.
86   Kane, *Bloody Sunday*.

news spread: *"La Garde recule. Sauve qui peut!"* ("The Guard retreats. Save yourself if you can!"). Wellington then stood up in Copenhagen's stirrups, took off his hat and waved it in the air three times to signal an advance of the Allied line. With a deafening cheer, his troops charged forward just as the Prussians were overrunning the French positions to the east.

Wellington spurred Copenhagen into the action, calling on senior surviving officers of regiments to lead them in a decisive attack. Some French artillery were still firing from La Haye Saint and a round passed between Wellington's body and Copenhagen's neck as they stood just below the farmhouse. Lord Uxbridge, just next to the Duke cried out, "By God! I've lost my leg!" Wellington continued to look through his telescope and absent-mindedly replied, "Have you, by God?" Then he looked down and realized the ball had shattered Uxbridge's knee and he quickly reached over to support his friend until help arrived to carry him off the field. The Duke then urged Copenhagen forward and followed his advancing men, ignoring the erratic enemy fire and the pleas from his staff not to take unnecessary risks.

What remained of the French army finally abandoned the field in disorder and it was 9:00pm and nearly dark when Blücher and Wellington met one another at Napoleon's abandoned headquarters of the inn of La Belle Alliance, on the north-south Brussels road, which bisected the battlefield. It was agreed that Blücher and the Prussians should continue south and pursue the retreating French army back to France, while Wellington turned north, back to Waterloo. Accompanied by only five of his staff, he walked Copenhagen quietly back through the battlefield in the moonlight.[87] Wellington felt sickened by the slaughter and with his rider in a state of emotional shock, the faithful Copenhagen continued steadily on, reaching the Waterloo inn at about 11:00 p.m., having left nearly 18 hours earlier. Years later, the Duke told a friend:

> Well, on reaching headquarters, and thinking how bravely my old horse had carried me all day, I could not help going up to his head to tell him so by a few caresses. But, hang me if, when I was giving him a slap of approbation on his hind-quarters, he did not fling out one of his hind legs with as much vigor as if he had been in the stable for a couple of days![88]

The Duke avoided the hoof which was the last danger he would face, since man and mount had both fought their last battle.

The Duke was awoken at about 3:00 a.m. with the list of the casualties which made him lament, "Well, thank God, I don't know what it is to loose a battle; but certainly nothing can be more painful than to gain one with the loss of so many of

87   Kane, *Bloody Sunday.*
88   Kane, *Bloody Sunday.*

one's friends."[89] After a couple of hours work and breakfast, he called for Copenhagen in order to get an early start back to Brussels. They arrived in Brussels late that hot morning, Copenhagen going to a shady stable to lie down in the cool of his stall and munch corn, whilst the thoughts of his master turned to the care of the wounded. He visited as many in hospital as he could that day and the next day, again rode Copenhagen back to Mont Saint-Jean to arrange for the respectful burial of the corpses of men and horses who still littered the battlefield. By 3 July 1815 Napoleon had fled and Paris surrendered, leaving Wellington to enter the city on Friday, 7 July 1815 astride Copenhagen, to shouts of, *"Vive Villianton!"* from the Parisians lining the route.[90]

The Paris Peace Conference began on 12 July 1815 and Copenhagen remained in Paris with Wellington, who in October was made Commander-in-Chief of the British Army of Occupation. The Duke leased a country house in Mont Saint-Martin, about a dozen miles from his headquarters at Cambrai and Copenhagen was happier in the country than in the city since his master had his brother-in-law send over a pack of hounds from England and was able to resume their hunting partnership. Occasionally, they even had a wild boar brought in to special hunt just as they had enjoyed in Spain. The Treaty of Paris was signed on 20 November 1815, and as the Duke's duties settled into a routine he found many more opportunities for hunting parties.[91]

In July 1817, Strathfield Saye in Hampshire, about 45 miles southwest of London was chosen as the site for the house and estate which the British government gave to the Duke in recognition of his exceptional service. At the end of 1818, the Army was withdrawn from France and it was the first time in five years that Copenhagen had set his hooves on British soil. Fortunately, his voyage across the English Channel was far shorter than his trip from England to Lisbon. Now he was not just any cavalry horse being shipped home but a national equine hero and everything was done to ensure his comfortable return home. The English in the era were a nation of horse-lovers and the story of his bold leap into the square of the 92nd Highlanders at Quatre Bras was famous across the land. He was also celebrated for his stamina in carrying Wellington "from dawn to midnight" on the field of Waterloo.[92] Very soon, the well-connected ladies of London Society began requesting a ride on the fearless thorough-bred, descendent of the legendary Eclipse. Soon it was the fashion to wear jewellery which incorporated hair from Copenhagen's mane or tail and Kitty, the Duchess of Wellington, is known to have sported such a braided bracelet from his hair and to give similar gifts to her friends.[93]

89   Kathryn, Kane, *From Paris to Stratfield Saye: Copenhagen as a Civilian* (Posted on 28 January 2011). See <https://regencyredingote.wordpress.com/2011/01/28/from-paris-to-strathfield-saye-copenhagen-as-a-civilian/ > (Accessed 2 January 2018).
90   Kane, *From Paris to Stratfield Saye.*
91   Kane, *From Paris to Stratfield Saye.*
92   Kane, *From Paris to Stratfield Saye.*
93   Kane, *From Paris to Stratfield Saye.*

At the end of the Battle of Waterloo, Napoleon's horse Marengo, in his red and gold shabraque, elegantly plaited harness and gold-plated bit and buckles, had eventually received disabling wounds in his hip, and had to be abandoned in the midst of the carnage when one of Wellington s officers saw the horse's plight and rescued him. Marengo was transported to England where, like Copenhagen, he also inspired the British public. When he was paraded in Pall Mall, 1,000s admired Napoleon's personal charger who carried the scars of five wounds and a bullet permanently lodged in his tail. After his public ceremonial duties were done, Marengo was sold and went to stud near Ely, where he outlived Napoleon by eight years and died of old age in 1831, at the age of 38. His remains were preserved and displayed as a trophy, becoming a popular public exhibit at the then Royal United Service Institution Museum. The hide with the 'N' brand was lost, but his skeleton is now on display in England's National Army Museum in Chelsea. It lacks one hoof which was presented to the officers of the Brigade of Guards for use as a snuffbox in the officers' mess. It plays a role amongst the regimental silver at St. James Palace, where each day the Captain in charge of the Guard lunches in the Officer's Mess with the hoof in front of him. On the silver hinged lid are the words: Hoof of Marengo, Barb charger of Napoleon, ridden by him at Marengo, Austerlitz, Jena, Wagram, in the campaign of Russia and lastly, Waterloo.

In London, Wellington had purchased Apsley House, near Hyde Park Corner, and the mews were only a short distance from the east end of Rotten Row which was perfect for exercising Copenhagen. Alternatively, Wellington would ride Copenhagen through Green Park and on through St. James's Park or The Mall to the Horse Guards, before returning Copenhagen to the mews of Apsley House. In 1819, Wellington joined the Cabinet and with increasing responsibilities he sent Copenhagen out to the country at Strathfield Saye. His stables were "pink-washed" and encrusted with many "rococo curves" and the stallion had the best paddock on the estate, known as the Ice House Paddock, to himself.[94] The Duchess who also stayed in the country, visited him almost every day to give him bread or sponge cakes, so that he developed a Pavlovian association with the arrival of ladies and an expectation of an offering of sweet cakes.

In 1828 when Wellington became Prime Minister he brought his old war companion out of retirement to celebrate his elevation to the highest office in the land. The Iron Duke, as he was lovingly known by the nation, rode Copenhagen from Apsley House along Constitution Hill and through St. James's Park to No. 10 Downing Street on the day he officially took the keys to the most famous front door in Britain. After his historic ride through the cheering crowds, Copenhagen returned to Strathfield Saye where he would remain in retirement. The Duke visited Copenhagen whenever he was at Strathfield Saye, often taking him some sweet treat, and would walk out to Copenhagen's paddock to spend time with him, as the last thing he did any time he left the estate, undoubtedly aware that it could, at Copenhagen's advanced age be his last farewell.

94   Kane, *From Paris to Stratfield Saye.*

Copenhagen became progressively deaf and blind, but he was well-cared for and lived to the ripe old age of 28, dying on Friday, 12 February 1836, in his stall at Strathfield Saye. The Duke was away but returned as soon as he heard the news. He went out to the stables early in the morning to have one last look at his old faithful companion but flew into a rage when he saw that his right forefoot had been cut the hoof. A servant had taken it as a souvenir, not thinking the Duke would mind, so, terrified by the Duke's anger, hid it and kept silent. He eventually returned it to the second duke 30 years later who had it made into an inkstand.[95]

Copenhagen was buried by order of the Duke, in the Ice House Paddock at Strathfield Saye with full military honours, including a salute fired over his grave. However, he did not allow the grave to be marked, to protect Copenhagen's remains from any souvenir hunters. Shortly afterwards the United Services Museum approached the Duke about disinterring Copenhagen's remains, since they wanted his skeleton in an exhibition to accompany the skeleton of Marengo. Wellington would not allow such sacrilege, thwarting the plan by saying that he was not sure where Copenhagen had been buried.[96] They never heard back from him and thus the Iron Duke ensured his old war horse and friend the dignity of the grave.

In 1846, to honour the hero of Waterloo and his famous charger, the largest equestrian statue ever created in Britain to that time,[97] was placed on top of a triumphal Constitution Arch opposite Apsley House, at the west end of Constitution Hill by Hyde Park Corner. The statue of Wellington astride Copenhagen was thus on the favourite hacking route which the pair had taken on their daily rides while the chestnut stallion was resident in the Apsley House mews. However, the statue impeded Queen Victoria's view of the London skyline from Buckingham Palace, and to many it appeared out of proportion to the arch which supported it. The portrayal was ridiculed in the press and by the public with one French wit saying, "We have been avenged!" and a young soldier describing it as "warning ambitious young officers

95 Kane, *From Paris to Stratfield Saye*. According to a different source, a farmer bought the hoof for a little over three shillings and returned the hoof directly to the Duke.
96 A false statement given that the Duke had witnessed Copenhagen's burial.
97 Matthew Cotes Wyatt designed and caste the great monument from the French cannon captured at Waterloo. In 1840, the Duke sat for Wyatt's son, James, who did the modelling work. Since Copenhagen had already passed away, he based the statue on the conformation and measurements of a substitute Thoroughbred racehorse, a mare named Rocovery. The Duke said she looked a bit like the chestnut stallion. Many of his friends privately disagreed and the press thought the rendition of Copenhagen's face with prominent flared nostrils was "something like a pig's snout". However, Sir Edwin Landseer, who had painted Copenhagen several times, and the second duke, who had known the chestnut stallion for much of his life both asserted it was an accurate portrayal and "very like Copenhagen." The 40-ton (40,000 kilogram), 8 metre-long and 9 metre-high statue was unveiled on 28 September 1846. Copenhagen's belly had a girth of 22 feet and eight inches and the section was used to host a "celebratory dinner" for Wyatt before the work was completed.

of the fate that awaits them if ever they are so unfortunate as to achieve greatness." However, Wellington was a much loved and respected septuagenarian so the statue remained in place on the arch for the rest of his life. In 1882, the Wellington Arch had to be moved when the roads in the area were widened so the Army, who still revered Wellington, and Parliament, agreed to the move it to Aldershot, the Home of the British Army. On 19 August 1885, the statue was placed on Round Hill, near the Royal Garrison Church, less than 15 miles southeast of Strathfield Saye where it stands to this day.

In 1843 the house-keeper at Strathfield Saye had planted an acorn in the Ice House Paddock which grew into the great Turkey Oak and shaded Copenhagen's gravesite. Some years after the Duke died, in 1852, his son, the second Duke of Wellington, placed a simple white marble tombstone under the spreading Turkey Oak which shaded Copenhagen's grave. There were two inscriptions on the stone, the first written by the second duke:

Here lies
COPENHAGEN,
The charger ridden by
the Duke of Wellington
The entire day at the
Battle of Waterloo.
Born 1808, Died 1836.[98]

The second epitaph was a couplet written by the English poet and sportsman, Rowland Egerton-Warburton,[99] at the request of the second duke:

God's humbler instrument, though meaner clay,
Should share the glory of that glorious day.[100]

Loyal and courageous, Copenhagen, the grandson of Eclipse, remains one of the most celebrated war horses of all time. His brave leap over the heads of the 92nd Highlanders at Quatre Bras saved Wellington's life. This action and his steadfastness, endurance and durability throughout Spain and the Waterloo campaign, enabled Wellington to deliver his victory at Waterloo. He was an obvious candidate for the first chapter in the book. Other chapters will celebrate less well known but equally worthy heroic and hard horses.

---

98   Kane, *From Paris to Stratfield Saye.*
99   14 September 1804–6 December 1891
100 Kane, *From Paris to Stratfield Saye.*

2

Ronald: The Leader

At Balaclava in the Crimea on 25 October 1854, Lord Cardigan,[1] astride his handsome, chestnut, Thoroughbred horse, Ronald, rode up to his superior officer to receive his orders. He listened to the instruction to advance down the valley to his front, with Russian guns on both flanks and ahead. He then saluted and raised his sword whilst remarking "Certainly, sir; but allow me to point out to you that the Russians have a battery in the valley to our front, and batteries and riflemen on each flank". When he was told that orders were orders he wheeled Ronald away and muttered disgustedly, "Here goes the last of the Brudenells"[2].

Lord Cardigan was Commander of the Light Brigade and this was the black day of the 'Charge' when, mounted on Ronald, he led his men straight into the jaws of the massed Russian canon. The general consensus of history is that Cardigan was, at best, a flawed character and perhaps it would not be too harsh to sum him up as an arrogant, over privileged, and psychologically challenged cad! So uniquely in this book, the author can have little praise for the horse's rider. This makes the achievements of Ronald all the more remarkable in that despite the rider, Ronald has his place in history at the front of possibly the most famous cavalry charge ever recorded and certainly the most celebrated in the literature of the English Language.

Ronald was born in England about 1850 having been bred by the Earl at Deene Park in Northamptonshire, the Brudenell family home. A chestnut thoroughbred with white socks, standing 15.2 hands high, the Earl had selected him as his personal charger and, along with other army horses, Ronald was shipped to the Black Sea. He was, however, lovingly transported to the Crimea in conditions appropriate for a rich Earl's horse. The journey was torturous enough for Ronald, but the average cavalry mount had to cope with 2,300 miles of rough seas and horrendous conditions aboard

---

1   Lieutenant General James Thomas Brudenell, 7th Earl of Cardigan, KCB (16 October 1797–28 March 1868).
2   Saul David, *Victoria's Wars* (London: Penguin, 2006), pp.230-231.

the small ships and many horses died long before they reached dry land or the battle field. Ronald survived and was soon reunited with the Earl.

In the 17th century, farmers and landowners in England had become increasingly interested in racing and in the search for success, both on the track and in their gambling pursuits, started the selective breeding which was to lead to the modern Thoroughbred breed. Charles II[3] had imported Barb Turk and Arab horses to improve the blood lines of his stable which became known as "the King's Mares".[4] The native British horses provided stamina but lacked speed so from 1689 to 1729 horses were brought in from the Middle East to improve English stock and the modern Thoroughbreds can thus be traced to three key stallions of the period.[5] The Byerley Turk was captured by Colonel Robert Byerley at the siege of Buda (Budapest) in 1688 from a Turkish officer,[6] whilst the Darley Arabian was bought by Thomas Darley in Aleppo, Syria in 1704.[7] Finally, the Godolphin Arabian was bought by the Earl of Godolphin[8] by way of the King of Tunis and the King of France in 1729.[9] All had long careers at stud and between them established the three key racing bloodlines of Herod, Eclipse and Matchem. The stallions brought speed and spirit to the breed whilst the mares gave size and strength.

By the Napoleonic period the breed characteristics were well established, averaging 16 hands high with defined withers, deep, sloped shoulders and a deep girth, although the name Thoroughbred did not appear until 1821.[10] The breed is truly beautiful and athletic, with long clean limbs, fine, silky coat, elegant profile, muscular body, finely sculpted ears and eyes that are always large and intelligent. Being bold, honest and courageous over fences they were also ideal for flat racing, steeplechases and the hunting field, being fast with endurance and nimble for jumping. The breed was used to improve the blood of hundreds of other breeds, in particular, the "Hunter Type". This was a British invention which could range from 14.2 to 17.3hh with any number of native horse and pony blood in the mix,[11] reflecting the terrain of the particular area of the country. The Hunter needed to be tough versatile, safe and mannerly horses capable over jumps, and thus the Thoroughbred blood was often to be found in the Hunter Type which was often crossed with an Irish Draught of Cleveland Bay. The British Army officer class were keen fox hunters and the Thoroughbreds, like Ronald, and Thoroughbred Hunters became their preferred mounts. Many were from Irish

---

3   Reigned 1660-85.
4   DiMarco, *War Horse*, p.209.
5   A. Fitzpatrick, *The Ultimate Guide to Horse Breeds* (London: Hermes House, 2011), p.276.
6   1660-1714.
7   Thomas Darley (born 19 May 1664) served as Her Majesty's Consul to the Levant (Syria) during the reign of Queen Anne.
8   Francis Godolphin, 2nd Earl of Godolphin, PC (3 September 1678–17 January 1766) was a British politician, styled Viscount Rialton between 1706 and 1712.
9   DiMarco, *War Horse*, p.209.
10   Fitzpatrick, *The Ultimate Guide*, p.276.
11   Fitzpatrick, *The Ultimate Guide*, p.298.

breeders and they had superior power in the charge but after being launched tended to run away with their riders.

Cardigan was an excellent rider and, inspired by the heroism of cavalry at the battle of Waterloo, his wish as a young man was to purchase a commission in a fashionable cavalry regiment. However, his father sent him up to Christ Church, Oxford in 1816 where, despite showing some aptitude, he did not take a degree. In February 1811 his father inherited the Cardigan earldom, along with the family seat of Deene Park and the immense estates and revenues that went with it. James took up residence in the grand household at the age of 14 and throughout his life played the part of the archetypal extravagant aristocrat. He was educated at Harrow but after a fight, his father removed him from the school, not for fighting, since fist fights were allowed at Harrow, but for playing truant while having a broken bone in his hand treated by a London surgeon. Subsequently educated at home, as the only son among seven sisters, he developed into something of a spoilt brat, accustomed to getting his own way. Some psycho-analysts might use this to explain his arrogance and stubbornness in later life.

In February 1818, during his last term at Oxford, he became Member of Parliament for Marlborough, a pocket borough "owned" by his cousin Charles, Earl of Aylesbury. Taking his seat on the ruling Tory side of the House of Commons, he made a stand in 1829 against his patron, Charles, in support of his party's bill allowing limited Catholic emancipation. This was because of his admiration for Wellington, the bill's sponsor, but as a consequence he was thrown out of his seat and had to buy the "rotten borough" of Fowey, Cornwall, at a cost of at least £5,000,[12] only to have the seat abolished by the Great Reform Act of 1832. He then fought the family's local constituency of Northamptonshire North where despite his family's patronage and distributing about £20,000 among the electorate,[13] he only just won the seat, before in 1837 he inherited the earldom from his father, and moved to the House of Lords.

At the age of 22 he had formed his own troop of Yeomanry in Northamptonshire and in 1824, at the age of 27, he joined the 8th King's Royal Irish Hussars. His progression through the Army was greatly aided by his wealth. He purchased a commission as a Lieutenant in January 1825, a Captain in June 1826, a Major in August 1830 and a Lieutenant-Colonel, only three months later, on 3 December 1830. Finally, he obtained command of the 15th The King's Hussars for a premium in March 1832. His youth and inexperience contrasted with the battle-tested officers whom he led and manifested itself in petty bullying. In 1833 he was publicly censured in a court martial for charges he had made against a subordinate and was dismissed, by order of King William. However, he had influence at court and got the decision reversed. Then he pestered senior officers and politicians until in March 1836 he was allowed to command the 11th Light Dragoons (later restyled the 11th Hussars), despite the

---

12   About £380,000 in today's money.
13   Equivalent to some £1,550,000 today.

view of his commander-in-chief, Lord Hill[14], that he was "constitutionally unfit for command". He joined his new command in India in October of the following year, before seeing the regiment off for Britain at the end of its long posting. He returned in a hired vessel, rather than sharing the discomforts of the warship carrying his troops, and of the two years following his appointment, only four weeks were spent with his regiment.

Brudenell set about using his own money to purchase brilliant new uniforms for his men. This was very unpopular with his professional officers who had to match the men's attire with even more costly uniforms, out of their own pockets. He wished his officers to be as aristocratic, flamboyant and stylish, as he was himself, and as a consequence he had no time for those "Indian officers" who had learnt their profession over many years of service with the 11th during its long posting in India. Brudenell had forbidden the serving of porter, the beverage of choice among the professional officers, and when at a formal mess dinner a visitor had requested moselle wine, which was served in a "black bottle" similar to that of porter, he decided that the "Indian" Captain John Reynolds, who had ordered it for the guest, should be arrested. Cardigan came in for much public criticism and ridicule in the press for this incident and furthermore, was prosecuted in 1841 for a duel with one of his former long-serving professional officers. However, he was acquitted on the most slender of legal technicalities, by a jury 120 of his peers, in the House of Lords, adding to his unpopularity, with *The Times* alleging that "in England there is one law for the rich and another for the poor".

Whilst Cardigan had been advancing his military career in his own idiosyncratic manner, a war had been brewing up. As the Ottoman Empire weakened, Russia had taken advantage by expanding south in search of warm water naval and merchant ports on the Black Sea that did not freeze over like its handful of northern ports. They also saw themselves as the protector of Orthodox Christians living under Ottoman control, and sought a free hand in dealing with the Ottoman Empire, by then known as the "sick man of Europe". Britain was eager to preserve her commercial interests and could not tolerate Russian dominance as that would challenge her own naval dominance in the eastern Mediterranean and might threaten India.

Furthermore, the ambitious slightly unhinged French head of state Napoleon III,[15] wanted to restore the grandeur of France by provoking a fight with Russia over the 'custody' of Christian land-marks and relics in the Holy Land. He thought he would get Catholic support if he attacked Eastern Orthodoxy, so he demanded French protection of the Roman Catholic rights to visit the holy places in Palestine. By sending a ship of the line to the Black Sea he forced the Turks to accept a new treaty, confirming France and the Roman Catholic Church as the supreme Christian

---

14   General Rowland Hill, 1st Viscount Hill, GCB GCH (11 August 1772–10 December 1842).

15   Louis-Napoléon Bonaparte (20 April 1808–9 January 1873) was the only President (1848–52) of the French Second Republic and, as Napoleon III, Emperor (1852–70) of the Second French Empire. He was the nephew and heir of Napoleon I.

authority with control over the holy places and possession of the keys to the Church of the Nativity.[16]

By previous treaties, the Sultan was committed to protect the Eastern Orthodox Christian religion and its churches and so Tsar Nicholas I deployed his 4th and 5th army corps along the River Danube,[17] as a direct threat to the Ottoman-controlled Danubian Principalities of Moldavia and Wallachia south of the river. He demanded a Russian protectorate over all 12,000,000 Orthodox Christians in the Empire. A compromise was reached regarding Orthodox access to the Holy Land, but in February 1853, the British government of Lord Aberdeen,[18] convinced the Sultan to reject the Russian treaty proposal, since it compromised the independence of the Turks. At the end of June 1853 Russia used the Sultan's failure to resolve the issue as a pretext for occupation, and in July the Tsar sent his troops across the Pruth River into the Danubian Principalities.

In response, Britain and France sent their fleets to the Dardanelles, and Sultan Abdulmecid I formally declared war on Russia.[19] The Ottomans managed to achieve some early victories on the Danubian front, and to stand their ground in the Caucasus. Then on 30 November 1853 the Russians sent a fleet to Sinope in northern Anatolia and destroyed a squadron of Ottoman ships at anchor in the port. Public opinion in Britain and France was outraged and demanded war against Russia. On 28 March 1854, after Russia ignored an ultimatum to withdraw from the Danubian Principalities, Britain and France formally declared war.

The Austrians entered the war on the side of Turkey with an attack against the Russians in the Principalities in June and they were joined in the same month by the Allied expeditionary force who landed at Varna, on the Black Sea's western coast (now in Bulgaria). When in July the Turks crossed the Danube into Wallachia and threatened Bucharest the Russians evacuated the Danubian principalities thus removing the original grounds for war, but war fever among the public in both Britain and France had been whipped up by the press to such a level that politicians could not resist. The allies realized that if they captured the key Russian naval base at Sevastopol, on the Crimean peninsula, they would control the Black Sea, teach the Russians a lesson and win the war. Hence, in September 1854 a large French army and a smaller British army boarded ships at Varna to invade the Crimean and landed on the sandy beaches of Calamita Bay on the south west coast of the Peninsula. After crossing the Alma River on 30 September 1854, the allies moved on to besiege Sevastopol, whilst the Russian army retreated to the interior. However, Britain had not fought in a European

16   Previously held by the Greek Orthodox Church.
17   Nicholas I (6 July 1796–2 March 1855) was the Emperor of Russia from 1825 until 1855.
18   George Hamilton-Gordon, 4th Earl of Aberdeen KG, KT, FRSE, FRS, PC, FSA Scot (28 January 1784–14 December 1860), served as Prime Minister from 1852 until 1855.
19   Abdülmecid I (23/25 April 1823–25 June 1861) was the 31st Sultan of the Ottoman Empire and succeeded his father Mahmud II on 2 July 1839.

theatre since the Battle of Waterloo in 1815, and the army had become bureaucratic, inefficient and would soon discover its own shortcomings.

A Russian assault on the allied supply base at Balaclava precipitated the battle of the same name which is still remembered in England for two British actions. On the morning of the 25 October the 93rd Highlanders held out against repeated attacks by a larger Russian cavalry force and became immortalised as the "Thin Red Line". The second memorable action was by the Light Cavalry Brigade, under the command of Cardigan, who was sent an ambiguous order from Lord Raglan, carried by the eager Captain Nolan[20], which precipitated their near suicidal charge into the north Valley of the Balaclava battlefield. This brings us back to our opening scene of Lord Cardigan on Ronald at the entrance to the Valley of Death.

Having had his orders confirmed by Lord Lucan, his immediate superior, Lord Cardigan rode up on Ronald to the 4th Light Dragoons and said to their commander, Lord George Paget, 'Lord George, we are ordered to make an attack to the front. You will take command of the second line, and I expect your best support-mind, your best support'.[21] Rather irritated by this repetition, Lord George replied just as loudly, 'You shall have it, my lord.' Lord Cardigan now galloped to the head of his brigade with the 13th Light Dragoons, 11th Hussars and the 17th Lancers in the first line and the 4th Light Dragoons and the main body of the 8th Hussars in the second[22].

Among the officers in the 17th Lancers was Godfrey Charles Morgan, 1st Viscount Tredegar[23], an aristocrat from Ruperra Castle in Glamorganshire. After being educated, like Cardigan, at Eton, Lord Tredegar, or the Honourable Godfrey Morgan as he was then, joined the 17th Regiment of Light Dragoons (Lancers), the "Death or Glory Boys", as a lieutenant in 1853. When the Crimean War broke out Tredegar, at the age of 22, held the rank of a captain and commanded a squadron of about 140 men and horses. Lord Tredegar and his brother Colonel Freddy Morgan were keen steeplechase riders, often racing against each other and staging National Hunt races at Tredegar Park. Steeplechasing has its roots in Ireland in the late 17th century when owners held Pounding Matches over chosen country to see who had the fittest and boldest horse. The aim was to outlast your opponent over rough ground and by the mid-18th century chosen courses from known landmark to known land-mark, often the steeple of a church, became common. For example, in 1752 there was a 4 ½ mile race from Buttevant Church in County Cork to the spire of St Leger Church between the horses of Edmund Blake and Mr O'Callaghan.[24] In England, as the Industrial Revolution consumed forests, stag hunting gave way to fox hunting and the slower horses could not keep up with the swifter fox across open country.

---

20   Louis Edward Nolan (4 January 1818–25 October 1854)
21   16 March 1818–30 June 1880.
22   M. Adkin, *The Charge: The Real Reason Why the Light Brigade were Lost* (London: Pimlico, 2004), p.2.
23   28 April 1831-11 March 1913
24   Whetstone & Welch, *The Little Book of Horse Racing*, p.105.

Hence huntsmen needed faster horses which could jump, and Thoroughbred crossed on mares made for faster animals who could also excel at Steeplechasing. One of the earliest races in England was in the 1790s between Loraine Hardy and the Honourable Mr Willoughby's horse for 1,000 guineas over a nine-mile course from Melton Mowbry to Dalby Wood.[25] Later on, flags were used to show the route and in 1813 the County Roscommon Course in Ireland covered six miles including six walls over five foot high. The first Steeplechase course in England was at Bedford where in 1810 there were eight fences of 4ft 6in and other courses were established at St Alban's in 1830 and Cheltenham in 1841.[26] A flat course was established at Aintree in 1829 but the Grand Liverpool Steeplechase, which from 1847 became known as the Grand National, was first run in 1839 with its' 4.5 miles and 30 fences.[27] The professional sport of National Hunt Racing was recognised by the Jockey Club in 1866 but the local hunts continued with their amateur Point-to-Point races under rules drawn up by the Master of Hounds Association,[28] which still do not allow professional riders or licensed trainers. National Hunt racing itself grows from strength to strength with Hurdling races from two or three miles over small, collapsible obstacles and Steeplechasing over bigger fixed fences and distances from two to 4.5 miles.[29]

In 1851 Godfrey Morgan had bought, a champion racehorse called Briggs who was born in South Wales in 1846 and was chestnut with black stockings, standing 15 hands high.[30] He was named after a family servant and had carried Lord Tredegar to victory in his purple and orange racing colours in a steeplechase over the old Cowbridge Hunt Steeplechase course at Penllyne in the same year.[31] This, the Lord would later say, gave him the pedigree to jump over the Russian cannons, and after showing remarkable bravery at Balaclava the horse would unofficially be knighted and be known henceforth as *Sir Briggs*.

The kindest thing would have been to send horses and men by steam ship to the Black Sea, but Morgan's horse *Briggs* set sail from Portsmouth in 1854 on board the Edmundsbury, a sailing ship carrying forty horses, four of which belonged to Godfrey. They lost horses to seasickness, including *Atheist*, Captain Morgan's second charger,

25 Whetstone & Welch, *The Little Book of Horse Racing*, p.105.
26 Whetstone & Welch, *The Little Book of Horse Racing*, p.105.
27 Including the massive Chair, The Canal Turn and Beecher's Brook with its take of side higher than the landing.
28 Whetstone & Welch, *The Little Book of Horse Racing*, p.90.
29 Whetstone & Welch, *The Little Book of Horse Racing*, p.71. Horses may go hurdling from the year in which they turn three on 1 July and must be over 4 to go chasing. The season proper runs from mid-October with the Charlie Hall Chase at Wetherby followed by the Open Meeting at Cheltenham (including the Paddy Power Gold Cup) with the highlighted of the season being the magnificent Cheltenham Festival in March.
30 Today if you visit the National Army Museum there is an oil painting of Sir Briggs by the artist, Alfred Frank de Prades, who visited the Crimea in 1854 and is particularly noted for his equestrian and sporting paintings.
31 Penlline or Penlynne

who was thrown overboard. The vessel stopped briefly at Malta, and by 19 May had reached the Dardanelles. By the time the vessel anchored at Constantinople the regiment had lost 26 horses, and others continued to die. The troops then embarked for the Bulgarian port of Varna. When the Bulgarian phase ended they moved to the Crimea, where the cavalry remained largely inactive, notably at the Battle of the Alma, and it was not until Balaclava that action was seen.

At the last moment before the charge Lord Lucan interfered with Cardigan's dispositions, ordering the 11th Hussars to fall back in support of the first line, so that there were now three lines, with the 13th Light Dragoons and the 17th Lancers of Godfrey Morgan leading. Lord Lucan's interference was probably designed to annoy Cardigan since the 11th was Cardigan's own regiment, while the 17th Lancers, Lucan's old regiment, remained in the front. The two men were barely on speaking terms as Lucan was married to one of Cardigan's sisters and Cardigan thought he did not treat her well. Lord Cardigan astride Ronald placed himself alone, two lengths in front of his staff and five lengths in advance of his front line. He drew his sword and raised it, a trumpet sounded, and in a quiet voice he gave the orders to advance, and the three lines of the Light Brigade began to move, followed after a few minutes' interval by the Heavy Brigade, led by Lord Lucan.

The North Valley was over a mile long and just under a mile wide. On the Fedioukine Hills, to the north, there were eight battalions of infantry, four squadrons of cavalry and 14 guns; whilst to the south on the Causeway Heights were 11 battalions, with 30 guns and a field battery.[32] At the end of the valley, facing the Light Brigade, the bulk of the Russian cavalry which had been defeated by the Heavy Brigade earlier in the day, was drawn up in three lines, with 12 guns, strengthened by six further squadrons of Lancers, three on each flank.[33] The Light Brigade was advancing into a three-sided trap.

The Brigade of five regiments numbering less than 700 men trotted across the short turf,[34] drilled and disciplined, and determined to show the 'damned Heavies' what the Light Brigade could do. As they headed to their doom, a sudden silence fell over the battlefield as for a moment gun and rifle fire ceased, and it became so quiet that the jingle of bits and equipment could be clearly heard. Lord Cardigan, alone at their head, rode Ronald quietly, stiff and upright in the saddle, never once looking back. He was performing a task which asked for no power of reflection or intelligence, only the physical courage expected of his breed. Astride Ronald, his beautiful chestnut thoroughbred, he wore the vibrant cherry and royal blue uniform of the 11th Hussars, decorated with fur, plume and lace, all preserved in pristine splendour due to the comfortable living conditions on his yacht. He was wearing his gold-laced pelisse as

32   Cecil Woodham-Smith, *The Reason Why* (New York: McGraw-Hill, 1953), p.243.
33   Woodham-Smith, *The Reason Why*, p.243.
34   David, *Victoria's Wars*, states 676.

a coat, rather than dangling from his shoulders, which showed of his slender figure, belying his 57 years.

Before the Light Brigade had advanced 50 yards the silence was broken as the Russian guns thundered out. A moment later, with the advance still proceeding at a steady trot, Captain Nolan, in a serious breach of military etiquette, galloped forward in front of Lord Cardigan. Turning in his saddle, he shouted and waved his sword to address the Brigade, but with the guns firing not a word could be heard. Maybe he had realised that his interpretation of the order had been wrong, and that he had directed the Light Brigade up the wrong valley but we will never know because at that instant, a shell burst through Nolan's chest, exposing his heart. As the sword fell from his hand, his right arm still reaching up, his body remained rigid in the saddle whilst his horse wheeled and galloped back through the Brigade, his body emanating an appalling cry. His terrified horse carried him through the 4th Light Dragoons, before he at last tumbled dead from the saddle. Lord Cardigan, unaware of Nolan's death, was furious, believing that he had been trying to take command of the Brigade and lead the charge himself. When asked later what he thought about as he advanced towards the guns, Cardigan replied that his mind was entirely occupied with anger against Nolan.

For the first few 100 yards of the attack the Russians assumed that the redoubts on the Causeway heights were the objective, but the Light Brigade horsemen continued straight on down the North Valley. The Russians on the Heights could not believe that this small force intended to attack the battery at the end and expose itself to deadly cross fire but after a moment's pause, battalions of riflemen and multiple gun batteries poured down fire on the Light Brigade from both sides. Caught in a lethal cross fire, the pace quickened, but Lord Cardigan restrained the Brigade to ensure the line advanced with parade-ground perfection, speaking only once in the course of the whole charge to say, 'Steady, steady, Close in!'. [35]

At the end of the valley was a white bank of smoke, through which flashed great tongues of flame marking the position of the guns. Cardigan chose one at the centre of the battery and rode Ronald for it, upright and unflinching, a cad maybe, but a courageous and disciplined one. As a man or horse dropped, the riders on each side opened out until clear and then closed again. On the heights old soldiers were moved to tears as the Brigade rode on down the valley, its numbers dwindling as it went, prompting the French General, Bosquet to observe, 'C'est magnifique mais, ce n'est pas la guerre'. [36]

The first line was now within range of the guns at the end of the valley, and round-shot, grape and shells began to mow swathes of men down. The pace quickened to a canter as the men and horses could no longer be restrained. The slower Heavy Brigade, weary from their earlier charge, were being left behind and the gap widened.

---

35   David, *Victoria's Wars*, p.232, and Adkin, *The Charge*, p.161.
36   "It is magnificent, but it isn't war." Adkin, *The Charge*, p.168.

Soon the Heavy Brigade came under the cross-fire and Lord Lucan, leading them, was wounded in the leg and his horse was hit in two places. One of his aides was killed, two of his staff were wounded and he saw that his two leading regiments,[37] the Greys and the Royals, were taking heavy casualties. Lucan had to decide whether to continue and destroy the Heavy Brigade, or halt and leave the Light Brigade to its fate without support? He turned to Lord William Paulet, who had just had his forage cap torn off his head by a musket ball and said, 'They have sacrificed the Light Brigade: they shall not the Heavy, if I can help it'.[38] Ordering the halt, he retired the brigade out of range and waited, to protect the Light Cavalry against pursuit on their return.

So the Heavy Brigade watched the Light Brigade go on alone down the valley and vanish into the smoke. The French Chasseurs d'Afrique, mounted on Algerian horses, could do nothing to help the charge, but charged the batteries and infantry battalions on the Fedioukine Hills. Galloping over broken and scrubby ground in a loose formation learned in Atlas mountain campaigns in Morocco, they forced the Russians to retreat, so that the remnants of the Light Brigade would now only suffer fire from the Causeway Heights.

Cardigan, Ronald and the first line of the Light Brigade were now more than halfway down the valley, and casualties were so heavy that formation was lost and the front line broke into a gallop. The men shot forward in front of their officers as regiments raced each other to death. Cardigan was forced to increase his pace, with the troopers' cheers changing to death-cries and horses falling and screaming. The first line was closely followed by the second line of Lord George Paget, who had increased the pace of the 4th Light Dragoons, and caught up along with the 11th Hussars. Meanwhile, the 8th Hussars were kept in hand by Colonel Shewell and advanced at a steady trot to the right rear.

The second line charged into the same hell across ground strewn with casualties, human and equine, dead and alive, crawling, screaming and writhing. They had to avoid riding over their comrades, while rider-less horses, some horribly injured, tried to force their way into the ranks. Horses in battle, as long as they are in company, will gallop with the herd, just like the horse of a fallen rider in a steeplechase, and when Lord George Paget's charger was hit, he was astonished to find the horse showed no sign of panic. However, once deprived of his rider, a horse, crazed with terror, seeks the safety and companionship of other horses, and attempts to attach himself to the herd and force himself into the ranks of the nearest squadrons. Lord George, riding in advance of the second line, found himself riding in the midst of seven rider less horses, who pushed against him as round-shot and bullets came by, covering him with blood from their wounds, and nearly unhorsing him.

Eight minutes had now passed since the advance began, and Lord Cardigan, with the survivors of the first line hard on his heels, was galloping furiously to within a few

---

37   Adkin, *The Charge*, p.170.
38   Adkin, *The Charge*, p.171.

yards of the battery and selected a space between two guns. Still sitting rigid in his saddle, he waved his sword over his head and at that moment there was a roar as huge flashes of flame shot out. The salvo from the Russian guns burst into the first line of the Light Brigade at a distance of 80 yards. The line ceased to exist and the second seemed to dissolve. Cardigan was only two or three lengths from the gun muzzles and Ronald was blown sideways by the blast, as flames scorched down his right flank. Wrenching Ronald's head round, the Earl drove into the smoke and, charging through the space he had previously selected, was the first man into the battery. Smoke hung like a curtain over the end of the valley as through their telescopes the watchers saw rider less horses gallop out and men stagger into view to fall among the corpses of their comrades littering the ground.

Only 50 men had survived from the first line and in the smoky gloom the frenzied British troopers cut, thrust and hacked,[39] while the Russian gunners fought to remove the guns. While the struggle went on, the survivors of the 17th Lancers outflanked the battery on the left, and emerged from the smoke to be confronted by a host of Russian cavalry to the rear of the guns. They charged into the stationary Russians who broke and retreated in disorder, but within a few seconds an overwhelming body of Cossacks came up and the 17th were forced to retreat, fighting the encircling swarm as they fell back towards the guns. In the midst of the struggle for the guns, Colonel Mayow, the Brigade Major, saw an overwhelming body of Russian cavalry preparing to descend in force. He collected the remaining survivors of the 17th and all that was left of the 13th Light Dragoons and charged out of the battery, driving the Russians before him until they were some 500 yards away.

At this moment the second line arrived, and the 4th Light Dragoons under Lord George Paget thrust into the smoke which obscured the battery. The Russian gunners persisted in their attempt to take the guns away, but the Dragoons, with their blood up, fell on them in a savage, hand-to-hand combat, and secured every gun. Meanwhile, Colonel Douglas, outflanking the battery with the 11th Hussars, had successfully charged a body of Russian Lancers on the left, only to find himself confronted by the main body of the cavalry and infantry and had to retreat with a large Russian force in pursuit. With the smoky battery heaped with a mass of dead and dying, the 4th Light Dragoons pressed on beyond the battery and collided with the retreating 11th. The two groups, numbering not more than 70 men,[40] joined together. Advancing on them within a few 100 yards were Russian cavalry, but Lord George noticed the great mass was disorderly and displaying signs of hesitation. Reining in his horse, he halted the 11th, turned to his major and said, 'We are in a desperate scrape; what the devil shall we do? Has anyone seen Lord Cardigan?'.

When Lord Cardigan and Ronald had led the brigade into the murky smoke of the battery they had passed in-between the two guns unhurt but did not pause.

39   Woodham-Smith, *The Reason Why*, p.251.
40   Woodham-Smith, *The Reason Why*, p. 255.

Cardigan later stated, it was 'no part of a general's duty to fight the enemy among private soldiers'. He galloped on clear of the smoke, until he saw the Russian cavalry. Ronald's Thoroughbred blood was up and he carried Cardigan to within 20 yards of the Russians who stared in astonishment at the arrival of this solitary, gilded horseman. By a coincidence of 19th century aristocracy, one of the officers, Prince Radzivill, recognised Lord Cardigan, having met previously in London at dinners and balls, and detached some Cossacks to capture him alive. However, after a brief encounter, during which he received a slight wound on the thigh, Cardigan wheeled Ronald and galloped back through the guns coming out where he had charged in.

Cardigan, now facing back up the valley could see no sign of his brigade in the casualty strewn valley where small groups of men, wounded or unhorsed, were struggling back to the British lines. He rode Ronald out of the fray never once looking back, and had no idea of the fate of his brigade. In his own words, having 'led the Brigade and launched them with due impetus, he considered his duty was done.'[41] With extraordinary indifference to danger he had led the Light Brigade down the valley on Ronald as if he were leading a charge in a review. By another miracle he was untouched by the fire from the Causeway Heights, which was still raking the unfortunate survivors of the charge in the valley. As he rode back slowly, most of the time at a walk to avoid any undignified appearance of haste, he continued to fume about Nolan, and when he reached the Heavy Brigade, he rode up to General Scarlett and immediately complained of his insubordination, finishing contemptuously, 'Imagine the fellow screaming like a woman when he was hit'. General Scarlett checked him: 'Say no more, my lord; you have just ridden over Captain Nolan's dead body.'[42]

Meanwhile the survivors of the 4th Light Dragoons and 11th Hussars under Lord George Paget, wheeled about, and spurred their exhausted horses to charge the Russian Lancers blocking their retreat. As they approached, the Russians drew back their right, presenting a sloping front, allowing the British to brush past at a distance of a horse's length, parrying thrusts from the lances. The Russians, having witnessed the destruction of the main body of the Light Brigade, seemed un-bothered by the handful of survivors, so, without the loss of a single man, they escaped and began the painful retreat back up the valley.

Beyond the guns, the 8th Hussars, under Colonel Shewell, had reached the battery in beautiful formation to find the 4th Light Dragoons had silenced the guns. Shewell led his men through the battery and halted on the other side, enquiring, like Lord George Paget, on Cardigan's whereabouts. For about three minutes the 8th Hussars waited, before on the skyline appeared lances. The 15 men of the 17th Lancers,[43] who with the few survivors of the 13th Light Dragoons had charged out of the battery before the second line attacked, were now retreating, with a large Russian force in

41   Woodham-Smith, *The Reason Why*, p.254.
42   Woodham-Smith, *The Reason Why*, p.255.
43   Woodham-Smith, *The Reason Why*, p.256.

pursuit. At that moment Shewell saw that he too was not only menaced in front but that a large force of Russian cavalry was preparing to cut off his retreat. Assuming command, he wheeled the little force into line and gave the order to charge. He himself, discarding his sword, gripped his reins in both hands, put down his head and rushed at the Russian commanding officer whose horse flinched clear as Shewell burst through the gap to the other side. Riding for their lives, his troopers galloped after him through the confused Russians to safety.

The chaotic remnants of shattered men and wounded horses made their way back up the valley. Troopers who had become attached to their horses refused to leave them behind and men staggered along, dragging their wounded and bleeding horses with them. The rabble who limped painfully along at a achingly slow pace were mostly on foot in little groups, dragging along step by step, leaning on each other. At first Russian Lancers made harassing attacks, swooping down on stragglers and taking prisoners, but when the retreating force came under fire from the Causeway Heights the Russians withdrew to avoid casualties from their own guns. For nearly a mile under fire, the straggling trail of men offered a poor target compared to the formed squadrons which had charged down the valley. As groups stumbled in men ran down to meet their comrades, shook them by the hand, and congratulated the survivors for their escape from hell and cheating death.

When the last survivors had trailed in, the remnants of the Light Brigade re-formed on a slope looking southward over Balaclava. The charge had lasted 20 minutes from the trumpet sounding to the return of the last survivor. Lord Cardigan addressed the survivors saying, 'Men, it is a mad-brained trick, but it is no fault of mine',[44] and a voice answered, 'Never mind, my lord; we are ready to go again'. The roll-call was punctuated by the heart-breaking sound of pistol-shots despatching ruined horses. It is an accurate reflection of fact that the Charge is often considered a futile and costly mistake. However, there is no denying that it was gloriously heroic and it achieved its objective to smash through the Russian guns and demoralize their cavalry.

One of the last to return was an angry Lord George Paget, who challenged Cardigan to account for himself. Unsatisfied with the response, he later wrote an official complaint to the new Commander-in-Chief, the Duke of Cambridge[45] who forwarded it to Cardigan. Cardigan's reply in turn complained that Paget had not taken his regiments into the attack, and claim and counter-claim followed, until Cardigan's protestations were diverted to more public allegations when Colonel the Hon. Somerset John Gough Calthorpe's book *Letters from a Staff Officer in the*

---

44   Woodham-Smith, *The Reason Why*, p.258.
45   Prince George, 2nd Duke of Cambridge, KG KT KP GCB GCH GCSI GCMG GCIE GCVO VD PC (Ire) (George William Frederick Charles; 26 March 1819–17 March 1904). Served as Commander-in-Chief of the Forces (head of the British Army) from 1856 to 1895.

Crimea went on sale.[46] Thus, the debates and blame shifting about the Charge began. However, the extent to which Lord Cardigan was to blame is unproven, since it is indisputable that he received a direct order in front of the troops from his immediate superior, Lord Lucan, and he openly expressed his doubts before obeying orders.

These debates have been fuelled over the years by books, poetry and film and the Charge has been celebrated and criticised in equal measure. The two ends of the spectrum are well illustrated by the two best known and most shown feature films on the subject. *The Charge of the Light Brigade* is a 1936 American historical romp made by Warner Brothers[47] with Errol Flynn[48] and Olivia de Havilland[49] in the leading role, alongside a young David Niven.[50] Warners were inspired to make the film after *Lives of a Bengal Lancer* (1935) had been released to great popularity, ushering in a series of British Empire adventure tales and it mashes up the Indian Mutiny with the Crimean war in the most cavalier manner, in both senses of the word. They wanted an all-British cast, hence Niven and de Havilland, but Errol Flynn, who was an Australian (considered Irish by Warners) had made such a strong impression in *Captain Blood* that he was selected to play the lead.

The story is very loosely based on the famous Charge with additional story line seemingly from the Siege of Cawnpore during the Indian Rebellion of 1857. However, when someone pointed out that the Sepoy Rebellion took place three years after the Battle of Balaclava, the name of Cawnpore was hastily changed to Chukoti, and the rebellion was turned into an imagined uprising led by the fictional Surat Khan, the leader of the vaguely Turkish country of Suristan.[51] The plot is set in 1854 with Major Geoffrey Vickers (Flynn) and his brother, Captain Perry Vickers stationed at Chukoti with the 27th Lancers.[52] Perry has secretly betrayed Geoffrey by stealing the love of his fiancee Elsa (Olivia de Havilland). During an official visit to local tributary rajah, Surat Khan, Geoffrey saves the rajah's life. Later, Surat Khan massacres the inhabitants of Chukoti (mainly the dependents of the lancers), and allies himself with the Russians. Fortunately for the plot, he spares Elsa and Geoffrey as they flee the slaughter to repay his debt to Geoffrey.

---

46   Somerset John Gough-Calthorpe, 7th Baron Calthorpe, KCB (23 January 1831-16 November 1912).
47   Directed by Michael Curtiz and produced by Samuel Bischoff, with Hal B. Wallis as executive producer, from a screenplay by Michael Jacoby and Rowland Leigh, from a story by Michael Jacoby based on the poem *The Charge of the Light Brigade* by Alfred Lord Tennyson. The music score was by Max Steiner and the cinematography by Sol Polito.
48   20 June 1909–14 October 1959.
49   This was the second of nine films that Errol Flynn and Olivia de Havilland Olivia Mary de Havilland (born 1 July 1916) starred together.
50   1 March 1910–29 July 1983.
51   Suristan is in fact an ancient Persian name for Syria.
52   The 27th Lancers are fictional: A "27th Lancers" were not a part of the British Army until 1941.

Subsequently posted to the Crimea and aware that Surat Khan is inspecting the Russian position opposite the 27th Lancers, Geoffrey Vickers secretly replaces the written orders of his Commander with orders for the famous suicidal attack thus enabling the lancers to avenge the Chukoti massacre. He writes a note explaining his actions and forces his brother Perry to deliver it, sparing him from almost certain death. The film comes to a climax at the Battle of Balaclava, when the lancers charge into the valley, with text from Lord Tennyson's[53] poem *The Charge of the Light Brigade*, superimposed on the screen. Vickers finds and kills Surat Khan, at the cost of his own life but after receiving Vickers' note, the honourable Commander takes responsibility for the charge and burns the note to protect Vickers' good name.

Scenes were shot in California with the Sierra Nevada mountains used for the Khyber Pass and Director Michael Curtiz, who did not have an excellent command of English, shouting "Bring on the empty horses", meaning "rider less horses".[54] The battlefield set was lined with trip wires to fell the cavalry horses and dozens were killed during filming, forcing U.S. Congress to ensure the safety of animals in motion pictures and ban trip wires from films. Unlike the rest of Flynn's blockbuster films, because of the use of trip wires and the number of horses killed, it was never re-released by Warner Brothers.

At the other end of the spectrum comes the 1968 British version of the battle by the same name, *The Charge of the Light Brigade*.[55] It aimed to be brutally authentic, based in part on the research in Cecil Woodham-Smith's *The Reason Why* (1953).[56] The film was produced during the Vietnam War era and is a warning against the folly of war and military interventions in other lands. The central character is a relatively competent Captain Nolan (David Hemmings),[57] who is unusual in the hierarchy of his day for having acquired his commission through merited promotion as opposed to purchase. As such he looks on with contempt at many of his mostly aristocratic colleagues. Lord Cardigan (Trevor Howard)[58] treats the regiment as his personal

---

53 Alfred Tennyson, 1st Baron Tennyson, FRS (6 August 1809–6 October 1892) was Poet Laureate of Great Britain and Ireland during much of Queen Victoria's reign.

54 David Niven used this as the title of his book about the Golden Age of Hollywood.

55 Made by Woodfall Film Productions and distributed by United Artists, directed by Tony Richardson and produced by Neil Hartley. The screenplay was written by Charles Wood from a first draft (uncredited) by John Osborne.

56 There was a lawsuit when John Osborne refused to alter his script for being too close to Woodham-Smith's book. *The Reason Why* (1953) and the 1968 film based on Woodham-Smith's research, did serious harm to the Earl's posthumous reputation. Another critical assessment of his career is *The Homicidal Earl*, by Saul David. Conversely, Terry Brighton in *Hell Riders: The Truth about the Charge of the Light Brigade* (London: Penguin 2004) is critical of Cardigan as Brigade Commander but finds him in no way to blame for the Charge.

57 David Edward Leslie Hemmings (18 November 1941–3 December 2003).

58 Trevor Howard (born Trevor Wallace Howard-Smith; 29 September 1913–7 January 1988).

property and Nolan gets into a highly publicised feud with Cardigan over the 'black bottle' affair,[59] which for plot purposes, the film incorrectly portrays Nolan at the centre of. As Raglan's aide, he is glad to get away from England to escape the morally uneasy affair he has been having in England with Clarissa (Vanessa Redgrave),[60] the wife of his best friend William Morris.

Raglan, the Waterloo veteran Fitzroy Somerset who had risen to high rank since we last met him jumping the over heads of the 92nd Highlanders with the Duke of Wellington at Waterloo, is played by John Gielgud[61] as an amiable, vague-minded man who proves a poor commander. British and French forces win at the Alma, but Lord Raglan refuses to allow the cavalry to press the advantage, so concerned is he with keeping his cavalry commanders, Lord Cardigan and his equally unpleasant arch-rival Lord Lucan, from having to work with one another. As the war progresses Lord Cardigan retires nightly to the yacht he keeps on the coastline to hold formal dinners, at one of which he seduces Mrs. Duberly, a minor officer's adventurous wife also travelling with the British command, who wants to observe battle first-hand and to be near Lord Cardigan, with whom she is infatuated.[62]

Captain Nolan, increasingly exasperated with Raglan's ineptitude and dithering, reaches boiling point at Balaclava when the Russians capture a British redoubt and Raglan is slow to respond. Nolan insists that Raglan should take steps to recover the guns, who then issues badly worded orders, which Nolan delivers personally and gains permission to ride with the light brigade. To Raglan, from his high vantage point, the lay of the land is obvious but Cardigan, at his lower level, can only see the valley the cannons at the end of the valley of death. The ensuing charge scene, filmed in Turkey, is one of the best and most colourful ever committed to screen and captures the glory and horror in a most memorable few minutes of action.[63] The film received generally positive reviews but proved a box office flop and compares and contrasts with the heroic Errol Flynn fantasy which was a box office hit.

The exact numbers taking part in the charge remains controversial, but is put between 661 and 674.[64] Of these only 195 men[65] and horses were still fit for duty, the rest killed, horribly wounded or taken prisoner. It cost the lives of about 107,[66] although others may have died of wounds later on. The 17th Lancers were reduced to 37 troopers, and the 13th Light Dragoons could muster only two officers and eight

59   The officer actually concerned was Captain John Reynolds.
60   Vanessa Redgrave, CBE (born 30 January 1937).
61   Sir Arthur John Gielgud, OM, CH (14 April 1904–21 May 2000).
62   The film was later criticised because although she was in the Crimea, she did not have an affair with Cardigan and was portrayed as eager for carnage.
63   In the film all of the Light Brigade regiments wore cherry coloured breeches which, in reality only the 11th Hussars wore. The other four regiments wore dark blue breeches, with double yellow stripes; the 17th Lancers wore double white stripes.
64   David, *Victoria's Wars,* p. 231, puts the figure at 676.
65   David, *Victoria's Wars,* p. 234.
66   David, *Victoria's Wars,* p. 234. Also 187 wounded.

mounted men. Of their horses, around 400 were killed or had to be destroyed.[67] Fortunately, Ronald and Sir Briggs were not among that number.

The failure of the British and French to follow up on the Battle of Balaclava led directly to the much more bloody Battle of Inkerman[68] in November when the Russians attempted to raise the siege at Sevastopol. In the week following the battle the remnants of the Light Brigade had been posted inland to high ground surrounding Inkerman and Cardigan, who had spent most nights of the campaign aboard his luxury steam yacht *Dryad* in Balaclava harbour, found this move a great inconvenience. As winter set in, with the allied armies hemmed in by the Russian army, food, fodder, clothing and shelter were in short supply on the high ground despite being available at the coast. However, Cardigan did nothing and refused to release any men and horses to carry up stores in case of a surprise attack, despite the pleas of his officers. Cardigan had more horses than men to ride them, but for want of fodder many horses died.

On 5 December 1854, citing ill-health, Cardigan and Ronald set off for England where newspaper accounts of the gallant charge ensured him a rapturous welcome. The indestructible duo had become the icons of the war and in January an enthusiastic London crowd mobbed them. They were received at Windsor by Queen Victoria who noted how "modestly" he presented his story. However, in public he gave a highly exaggerated account of his part in the charge at a banquet held in his honour at the Mansion House in February, where he arrived on Ronald, wearing the uniform he had worn a Balaclava.[69] The cad in him now took over and in the same month, at a speech in his home town of Northampton, he went even further, describing how he had lived the "whole time in a common tent" and how, after the charge, he had rallied his troops and pursued the fleeing enemy artillerymen as far as the Tchernaya river. He was made Inspector-General of Cavalry and was invested as a knight in the Order of the Bath. Merchants sold pictures depicting his role in the charge and his own account was rushed into print. It was at this time that the "cardigan", a knitted waistcoat supposedly as worn by the earl on campaign, became fashionable.

In contrast, Lord Lucan, had been recalled in disgrace, largely because the commander-in-chief, Lord Raglan wished to displace blame from himself. In England, as "Lord Look-on",[70] little regard was given to his version of events[71] whilst

---

67   David, *Victoria's Wars*, p.234.

68   Cardigan missed the Battle of Inkerman, casually asking journalist William Russell "What are they doing, what was the firing for …?" as he rode up from the harbour at noon on the first day. The decisive stages of the battle were on the second day and again Cardigan was absent.

69   Adkin, *The Charge*, p.244.

70   An unfortunate pun on his name earned while held in reserve during the earlier Battle of Alma and much exploited by Cardigan

71   Lucan, later giving evidence recalled that Cardigan had been galloping back, only slowing to walk when he realised he was being watched. This hurried retreat was also noticed by officers and men of the second and third lines who were still advancing at the charge.

Cardigan enjoyed many months of adulation. However, doubts about his conduct emerged in July 1855 when officers who had taken command in the aftermath of the charge heard of Cardigan's reception in England and were anxious to put the record straight. The doubts grew until in the following year the official enquiries of Colonel Tulloch and the publication of Calthorpe's *Letters*, provided proof that Cardigan had not been telling the truth.

Military inefficiency saw far more troops killed by disease than enemy action and public dissatisfaction with the conduct of the war was growing, aggravated by reports of military fiascos and incompetence. Aberdeen lost a vote of no confidence in Parliament and resigned as prime minister on 30 January 1855 to be replaced by the veteran former Foreign Secretary Lord Palmerston[72] who wanted to expand the war, foment unrest inside the Russian Empire, and permanently reduce the Russian threat to Europe. In September 1855 Sevastopol fell after a year-long siege and the neutrals, Sweden and Prussia, aligned with the allies leaving Russia isolated and facing a bleak prospect if the war continued. They finally signed the Treaty of Paris on 30 March 1856, which ironically, left the Turks worse off than the Russians, and Britain and France hardly gained anything of value. The treaty returned the occupied territories to their original owners and the Tsar and the Sultan agreed not to establish any naval or military arsenal on the Black Sea coast, weakening Russia, and removing the naval threat to the Ottomans. The principalities of Moldavia and Wallachia became, in practice, independent but the Great Powers pledged to respect the independence and territorial integrity of the Ottoman Empire.[73]

The Crimean War was now symbolic of logistical and medical mismanagement and of tactical failures and public opinion was outraged. The newspapers demanded drastic reforms, and parliamentary investigations demonstrated the multiple failures of the Army, but the traditional aristocratic leadership of the Army pulled itself together, and blocked all serious reforms. As with more recent wars and conflicts, no one was ever punished for failure, although Florence Nightingale[74] achieved professionalization of modern nursing and the war eventually led to the abolition of the sale of commissions.

Cardigan remained in the army and applied his standards of dress and parade to the whole cavalry. He was made Colonel of the 5th Dragoon Guards in 1859, but was most pleased when, after his formal retirement in 1860, he became colonel of his favourite regiment, the 11th Hussars, which he had first commanded in 1836. After his retirement in 1866 he lived happily at Deene, enjoying horse-racing, hunting and

---

72   Henry John Temple, 3rd Viscount Palmerston KG GCB PC (20 October 1784–18 October 1865) served twice as Prime Minister.

73   The Treaty stood until France was defeated by Prussia in the Franco-Prussian War of 1870–1871 and abandoned its opposition to Russia.

74   Florence Nightingale, OM, RRC (12 May 1820–13 August 1910) was a celebrated English social reformer and statistician, and the founder of modern nursing.

shooting. Perhaps appropriately, he died from injuries caused by a fall from another of his horses on 28 March 1868, possibly following a stroke.

Ronald also returned safely to Deene Park where he outlived Cardigan. His last service to his master was to follow the coffin in his funeral cortege. However, the old horse, having endured ghastly sea journeys, life on the foreign front, the atrocity of battle, near starvation and probably deep terror, found the whole prospect of a funeral procession far too exhilarating and became boisterous. To avoid the solemn pageantry of the day being ruined by the over-excited horse, they administered laudanum, but the dose must have been overdone because no one could move the dozing charger. Eventually someone sounded a cavalry charge which stirred Ronald to duty, and he jumped to and set off as required.

Morgan, who put his survival down to Sir Briggs, also got back from the charge more or less unscathed, although Sir Briggs received a sabre cut to the ear and the forehead. Soon after Inkerman Godfrey Morgan became sick and returned to Constantinople but Sir Briggs remained in the Crimea with Morgan's brother Frederick, as his staff horse. In 1855, after Sebastopol fell, Sir Briggs won the military steeplechase at Sebastopol when he was ridden by Sir William Gordon of the 17th Lancers. Later in 1855 Sir Briggs returned to England and was ridden for two seasons in Leicestershire, before he came home to Tredegar House for the rest of his life. Sir Briggs died at the age of 28 in 1874 and Morgan was so grateful to have survived the Crimea that he had Sir Briggs buried in the Cedar Garden at Tredegar House. A monument still stands there today with an inscription that reads:

In Memory of Sir Briggs
Favourite charger. He carried his master the Hon. Godfrey Morgan, Captain
17th Lancers boldly and well at the Battle of Alma, in the first line of the Light
Cavalry Charge at Balaclava and the battle of Inkerman, 1854. He died at
Tredegar Park February 6th, 1874. Aged 28 years.

Morgan sold his commission in January 1855 but continued to serve in the Royal Gloucestershire Yeomanry until 1875, and as Honorary Colonel of the Royal Monmouth Engineer Militia from 1885. He was Member of Parliament for Breckonshire from 1858 until 1875 when he succeeded his father as 2nd Baron Tredegar and thus relinquished his seat. Made a Viscount in 1905, he become the first Freeman of Newport in 1909, and had a statue erected in his honour astride Sir Briggs in the same year. It is still there in Gorsedd Gardens, Cardiff, in the front of the City Hall. He died on 11 March 1913 aged 81.

Four years after Cardigan's death, on 28 June 1872, Ronald died. The Brudenell family honoured the valiant old horse by preserving his tail and his stuffed head at Deene Park. To this day, in the White Hall, his preserved eyes gaze upon the daily sightseers to the historic house. Another memento of this loyal and magnificent horse was made from one of Ronald's hooves which was placed on a bronze pillow, surmounted by a small statue of Lord Cardigan riding Ronald, an artefact which can still be seen at the King's Royal Hussars Museum, Peninsula Barracks, Winchester. There are also several magnificent paintings of the charge and its participants but the charge is most notably memorialised in the famous poem by Alfred Lord Tennyson, *The Charge of the Light Brigade*. It is no less than Ronald and Sir Briggs deserve:

> Cannon to right of them,
> Cannon to left of them,
> Cannon behind them
> Volleyed and thundered;
> Storm d with shot and shell,
> While horse and hero fell,
> They that had fought so well
> Came thro the jaws of Death
> Back from the mouth of Hell,
> All that was left of them,
> Left of six hundred
> When can their glory fade?
> O the wild charge they made!
> All the world wondered.
> Honour the charge they made,
> Honour the Light Brigade,
> Noble six hundred.

3

Tartar, Old Baldy, Dandy and Other Battlers: Equine Heroes of the American Civil War and the West

In early July 1857, Captain John W. Phelps,[1] commanding officer of Battery B, 4th Regiment of Artillery, at Fort Leavenworth, Kansas, was acquiring horses for his battery's planned expedition to Utah to put down the Mormon rebellion. Being part of the frontier Army was not an easy lot for horse or rider in the 1850s, and it was especially gruelling as an artillery horse. The cavalry or mounted rifles would have been preferable for the horse rather than being chosen to pull a field piece and limber and face exhausting labours in the mountains, along with the challenge of becoming conditioned to the roar of cannon fire. One of the horses acquired by the U.S. Army at Fort Leavenworth was a four-year-old named Tartar, who was branded on the flank with a "U.S" and assigned to Sergeant James Stewart.[2] Stewart emigrated to the United States to join the US Army as a private in 1851 and chose Tartar as his mount because, "There was something about the animal." This prophetic statement would be verified in the course of the Mormon campaign and in his subsequent military service in the American Civil War.

Members of The Church of Jesus Christ of Latter-day Saints, often called Mormon pioneers, began settling in what is now Utah in the summer of 1847 after a series of conflicts with neighbouring communities in Missouri and Illinois. Mormon leaders believed that the remoteness of Utah would secure their freedom to practice their religion within the political structure of the United States. However, when gold was discovered in California sparking the Gold Rush of 1849, thousands of migrants began moving west on trails that passed through Mormon territory, ending their short-lived isolation.

The Mormons primary concern was to be governed by men of their own choosing rather than Washington appointees, and, as part of the Compromise of 1850, the U.S.

1   13 November 1813– 2 February 1885.
2   Born in Edinburgh, 18 May 1826.

Congress created the Utah Territory and selected Brigham Young,[3] President of the Mormon Church, as the first governor of the Territory. Unfortunately, at this time, the Mormons supported polygamy, which the rest of American society abhorred, and during the Presidential Election of 1856 the newly formed Republican Party pledged "to prohibit in the territories those twin relics of barbarism: polygamy and slavery." Many east-coast politicians, including President James Buchanan[4], were alarmed by the semi-theocratic dominance of the Utah Territory, whilst newspaper articles sensationalised Mormon beliefs and gave exaggerated accounts of conflicts with frontier settlers. Consequently, the President chose federal officers for the territory without the approval of the inhabitants, and soon the relationship between "Gentile" (non-Mormon) federal appointees and the Mormon leaders deteriorated.

Many of the federal officers had severe difficulties adjusting to the Mormon-dominated territorial government and the unique culture, and a number of them, some claiming that they feared for their physical safety, left their Utah appointments for the east. The stories of these "Runaway Officials" convinced President Buchanan that the Mormons were nearing a state of rebellion against the United States, and so under massive popular and political pressure, he decided to take decisive action. After his inauguration on 4 March 1857, he appointed a new governor, Alfred Cumming[5], to replace Brigham Young, who only became aware of the change through press reports and received no official notification until Cumming arrived in the November. Buchanan also decided to send a force of US Army troops to build a post in Utah and to act in a policing role under the direction of new governor.

Although the Utah Expedition had begun to gather as early as May, the first soldiers did not leave Fort Leavenworth until July 1857 and among them were the 4th Artillery, including Stewart on Tartar. They started their 1,200-mile trek over South Pass of the Continental Divide to Salt Lake City, Utah as part of a force consisting of two regiments of infantry, Phelps's battery, a heavy artillery battery, and six companies of the 2nd Dragoons. The Mormons, fearful that the large U.S. military force had been sent to annihilate them, made preparations for defence.

Tartar's first taste of action came when Stewart took him on a buffalo hunt to supply meat for the battery. Herds were plentiful in the 1850s, and Tartar and Stewart were soon charging into the mass of buffalo, keen to test marksmanship and courage against the celebrated bison. In late September before reaching the Green River in what is now Wyoming, Tartar was taken sick with "malignant distemper". Since the expedition expected trouble from Brigham Young, Captain Phelps ordered that Tartar be left to fend for himself, while the expedition moved on. However, the men did not shoot him because there was a slim chance he might get well and perhaps join a herd of wild horses.

3   1 June 1801–29 August 1877.
4   23 April 1791–1 June 1868.
5   4 September 1802–9 October 1873.

Winter was very severe on the plains that year, with temperatures plunging to minus 45 degrees, and on one brutal night, the expedition lost 600 animals,[6] horses, mules and oxen to cold and starvation. The army struggled to reach Fort Bridger in Wyoming, still well over a 100-miles short of their Salt Lake City goal. When spring finally came, Brigadier General Albert Sidney Johnston,[7] commanding the expedition, was short of horses and offered a $30 bounty for every stray carrying a government brand that was returned to camp.[8] One morning that spring two Indians came in with a couple of horses, one of which Stewart recognized as Tartar. They had found him in the Autumn near Green River, nursed him back to health and used him to haul tent poles. Stewart took him over to the battery where Phelps returned Tartar to duty, remarking that the horse had fared better with the Indians than other animals had with the battery.

The Mormons blocked the army's entrance into the Salt Lake Valley, and hindered their supply lines but, whilst the confrontation between the Mormon militia and the U.S. Army involved some destruction of property and a few brief skirmishes in south-western Wyoming, no actual battles occurred. However, at the height of the tensions, on 11 September 1857, a wagon train of California-bound settlers, including unarmed men, women and children, were killed in remote south-western Utah by Mormon militiamen who blamed the attack on Native Americans. This event was later called the Mountain Meadows massacre and in October the "Aiken massacre" took place, when the Mormons murdered six Californians travelling through Utah.[9] In the end the Utah War lasted a year before negotiations resulted in a full pardon and the transfer of Utah's governorship to Alfred Cumming, with the peaceful entrance of the U.S. Army into Utah.

From 1858, Tartar and Battery B had a relatively easy time for a couple of years in garrison at Camp Floyd, half way between Salt Lake City and Provo. However, in 1860 the field cannon were left in camp and the Battery formed to do duty as a mounted infantry company, keeping open the mail, emigrant, and pony express routes from hostile Native Indian raids between Salt Lake City and Carson City. Tartar's average work during this assignment included 40 to 50 miles a day.[10]

With the start of the Civil War, in July 1861, Battery B, then under the command of Captain John Gibbon[11] with Stewart as First Sergeant, received orders to move east. After a march across the plains the battery, including Stewart and Tartar,

6   Hal Schindler, (9 May 1994) *The Salt Lake Tribune: Tartar the War Horse.* See <www.sltrib.com> (Accessed 19 December 2017).
7   2 February 1803–6 April 1862
8   Schindler, *Tartar the War Horse.*
9   Other incidents of violence have also been linked to the Utah War, including an Indian attack on the Mormon mission of Fort Limhi in eastern Oregon Territory.
10   Dr. Greg Bradsher, *The Tale of Tartar the War Horse* <http://blogs.archives.gov/TextMessage/2013/10/23/the-tale-of-tartar-the-war-horse/> (Accessed 14 Jul 14).
11   20 April 1827–6 February 1896.

reached Fort Leavenworth on 1 October, and remained there for three days before heading for Washington, D.C., first by riverboat on the Missouri River, and then by railroad. It camped on Capitol Hill in mid-October where Stewart was commissioned 2nd Lieutenant a month later. Gibbon was appointed chief of artillery for a division in the Army of the Potomac, while still continuing to command his own Battery B, which was assigned to the defence of Washington. They moved against Confederate forces for the first time at Orange Court House on 26 July and then engaged the enemy throughout the month of August,[12] culminating in the Second Battle of Bull Run on 29/30 August. During the battle, Tartar was struck by shell fragments that tore both his flanks and carried away his tail. Stewart thought he could no longer use Tartar, and turned him into a small field, but the faithful Tartar was no readier to give up than he had been on the western plains and as the battery moved out the next morning, he pressed against the farmyard fence and neighed loudly. His master, who was riding a remount, looked over his shoulder to wave a sad farewell, but the gallant Tartar was not going to be left behind. He backed off, jumped the fence easily, and trotted after the battery. Tartar, it seemed, liked the Army life and Stewart rode him again as soon as the horse's wounds had healed.

When the Armies of the Potomac and of Virginia were combined under General George Brinton McClellan[13] in September 1862, Battery B were assigned to I Corps under Major General Joseph Hooker.[14] Both McClellan and Hooker rode famous and rather grand horses called *Daniel Webster*[15] and *Lookout*[16] respectively. Much less grand in appearance than *Lookout* and *Daniel Webster, Tartar* still had much hard soldiering to do. The battery fought gallantly at the Battle of South Mountain[17] at Turner's Gap, Maryland and in the Battle of Antietam on 17 September, during which *Daniel Webster* carried the commander safely throughout the day.[18] That day the battery was in the thick of the fight, with Stewart's section being the first Union guns deployed into the Cornfield, crucial in stopping the Confederate charge. The battery commanding officer was hit, along with 39 men and 33 horses who were killed or wounded.[19] Command of the battery fell to Lieutenant Stewart on Tartar, who would

---

12   Battle of Cedar Mountain 9 August, Rappahannock Station 21-23 August, Sulphur Springs 25-26 August and Gainesville 28 August.

13   3 December 1826–29 October 1885.

14   13 November 1814–31 October 1879.

15   Dark bay, 17 hands, pure bred, nicknamed that "Devil Dan" by the general's staff because of his speed and endurance which made him very hard to keep pace with.

16   Hooker rode this 17-hands, rich chestnut horse, in his campaigns where the grandeur of Lookout's height, long slender legs and equally long stride, earned this courageous warhorse a reputation as one of the finest chargers in the army.

17   14 September 1862.

18   After McClellan retired to private life, Dan became the family horse at Orange, N.J., where he died at the age of 23. McClellan said, "No soldier ever had a better horse than I had in Daniel Webster".

19   Bradsher, *The Tale of Tartar*.

command the battery for the remainder of the Civil War. Moreover, at Antietam that day was another "hard" horse who, like Tartar, was born and raised on the western frontier. After the first battle of Bull Run a bright bay horse with white face and feet stood alone and wounded, struck in the nose by a piece of an artillery shell, his rider seriously injured and hospitalised. The horse's name was Baldy and at the start of the Civil War was owned by Major General David Hunter.[20] Baldy was taken to recover from the wounds it received that day and soon after, in September 1861, he was purchased from the government by Major General George Gordon Meade[21] for $150. Named Baldy because of his white face, Old Baldy[22], as he was later to be called, was to be ridden by Meade in nine major battles and suffer many major wounds.

Despite Baldy's unusual, uncomfortable pace, Meade became devoted to him and rode him in all his battles through 1862 and the spring of 1863. Like Tartar, Old Baldy was wounded in the right hind leg at the Second Battle of Bull Run.[23] A few days later, Meade received command of the 3rd Division, I Corps, and distinguished himself during the Battle of South Mountain.[24] In the Battle of Antietam[25], Meade replaced the wounded Hooker in command of I Corps and performed well, but was wounded in the thigh whilst Baldy was wounded through the neck and left for dead on the field. Remarkably, in the next Federal advance, Baldy was discovered quietly grazing on that battleground, although he now sported a deep wound in his neck. Again, Baldy was warmly cared for and was soon fit for duty.

Famous horses of the war were not confined to the Union side and *Traveller*[26] was General Robert E. Lee's[27] celebrated dappled iron grey, Morgan cross Thoroughbred gelding. Standing 16 hands, *Traveller* was the son of *Grey Eagle*, a prominent thoroughbred four-mile racehorse, who sired both Saddlebreds and racehorses. Lee had inherited a love of horses from his father, "Light Horse Harry" Lee, who was known for his skilled horsemanship, and like many Southern gentlemen, Robert E. Lee started riding at a very young age. When Lee first saw *Traveller* in 1857, he took quite a fancy to him and,[28] after trying the 5-year-old in the spring of 1862, he finally bought him for $200. He renamed him *Traveller*[29] because he was such a fast walker and could easily carry Lee's weight at five or six miles an hour. Both Confederate and

20   21 July 1802–2 February 1886.
21   31 December 1815–6 November 1872.
22   ca. 1852–16 December 1882.
23   28–30 August, 1862.
24   14 September 1862.
25   17 September 1862.
26   1857-1871.
27   19 January 1807–12 October 1870.
28   Traveller was born and raised in the mountains near Blue Sulphur Springs in Greenbrier County. His dam, Flora, was a gaited Kentucky mare, and he was muscular, with a deep chest and short back, strong haunches and legs, small head, quick eyes, broad forehead, and small feet.
29   He was originally named *Greenbrier*.

Union soldiers knew the sight of the commander, astride the grey, his black points contrasting against his light colour, and long mane and flowing tail. The stoic steed withstood the hardships of the campaigns and would go on to carry Lee throughout the war.

In mid-November Major General Ambrose Burnside's[30] plan was to cross the Rappahannock River and race to the Confederate capital of Richmond before Lee's Army of Northern Virginia could stop him. Bureaucratic delays prevented Burnside from receiving the necessary pontoon bridges in time and Lee moved his army to block the crossings. When, finally, able to build bridges and cross under fire, the Battle of Fredericksburg[31] ensued which opened with street fighting on 11 December before Union troops could assault the Confederate defensive positions. The Union army's futile frontal attacks against the entrenched defences of the great Southern leader, Lieutenant General Stonewall Jackson[32] on the heights behind Fredericksburg is remembered as one of the most one-sided battles of the war, with Union casualties more than twice as heavy as those suffered by the Confederates. Baldy and Meade also charged at Fredericksburg where his division made the only breakthrough of the Confederate lines, spearheading through a gap in Jackson's corps at the southern end of the battlefield. For this action, Meade was promoted to major general, but his attack was not reinforced, resulting in the loss of much of his division.

On 15 December Burnside withdrew his army, ending another failed Union campaign in the Eastern Theatre. Tartar and the battery were part of the First Corps' 1st Division, and during the battle Tartar was wounded again. Thereafter, not surprisingly, it was difficult to get the fearless horse to stand under musket and rifle fire, having developed an understandably healthy aversion to explosions and fast-flying metal.

On 9 April 1863 President Abraham Lincoln[33] reviewed I Corps of the Army of the Potomac on a plain two miles back from the Rappahannock River, directly opposite Fredericksburg. As the battery passed Lincoln noticed the tailless Tartar and after the review he sent for the artillery officer and his mount. Stewart rode up on Tartar, and saluted whilst Lincoln, scanning Tartar's hindquarters, grinned and said to the general officers about him: "This reminds me of a tale," which he proceeded to relate to their great amusement. Unfortunately, Stewart was not in ear shot because his attention was distracted by Lincoln's 9-year-old son Tad, who, mounted on a pony, followed Stewart and insisted on trading horses. Impressed by Tartar, he begged Stewart to trade mounts, and was willing to give up any horse other than his own pony, based on his father's Presidential powers. "I had a hard time." Stewart later recalled, "to get away from the little fellow."[34]

30   23 May 1824–13 September 1881.
31   11-15 December 1862.
32   21 January 1824–10 May 1863.
33   12 February 1809–15 April 1865.
34   Bradsher *The Tale of Tartar*.

Less than three weeks later, as April turned to May, Stewart and Tartar were back at war. Battery B was engaged at Fitzhugh's Crossing,[35] Pollock's Mill Crossing,[36] and at the Battle of Chancellorsville,[37] where Meade led V Corps astride Old Baldy. The next month General Hooker, resigned from command of the Army of the Potomac and in the early morning hours of 28 June 1863, a messenger from Lincoln arrived to inform Meade, to his surprise,[38] of his appointment as Hooker's replacement. Lee's Army was invading Pennsylvania and Tartar and the battery now moved north toward Maryland to counter Lee who was moving his army up the Shenandoah Valley. Only three days after taking command, Meade confronted Lee at Gettysburg from 1 July 1863 to 3 July 1863, the battle that is considered the turning point of the war. Stewart was still riding Tartar on the road to Gettysburg and the valiant Tartar would have carried his master in the battle, but was lamed by a nail run into a fore hoof and had to stay in the horse lines.

The battle began almost by accident, as the result of a chance engagement between Confederate infantry and Union cavalry in Gettysburg on the first day. By the end of that first day, two Union infantry corps had almost been destroyed, but had taken up positions on favourable ground. Meade rushed the remainder of his army to Gettysburg and skilfully deployed his forces for a defensive battle.[39] Tartar, Stewart and Battery B went into heavy action on the afternoon of the first day, barely escaping capture, before finally falling back to Cemetery Hill. The next day it was hard at work under a very heavy fire, and, staying in position, had a similar experience on the final day. Stewart and another officer were wounded, along with 32 men and 32 horses killed,[40] wounded and missing. Throughout the battle, Meade reacted swiftly to fierce assaults on his line's left, right, and centre, culminating in Lee's disastrous assault on the centre, known as Pickett's Charge.

For two days Baldy was present at Gettysburg where, on the second day of the battle, he received his most severe wound from a bullet that passed through Meade's right trouser leg, lodged between the ribs and entered his stomach. He staggered and refused to move forward, defying all of Meade's directions. This was the first time he had refused to go forward under fire and, mercifully, Meade realised his combat days were through. Baldy was sent to the rear for recuperation where, because of Meade's great affection for the horse, he stayed until the following spring. In 1864,

35   26 April 1863.
36   from 29 April- 2 May 2.
37   4-6 May.
38   He had not actively sought command and was not the president's first choice. John F. Reynolds, one of four major generals who outranked Meade in the Army of the Potomac, had earlier turned down the president's suggestion that he take over.
39   In the film *Gettysburg*, an adaptation of Michael Shaara's novel *The Killer Angels*, Meade is portrayed by Richard Anderson. A monument to Meade by sculptor Henry Kirke Bush-Brown, on the Gettysburg Battlefield, located close to the point where Pickett's Charge was repulsed.
40   Bradsher *The Tale of Tartar*.

having returned to duty for the Overland Campaign[41] and the Siege of Petersburg,[42] Baldy was struck in the ribs by a shell at the Weldon Railroad[43] and Meade decided that Old Baldy should be retired. He was sent north to Philadelphia and then to the farm of Meade's staff quartermaster, Captain Sam Ringwalt, in Downingtown, Pennsylvania.[44]

After the Confederate defeat at Gettysburg, Stewart tried to ride Tartar in pursuit of Lee's Army, but the horse was still too lame and could not keep up the pace. Once more, for a third time, Stewart was forced to leave Tartar, on this occasion with a Pennsylvania farmer, along with a note explaining what command he belonged to. The battery followed the Confederate retreat towards Virginia and, in August one of Stewart's friends informed him that he had seen a tailless horse tied up with some cavalry mounts. Stewart went over, found and re-claimed his old friend and henceforward Stewart and Tartar would remain together until the end of the war and beyond.

The battery next saw action at Haymarket on 19 October and at Mine Run on 30 November. After that it was a relatively relaxing winter for Tartar until, in order to distract attention from a planned raid up the Peninsula on Richmond, the Union army, with Battery B, forced several crossings of the Rapidan River on 6 and 7 February 1864. The battery and Tartar participated in General Grant's offensive against the Confederate Army of Northern Virginia, fighting at the Battle of the Wilderness from 5-7 May and at Spotsylvania Court House on 12 May, and it was at this battle that Isaac Vandicar, who served as Stewart's orderly, and as such had taken care of Tartar, was mortally wounded. Some of his battery mates started to carry him away from the field in a blanket when he said, "I want to see the Old Man!" They called Stewart, who came to him and said, "Van, my poor boy, what can I do for you?" "Nothing, Captain," replied Ike, "I know I must die, but I wanted to say good-by to you, and I want you to see that 'Old Tartar' has good care after I am gone!" Vandicar would die that day. Stewart was honoured by brevet promotion to Captain on 1 August, 1864 for gallant and meritorious service in the battle and during the campaign before Richmond. The battery would see action at Po River on 20 May, North Anna River three days later, at Totopotomy Creek on 25 May, Bethesda Church,[45] White House on 15 June and at the battle before Petersburg on 18 June. Stewart was brevetted a Major on 18 August 1864 for gallant and meritorious service. After a peaceful winter, Battery B and Tartar were back in action at Lewis Farm, near Gravelly Run,[46] at Quaker Road on 30 March, at White Oak Road the following day, and at the Battle of Five Forks on 1 April. Union victory at Five Forks cut off Lee's lines of support, forcing him to

41   4 May-24 June 1864.
42   9 June-25 March 1865.
43   18-21 August 1864.
44   He was later relocated to the Meadow Bank Farm, owned by a friend of the Meade family, where he remained for several years.
45   1-4 June.
46   29 March 1865.

abandon his entrenchments around Petersburg and he retreated to Appomattox where on 9 April, finding himself surrounded, he surrendered his army.

When Lee rode to Appomattox Court House to surrender, he was astride *Traveller*. After the war Lee retired to Washington as president of Lee University and the veteran warhorse remained with him. In 1870, Lee died and *Traveller*, marching behind the hearse, escorted Lee to his last resting place. Two years later in 1872, turned out to pasture for grazing, Traveller stepped on a nail, succumbed to lockjaw (tetanus) and died. Traveller's bones were eventually returned to Washington and Lee University where they were put on display but eventually deteriorated. On 8 May 1971 after more than 60 years on exhibit, and a century after his death, *Traveller*'s remains were interred for the last time, encased in concrete, outside the Lee Chapel close to the Lee family crypt. The stable door to Traveller's stall at the College is traditionally left open to allow his spirit to wander at will.

In addition to Lee on *Traveller* many of our heroic horses were present at Appomattox where they waited outside while Lee and Grant brought the Civil War to a close.[47] At an early age, Grant emotionally bonded to horses, became an excellent horseman, and owned many horses in his lifetime. Grant's favourite horse called Cincinnati stood at 17 hands and was handsome and powerful. He was the son of Lexington, the fastest four-mile thoroughbred in the United States and the most successful sire during the second half of the 19th century. Cincinnati was also the grandson of the great Boston, who sired Lexington, and a half-brother to Kentucky. Cincinnati remained Grant's battle charger from the siege of Vicksburg until the end of the war and he rode *Cincinnati at Appomattox*.

After the surrender, Meade hurried to meet his faithful, and now fully recovered charger, *Old Baldy*. He was moderately active in retirement and Meade was able to ride him in several memorial parades. For many years, the horse and the general were inseparable companions, and when Meade died in November 1872, the bullet-scarred warhorse followed the hearse of his master. Baldy lived another 10 years but was euthanized on 16 December 1882, at the age of 30, when he became too feeble to stand. To honour this courageous steed, on Christmas Day of that year, two Union Army veterans[48] disinterred Baldy's remains and decapitated him, sending the head to a taxidermist. Baldy's stuffed head was mounted on a plaque in a glass case and displayed by the Grand Army of the Republic Civil War Museum and Library in Philadelphia where it can still be seen today.

Battery B and Tartar were also at Appomattox and perhaps Tartar might have seen General Grant's horse, *Cincinnati*, or Lee's *Traveller*, both famous horses but perhaps neither of them "hard" in the way that Tartar and Old Baldy were "hard". The battery

---

47   Grant went on to become the 18th President of the United States from 1869 to 1877. Cincinnati lived to enter the White House stables when Grant assumed the presidency in 1869. Cincinnati died at Admiral Ammen's Maryland farmstead in 1878.

48   Albert C. Johnston and H.W.B. Harvey

and Tartar moved to Washington, D.C. in May and took part in the Grand Review of the Army on 23 May. By the fall of 1865 most of the batteries of the 4th Artillery Regiment had been dismounted and the regiment was performing garrison duty. At some point in 1866 Battery B was sent to Fort Leavenworth. Stewart continued in Regular Army service, and was appointed Captain, 18th U.S. Infantry Regiment on 28 July 1866, leaving Tartar with the battery. Stewart would serve with the 18th Infantry Regiment until he retired on 20 March 1879. Tartar probably did not follow Battery B into the field in 1867 when it was engaged in a campaign against the Cheyenne Indians but ended his service at Fort Leavenworth where his career in the Army had begun in 1857. Tartar, who had earned his place in the Army with the Utah Expedition, and whose record showed service at Camp Floyd, Indian-fighting on the Overland Trail to Carson City and many major engagements of the Civil War, was wounded on three occasions and now became one of the most celebrated horses in the military. But as Stewart went off to war again, another horse was soon to prove himself "hard".

The Indians on the Great Plains had been generally peaceful during the Civil War until the discovery of gold in 1863 around Bannack, Montana encouraged white settlers to develop the Bozeman Trail[49] from Fort Laramie north east of the Bighorn Mountains to the Yellowstone, then westward over what is now Bozeman Pass. The trail passed through the Powder River hunting grounds of the Lakota Sioux, with its numerous rivers, including the Bighorn, Rosebud, Tongue and Powder, which flow north eastward from the Bighorn Mountains to the Yellowstone. This region was the last unspoiled hunting ground of the Northern Cheyenne and Arapaho and several of the seven bands of the Lakota.

In the summer of 1865, the Government sent over 2,000 soldiers on a march to prepare the way for the new road. What is now known as the Powder River Expedition moved into the Powder River country and destroyed an Arapaho village at the Battle of the Tongue River,[50] but harassed by the Sioux under Red Cloud, they withdrew and Indian resistance to white emigrants travelling the Bozeman Trail became more determined than ever. After the expedition, the U.S. tried to negotiate safe passage through Indian territory with some of the Lakota, Cheyenne, and Arapaho leaders, providing money in exchange for withdrawal from the overland routes. However, the signatories to these treaties were "Laramie loafers" who lived near Fort Laramie off Government handouts. Red Cloud had not signed and on 12 March 1866, he and his followers rode into Fort Laramie and committed to remain peacefully at the Fort until such time as the U.S.'s chief negotiator, E. B. Taylor, arrived.

49   Named after John Bozeman.
50   29 August 1865.

The negotiations began on 13 June 1866, but almost immediately Colonel Henry B. Carrington[51] commanding two battalions[52] of the 18th Infantry arrived at Laramie with construction supplies. He had orders to establish forts in the Powder River country using the 2nd Battalion of the 18th Infantry, chosen because it contained 220 veterans of the American Civil War. Red Cloud refused to acknowledge Carrington, accusing the U.S. of bad faith in the negotiations, and he departed Fort Laramie making clear that he would fight. Negotiations continued with the remaining Indian leaders and on 29 June, Taylor reported to Washington that a treaty had been concluded and that only about 300 warriors, led by Red Cloud, objected.

Carrington left Fort Laramie for the Powder River Country on 17 June 1866. Five hundred of Carrington's men were new recruits, and most were infantry, rather than cavalry. He also had scant ammunition and his men were armed with muzzle-loading Springfield rifles from the Civil War rather than new, faster-firing Spencer carbines and breech loading rifles. Carrington's opponents, the nomadic hunting societies of the Lakota Sioux, Northern Cheyenne, and Arapaho, had advantages in mobility, horsemanship, knowledge of the country, guerrilla hit-and-run tactics. Estimates for the number of Red Cloud's warriors vary, but it is unlikely that he could put even that many more than 1,000 men in the field at any given time since warriors had to spend much of summer and fall each year hunting buffalo and other game to feed their families. In the late winter and spring, they were limited in mobility until the grass turned green and their horses recovered from the severe winters of the northern Great Plains.

The Indians had few guns and little ammunition and their basic weapon was the bow and arrow. Designed for short-distance hunting from horseback, the short, stout Indian bow was deadly at close range, but had less than one-half the range of the English longbow which was effective to 200 yards. So Indian warriors could do little damage at ranges of more than 100 yards, whilst, in contrast, the foot soldier's issue Springfield Model 1861 muskets had an effective range of 300 yards or more, but with a much lower rate of fire.

Carrington's objective was to protect emigrants travelling the Bozeman Trail by establishing three forts along the trail. Carrington reached Fort Reno on 28 June 1866 and left two companies (about 100 men) there and proceeded north, on 14 July, to establish his headquarters at Fort Phil Kearny on Piney Creek, near present-day Buffalo, Wyoming. From there two companies of the 18th advanced 90 miles to the northwest, where on 13 August, they founded a third post, Fort C. F. Smith on the Bighorn River. Given the early and severe winters of the high plains, the middle of August was very late in the year to begin constructing forts, but Carrington was an engineer and used his manpower resources building fine, mathematically precise fortifications. Given the severity of the Wyoming winters, this strategy was not unreasonable, but many of his junior officers, anxious for battle, were infuriated. On 16 July two

---

51   2 March 1824–26 October 1912.
52   Approximately 1,300 men.

white civilians were killed and the campaign against the forts along the Trail began the next day. Red Cloud's warriors infiltrated the picket lines near the fort and stampeded over 100 horses and mules. The soldiers pursued the Indians in an unsuccessful running 15-mile fight, suffering two men killed and three wounded. Returning to the fort they found the bodies of six civilian traders killed by the Indians. Wagon trains were also attacked and nearly all civilian traffic on the Bozeman Trail ceased. Carrington could only be re-supplied with food and ammunition by heavily guarded wagon trains, and the Indians repeatedly attacked the wagon trains that sallied out of Fort Kearny to cut construction timber in a forest six miles away. Fifteen Indian attacks near Fort Kearny between 16 July and 27 September resulted in the deaths of six soldiers and 28 civilians and the loss of several 100 horses, mules, and cattle.

Carrington was under increased pressure from several of his junior officers to take the offensive and this pressure mounted when, on 3 November 1866, a cavalry company numbering 63 men, commanded by Lieutenant Horatio S. Bingham, arrived to reinforce the fort. With him were Infantry Captains Fetterman and James W. Powell, assigned from Fort Laranie, the headquarters garrison of Tartar's regiment, the 18th Infantry. Unlike Carrington, Fetterman had extensive combat experience during the Civil War, but lacked experience of fighting American Indians. Nevertheless, he was immediately critical of Carrington's defensive posture and contemptuous of the foe. He is reputed to have boasted, "Give me 80 men and I can ride through the whole Sioux nation."

On 25 November 1866, Carrington was ordered by his superior, General Philip St. George Cooke[53] at Fort Laramie to take the offensive. His first opportunity to strike back at the Indians came on 6 December when a wood train came under attack four miles west of the fort. Carrington told Fetterman to proceed west with a company of cavalry and a squad of mounted infantry to relieve the wood train. Worried about his officers' tendency to blindly follow Indian decoy parties, Carrington circled north with a mounted squad to attempt to cut off the Indian's line of retreat. During the movement, Lieutenant George W. Grummond of the 18th, also a vocal critic of Carrington, leading the cavalry, and 2nd Lieutenant Horace S. Bingham, commanding Company C, 2nd Cavalry became separated from Carrington, who found himself surrounded by 100 Indians. Fetterman arrived a few minutes later to rescue Carrington and the Indians retreated. Grummond eventually reached safety with seven Indians chasing him but Bingham's body and that of a sergeant were discovered several hours later and four soldiers were wounded, in the Indian's trap. Both Carrington and Fetterman were sobered by the experience.

Carrington intensified training and doubled the number of guards for the wood trains, keeping his remaining 50 serviceable horses saddled and ready to sally from dawn to dark. On 19 December, the Indians attacked another wood train and Carrington sent out his most cautious officer, Captain Powell, to relieve it with explicit

53   13 June 1809–20 March 1895.

orders not to pursue the Indians beyond Lodge Trail Ridge, two miles north of Fort Kearny. Powell returned safely, having accomplished his mission and Carrington reemphasized to his subordinates his policy of caution until reinforcements and additional horses and supplies arrived from Fort Laramie. Buoyed by success, Red Cloud now decided to attack Fort Kearny before winter snows forced them to break up their large village on the Tongue River. He decided to try the decoy trick again, this time with more than 1,000 warriors congregated and set a trap on the Bozeman trail north of Lodge Trail ridge, out of sight but only about four miles from the fort.[54]

On the clear and cold morning of 21 December 1866, at about 10:00 a.m., Carrington dispatched a wagon train to the nearest source of construction timber and firewood about five miles northwest. Almost 90 soldiers were detailed to guard it but less than an hour later, pickets signalled that it was under attack. Carrington ordered a relief party, composed of 49 infantrymen of the 18th Infantry and 27 mounted troopers of the 2nd Cavalry,[55] under the command of Fetterman. Carrington's other critic, Grummond, led the cavalry. The relief force totalled 81 officers and men. The infantry marched out first because the cavalry had to ready their mounts before they could follow and catch up. Carrington's orders were clear. "Under no circumstances" was the relief party to "pursue over the ridge, that is Lodge Trail Ridge". Within a few minutes of their departure, a Lakota decoy party including Crazy Horse appeared on Lodge Trail Ridge. Fetterman took the bait, especially since several of the warriors stood on their ponies and mooned their bare buttocks at the troopers. Fetterman and his company were joined by Grummond at the crossing of the creek, deployed in skirmish line and marched over the Ridge in pursuit. However, Fetterman took the Lodge Ridge Trail northward rather than the trail northwest toward the wagon train. Within a short time, the signal came that the wood train was no longer under attack. About 50 Indians appeared near Fort Kearny, but Carrington dispersed them with a few cannon shots. Those Indians and others then harassed Fetterman as he climbed Lodge Trail Ridge and disappeared out of sight of the fort.

Fetterman fired volleys at the small group of harassing, taunting Indians on his flanks but rather than turning east towards the wagon train, he advanced northward climbing Lodge Trail Ridge, drawn by the Indian decoys leading him onward. At the top of the ridge, in violation of his orders, he made the fateful decision to follow the Indian decoys north, advancing along a narrow ridge leading to a flat area along Peno Creek. His cavalry under Grummond took the lead, moving at a walk so the infantry could keep up but as the decoys led him onward, the cavalry left the infantry behind. About half a mile beyond the summit of Lodge Trail Ridge, the decoys gave a signal and the Cheyenne and Oglala concealed on either side of the trail sprang their trap.

---

54   The group of Indians chosen to decoy the soldiers included the young Oglala, called Crazy Horse (c. 1840–5 September 1877).

55   Stan, A Hoig, *Travel Guide to the Plains Indian Wars* (Albuquerque: University of New Mexico Press, 2006), p.72. The party consisted of three officers, 76 troopers and four civilians.

Fetterman's infantry had no escape and their 50 bodies were found facing outwards in a small circle, huddled together for defence among some large rocks. Grummond and most of the cavalry were a mile ahead of the infantry, possibly chasing the Indian decoys, and nearing the flat along Peno Creek. When attacked the cavalry retreated uphill and southward, toward Fetterman and Fort Kearny, but halted to fight in a flat area on the ridge 400 yards north of where the infantry lay dead. Here they too perished.[56]

About noon in the fort, Carrington and his men heard heavy firing to their north and immediately sent out a party under Captain Tenedor Ten Eyck, to investigate. Carrington mustered his remaining troops to defend the post as Ten Eyck advanced carefully up Lodge Trail Ridge, reaching the top, about 12:45 p.m. There they saw a very large force of Indians in the Peno Creek valley below. He sent back a message reporting that he could not see Fetterman's force, but the valley was filled with Indians taunting him to come down. Perhaps he should have marched straight to the sound of the battle but doing so would have resulted in the destruction of his force. When the Indians in the valley slowly dispersed Ten Eyck advanced carefully and found the bodies of Fetterman and all of his men scalped, stripped naked and mutilated in the valley. Eyes were torn out and laid on rocks, noses and ears cut off, teeth chopped out, brains taken out and placed on rocks, hands and feet cut off, and private parts severed.[57] That afternoon, wagons were sent to bring the bodies back to Fort Kearny but because of continuing threat, they could not recover those of the cavalry for two days.

Fetterman still had 119 soldiers inside the walls of Fort Kearny and now hunkered down, surrounded, outnumbered and under siege,[58] he prepared for an attack that evening, ordering all his men to stand watch, three to a porthole. All extra ammunition and explosives were deposited in a powder magazine ringed with wagons as a last redoubt. If the Indians attacked, the women and children at the fort were ordered to get into the magazine which Carrington would then blow to ensure that no whites remained alive to be captured by the Indians.

Carrington's only hope for reinforcements was to get word of the massacre to General Cooke at Fort Laramie, 236 miles to the south, requesting immediate reinforcements. The nearest telegraph was at Horseshoe Station, near present day Glendo, Wyoming 190 miles away on the North Platte and Carrington called for volunteers to carry the dispatch to that remote station in the sub-zero weather. A blizzard had

56   Estimates of Indian casualties vary; Historian Stephen Ambrose states 10 Lakota, 2 Cheyenne, and one Arapaho. Cheyenne-Anglo participant George Bent said 14 Indian warriors were killed. White Elk said two Cheyenne and 50 or 60 Lakota dead. Some estimates range up to 160 Indian dead and an equal number of wounded.
57   Mutilating the bodies of their dead foes was an Indian custom, ensuring, according to their religion, that their enemies were unable to enjoy the physical pleasures of an afterlife.
58   < http://wyominggravestones.org/view.php?id=34> *John "Portugee" (Famous) PHILIPS* (Accessed 10 January 2018).

swept down from the Arctic and temperatures had plummeted to minus 25 degrees with driving winds and blinding snow. A 34 year old civilian Portuguese immigrant, named John Phillips but known as Portugee Phillips or just Portugee, stepped forward to carry the news of the Fetterman Disaster through those 236 miles of frozen hostile Indian country.

John Phillips[59] had left the Azores at the age of 18 aboard a whaling vessel bound for California, where he planned to pan for gold. Subsequently he had followed the rumours of the next big gold strike to Oregon, and Idaho, reaching the Montana fields in 1865. In spring of 1866, he had joined a party of miners headed for the Big Horn Mountains, prospecting until the first snows of late summer, arriving at Fort Phil Kearny on 14 September where he worked as a water carrier for a civilian contractor. Phillips volunteered requesting the strongest and fastest horse on the post which was Colonel Carrington's own magnificent Kentucky Thoroughbred, Dandy. Sleek and black with three strikingly white socks, Dandy was stout and well-muscled and possessed extraordinary strength and stamina.[60] Carrington knew that if any horse could make the journey, it would be his battle-proven, faithful horse. So Carrington ordered Dandy to be saddled and Phillips was wrapped in a buffalo robe coat, scarf, gloves, head cover and boots and given a canvas bag of hardtack and a bag of grain for Dandy. They also gave him a Spencer repeating rifle, jammed into the scabbard of the McClellan saddle, and 100 rounds of ammunition which they strapped to his ankles in two separate cartridge belts, to help keep his feet firmly in the stirrups. With hundreds of Sioux warriors in the surrounding hills watching the trails leading from the fort, it was doubtful whether Phillips would be able to get through the first few miles without being slaughtered. However, Carrington was hopeful, and just before midnight on the 22 December 1866 Phillips mounted Dandy and prepared to leave. While the popular story is that he rode alone, Phillips was in fact accompanied by Daniel Dixon and they were both paid $300 for taking on a suicide mission.[61]

In the darkness Phillips and Dixon left the fort by the rear gate, staggering their departures to reduce the chance of being captured together. They managed to avoid the Sioux near the fort but Phillips was spotted at daybreak and narrowly escaped attack from a small band of warriors. However, the blizzard continued to whip the snow into drifts of five to 25 feet high and there was no trail to be followed. With all the country covered in snow, Phillips and Dixon met up and pushed on southward by dead reckoning, paralleling the Boozman Trail and riding at night through the blinding whirl, hiding in coulees. They took shelter from the driving wind during the day, rationing their meagre supply of hardtack and struggling to maintain their strength and core body temperature, shivering violently as their bodies tried in vain to

---

59   Manual Felipe Cardoso born, fourth of nine children, on 8 April 1832, in the town of Terra, on the island of Pico, in the Azores.

60   Gene Gade, *Ride of a Lifetime*. See <http://www.historynet.com/ride-of-a-lifetime.htm> (accessed 10 January 2018).

61   Gade, *Ride of a Lifetime*.

generate some heat. They knew their survival depended on willpower and the survival of Dandy and Dixon's horse, so they fed them generous portions of precious grain in their cupped hands while the steaming breath from the horses' nostrils warmed their numbed fingers.

The couriers reached Fort Reno in the early hours of 23 December 1866 where they received an additional message to carry to Fort Laramie from Lieutenant Colonel Henry Wessells. After some food and a brief rest, they set of again at midday, this time accompanied by another rider, Robert Bailey. It was still 130 miles to Horseshoe station where Phillips would be able to send the urgent telegram to Fort Laramie.[62] The cold, wind and fatigue was taking its toll on both horses and riders as the temperature remained at 25 below. Dandy's chest was caked with ice and bruised from constant battering against frozen snow drifts as he struggled to break through. Ice clung heavily from his muzzle and ears and sweat mixed with snow was packed and frozen from croup to withers. Driving on, Phillips, Dixon, and Robert Bailey arrived at the station by 10:00 a.m. on Christmas morning. In little more than three days, Dandy had covered 190 gruelling miles.[63] Phillips wired the telegram to the headquarters of the Department of the Platte in Omaha, Nebraska and to Washington, but he feared that the telegraph lines might be down, either from the weather or hostile Indians in the area. Therefore, he decided to ride on to Fort Laramie and deliver the message in person. At this point, exhausted from the physical effort and exposure, Dixon, Roberts and their horses declined to go on. Phillips and Dandy were made of sterner stuff. With nearly 50 miles to go and the Wyoming plains still in the grip of the raging blizzard, Phillips wearily climbed back in the saddle and once more rode into the blinding whiteout.

Phillips rode Dandy into Fort Laramie 13 hours later, at 11:00 p.m., where a full-dress ball was in progress. Dandy had carried Philips the 236-mile ride to Fort Laramie in four days.[64] With his hands, face, knees and feet frostbitten Phillips struggled to dismount and complete exhaustion reduced him to helplessness as the guards supported his shuffle into the ballroom to report the desperate situation at Fort Phil Kearny. The gaunt appearance of Phillips, cloaked in a buffalo overcoat, immediately silenced the festivities, and his message caused preparations for a rescue party.

The remarkable Dandy had given his all and the final 50 miles and sub-zero conditions had drained the life from the courageous steed. His feet and legs were stripped of hair from constant abrasion through the frozen snow, revealing blackened flesh, and the unbearable cold had ripped the tissue of his lungs to shreds as he gasped for breath with each gruelling step. His once strong heart was reduced to a weak and unsteady cadence before it finally gave way. As Phillips made his report, Dandy

62 Gade, *Ride of a Lifetime.*
63 Gade, *Ride of a Lifetime.*
64 The pay for the service was $300 apiece for Phillips and Dixon, which they received in January, 1867. In addition to receiving his pay, Phillips was given the best horse in Company F of the 2nd Cavalry.

crumpled to the frozen parade ground and died, the only casualty of the war that bitterly cold winter day, Christmas 1866. Nevertheless, the telegraph that Phillips had sent from Horseshoe Station had not arrive at Fort Laramie and so that final 50 miles of gruelling ride was not in vain and Dandy's sacrifice was not futile. However, due to the extreme weather conditions, the troops at Fort Laramie were not able to depart until 6 January 1867, 12 days after Dandy carried Portugee Phillips through the gates of the fort. Had Fort Phil Kearny been attacked, it would have long been over by the time the troops arrived. Fortunately for the Army, because of the brutally cold weather, the Sioux and Cheyenne gathered near Fort Phil Kearny did not attack and neither did they lay siege to the fort.

Dandy seems to have been forgotten except for the bronze plaque at Fort Laramie, dedicated in 1951, "In honour of the thoroughbred horse ridden by John 'Portugee' Phillips."[65] We can surmise that given the context of Phillips' message was of a fort under siege with women and children in peril, the priorities were the preparations of the troops for the rapid deployment to Fort Phil Kearny. As for Portugee, the surviving accounts tell that Phillips was taken to the post hospital and was there for two full weeks until he had recovered enough to leave. No doubt a detail was assembled to remove Dandy's frozen carcass from the snow-covered parade ground. With the raging blizzard and sub-zero temperatures no grave was dug in the iron-hard frozen ground and it's likely that a wagon team was harnessed and hitched to the stiff, lifeless form that was Dandy and dragged, unceremoniously, to the edge of the Platte and left as a feast for hungry prairie wolves. These actions were not intended to be disrespectful, but under the circumstances the simplest and most expeditious disposal was required. There is no confirmed burial site for Dandy, this extraordinary horse that accomplished the near impossible and died getting it done. Although of humble origins and not particularly successful in life,[66] Phillips was a national figure then and today he remains a symbol of courage and devotion to duty.

By 1 January 1867, Carrington's fears of an Indian attack on the fort had subsided as the snows were deep and the Indians were holed up for the winter. General Cooke, on receipt of Carrington's distress message, immediately ordered that he be relieved of command by Brigadier General Henry W. Wessells. Wessells arrived safely at Fort Kearny on 16 January 1867 with two companies of cavalry and four of infantry. Carrington left Fort Kearny on 23 January 1867 with his wife and the other women and children, including the pregnant wife of the deceased Grummond. They braved brutal temperatures during the journey to Fort Laramie and a half of his soldier escort suffered frostbite.

This battle was called the "Battle of the Hundred Slain" or the "Battle of the Hundred in the Hand" by the Indians and the "Fetterman Massacre" by the soldiers.

65   Gade, *Ride of a Lifetime.*
66   Phillips eventually moved to Cheyenne where he remained until his death 18 November 1883. He is buried in Lakeview Cemetery in Laramie County, Wyoming.

It was the Army's worst defeat on the Great Plains until the disaster on the Little Big Horn nearly ten years later. It soured the mood of the nation and newspaper stories blamed Carrington for the disaster, but both an Army court of inquiry and the Secretary of the Interior investigations absolved him of blame. General Ulysses S. Grant, commanding the U.S. Army, was not inclined to place all the blame only Carrington and he relieved Cooke on 9 January 1867. After a severe hip injury, Carrington resigned his commission in 1870 and spent the rest of his life defending his actions and condemning Fetterman's alleged disobedience in order to recover his tarnished reputation as a soldier.

After the Fetterman Fight, the Indians dispersed into smaller groups for the 1866-67 winter and conflict subsided. However, Wessells and his men at Fort Phil Kearny had a difficult time. Food was short, most of the horses and mules died from lack of forage, and scurvy was common among the soldiers. In April, Indian raids along the Oregon Trail in the North Platte River valley began. Most serious was the Indian threat to the construction of the First Transcontinental Railroad routed through southern Wyoming. Although army forces had been augmented along the Bozeman Trail and at Fort Laramie, resources were still insufficient to take the offensive against the Indians. The Army did not have the resources to defend both the transcontinental railroad and the Bozeman Trail from Indian attacks and increasingly sought a peaceful rather than a military solution to Red Cloud's War. The successful completion of the railroad took priority, and the military presence in the Powder River Country was both expensive and unproductive. Peace commissioners were sent to Fort Laramie in the spring of 1868, but Red Cloud refused to meet with them until the Army abandoned the Powder River forts, which they did in August 1868. The day after the soldiers left the forts and withdrew to Fort Laramie, the Indians burned them. The government finally gave up on defending the Bozeman Trail and in November that year Red Cloud signed a peace agreement with the U.S., the first time in history that the United States Government had negotiated a peace which conceded everything demanded by the enemy and which extracted nothing in return. The Fort Laramie Treaty created the Great Sioux Reservation, including the Black Hills and all of South Dakota west of the Missouri River. The treaty declared the Powder River country as "unceded Indian territory", as a reserve for the Indians who chose not to live on the new reservation, and as a hunting reserve for the Lakota, Cheyenne, and Arapaho. It also specified that no white person could settle on any portion of the Powder River country or pass through without the consent of the Indians "the Powder River country. That Indian sovereignty was to endure only eight years until the Great Sioux War of 1876 which was to bring fame to the next equine hero we will meet.

4

Comanche: The Survivor

As the burial party walked among the bloating, decaying bodies of their fallen US cavalrymen comrades on 27 June 1876, they bowed their heads in silent prayer before beginning their horrific duty. Suddenly the silence was broken by a faint whinny. They searched the rough terrain down by the river and found a horse struggling to get to its feet. Several of the men recognized the gelding as Comanche, the favorite mount of Captain Myles Keogh,[1] who had been with the men of I Company right up to the point when they were overwhelmed by the charge of Sioux warriors. A Mustang in the service of the US 7th Cavalry, Comanche was the sole survivor, man or beast, of the regiment who had confidently marched westward from Fort Abraham Lincoln in the Dakota Territory on 17 May in search of Sitting Bull and the Sioux nation. Now the horse was on its haunches, his coat matted with dried blood and soil, too weak to move any further having sustained at least seven wounds. Comanche was probably born around 1862, on what was once called the Great Horse Desert of Texas, a vast region that was home to 100s of 1,000s of Mustangs. The Mustang horse is the free-roaming horse of the American West that first descended from horses brought to the Americas by the Spanish. Small and compact with good bone and very hardy, Mustangs are often referred to as wild horses. However, the English word "mustang" comes from the Mexican Spanish word mestengo, derived from Spanish mesteño, meaning "stray livestock animal", and since they are descended from once-domesticated horses, they are probably better classified as feral horses. Comanche was captured in a wild horse roundup and he bore the markings of the early Spanish horses. He was a bay[2] gelding with the tell-tale black dorsal stripe down his back which today can still be seen on some wild horses in the high deserts of Nevada, Oregon, Wyoming, Utah, and Montana. He also had a small white star on his forehead and white patches in the saddle area. Weighing 925 to 950 pounds and standing 15 hands high,[3] he was an

---

1   25 March 1840-25 June 1876.
2   Although he is often and inexplicably referred to as dun or buckskin in many accounts.
3   DiMarco, *War Horse*, p.287.

odd-looking horse, with a big head and thick neck that were out of proportion for his body, and legs that seemed slightly too short.

An early breed of horse had once lived in the Americas but was extinct when Columbus arrived, so it is believed that the horse first returned to the American mainland with the Spanish conquistadors. Herman Cortez[4] bought 16 horses of Andalusian, Barb, and Arabian ancestry to Mexico in 1519 and others followed, such as Francisco Vásquez de Coronado,[5] who brought 250 horses of similar breeding to America in 1540. Many of these horses and their descendants escaped or were stolen, becoming the foundation stock of the American Mustang. By 1600, most Indians in New Mexico were mounted[6], the Navaho being the first to acquire horses. By 1700 the Comanche from Wyoming were raiding Navaho and Apache land, armed with guns from the French in search of horses and the period from 1750 to 1800 saw the birth of the American Indian horse culture turning the natives from sedentary hunter gatherers to nomadic horsemen. They quickly adopted the horse for transportation, battle, trade, and bison hunts. Starting in the colonial era and continuing with the westward expansion of the 1800s, horses belonging to explorers, traders and settlers that escaped joined the gene pool of Spanish-descended herds. Western ranchers also released their horses to locate forage for themselves in the winter and then recaptured them, as well as any additional Mustangs, in the spring. Some also attempted to "improve" wild herds by shooting the dominant stallions and replacing them with pedigreed stallions.

Tribes moved west in the face of the advancing whites, with the Sioux moving from Minnesota and trading their canoes for horses, bringing with them firearms that the eastern tribes had learned to use from the white settlers. Horses were acquired through trade and raiding southern tribes, by trading with the French or whites, and by breeding and the mounted warrior with bow or musket became the norm. There were also feral horse herds and it is estimated that 2,000,000 wild Mustangs were on the Great plains in 1806.[7] Among the most capable horse-breeding native tribes of North America were the Comanche, the Shoshoni, and the Nez Perce. The last in particular became master horse breeders, and developed one of the first distinctly American breeds,[8] the Appaloosa which we will hear a lot more about in the next chapter. Most other tribes did not practice extensive amounts of selective breeding, though they sought out and acquired desirable horses and quickly weeded out those with undesirable traits.

---

4   Hernán Cortés de Monroy y Pizarro, 1st Marquis of the Valley of Oaxaca; Born in 1485, died 2 December 1547.
5   Born in 1510, died 22 September 1554.
6   DiMarco, *War Horse*, p.275.
7   DiMarco, *War Horse*, p.276.
8   Alternatively, as we will see in the next chapter, recent DNA data suggests that the Appaloosa may have developed from indigenous stock which has great genetic similarity to extant wild herds in Kyrkaztan. If so the breed is pre-Columbian.

In the 19th century, European and American powers successfully expanded into the lands of indigenous peoples but west of the Mississippi, they experienced stiff resistance from the natives who had the tactical advantages of mobility of the horse and their superior horsemanship.[9] The Great Plains from the Missouri at Kansas City to the Rocky mountains and from Texas and New Mexico in the south to Montana and North Dakota in the north was a huge area of rolling grassland which made horses essential to the conduct of operations. With small ranges of hills and canyons, forests in the north and west, and desserts in the south west,[10] the Plains Indians lived in an area that was vast, largely unexplored by whites and blessed with horses and a nomadic lifestyle which enabled them to strike swiftly and avoid pursuit.[11]

In 1866 there were about 270,000 American Indians in the west living in about 125 distinct groups over an area of 120,000 square miles[12] and they were to fight a series of wars starting with Red Clouds War in Montana which we heard about in the last chapter. The 11 most powerful and hostile tribes numbered around 100,000 but they had no significant unity in the face of the US Army. Tribes were sub-divided into bands and, for example, the Sioux had seven different bands. Their weapons included the 6-7ft long lance and the bow from horseback and on foot. This was a single stave weapon although some were strengthened with bone and they were effective up to 100 yards with a good rate of fire and accuracy.[13] As the years went by, many carried quality firearms,[14] but the US had ammunition supply and artillery which the natives lacked and also had trains, telegraphs and steamship to aid the movement of troops and supplies. Importantly the US Army had political cohesion, military organisation and unlimited resources, including people, and they shifted units around to reduce the number of hostile tribes one by one.[15] Between 1866 and 1890, despite some defeats, the US Army were to gain control of the entire Western territories.[16]

The Indians were taught to ride from an early age but did not ride bareback as is often commonly supposed. Instead they used hand crafted saddles of wood and rawhide, to transfer weight from the horses' spin to either side of the back, or a simple pad saddle.[17] The warriors tended to use the pad saddle which had two hour glass shaped pieces of rawhide sown together and padded out with dear hair. There was additional padding for the seat to which stirrups were attached. These simple affairs could not match the US Army saddles which became prize possessions. Simple rope

9   DiMarco, *War Horse*, p.270.
10   DiMarco, *War Horse*, p.271.
11   DiMarco, *War Horse*, p.271.
12   DiMarco, *War Horse*, p.272.
13   DiMarco, *War Horse*, p.273.
14   At the battle of Little Big Horn, 29 different types were used and one warrior in every three had a rifle. DiMarco, *War Horse*, p.274.
15   DiMarco, *War Horse*, p.271.
16   DiMarco, *War Horse*, p.286.
17   DiMarco, *War Horse*, p.279.

bridles would be used with curb bits if they could get them, otherwise they made use of leather bridles and reins, whilst only the Apache used spurs, although all used a whip or quirt as an aid.[18]

Comanche was a born survivor, one of 1,000s of horses who grew up on the open plains before being captured and then sold to the army. It was probably in 1868 that he and an unknown number of horses were driven north, most likely following the Kickapoo Trace, a rutted and dusty by-way through the unfamiliar and rough terrain of Indian territory into Missouri. The trail ended at St. Louis where, just days after running free on the open range, the horses were funneled into crowded corrals, awaiting buyers from the army who purchased horses on the basis of health and stamina, rather than looks.[19] George Armstrong Custer's[20] 7th Cavalry unit had been stationed in Kansas to protect the Kansas-Pacific railroad which had begun in Fort Leavenworth in 1863.[21] The 7th had been formed in 1866 at Fort Riley, Kansas in order to patrol the Western plains against raiding native Americans and to protect the westward movement of pioneers. By that April of 1868 they had lost a number of horses so he sent his brother, First Lieutenant Tom W. Custer, to buy remounts. After looking them over in the corrals, he purchased 41, including the horse that would soon be named Comanche. On 3 April, 1868, Comanche was gelded and sold to the army for the average price of $90. A week later he and his herd mates were loaded onto railroad cars and shipped west to Fort Leavenworth, Kansas, where they arrived in mid-May and were branded with the letters US on the left shoulder, the regiment number on the left thigh and the letter C for cavalry.[22] Once again the horses were loaded onto a train, where they stood head to tail in crowded cars to be shipped the short distance to Hays City, near Ellis, Kansas where Custer and his troops were encamped.

The myths and legends surrounding Custer are part of the story the West and how that story is interpreted and re-interpreted reflects how America views itself. As such it remains highly contested. Whether he is a hero or villain, courageous, dashing and charismatic leader, or near psychopathic bully and deranged perpetrator of genocide against American natives, is a debate which still has relevance for Americans. Custer and the Little Big Horn story remains one which has the power to stimulate heated debate and continues to be the subject matter for cinema. The first movie about the battle, titled *Custer's Last Fight*, was released in 1912 and many followed including Robert Shaw[23] taking the lead in the 1967 film *Custer of the West* which is not a bad

18   DiMarco, *War Horse*, p.280.
19   DiMarco, *War Horse*, p.286.
20   5 December 1839–25 June 1876.
21   John Keegan, *War Paths: Travels of a Military Historian in North America* (London: Pimlico, 1995), p.260.
22   Sometimes the letter of the company to which the horse was assigned was added to the brand.
23   9 August 1927–28 August 1978.

romp, and *Little Big Man* in 1970 starring Dustin Hoffman,[24] which portrays Custer [25] as a manic and somewhat psychotic realizing to his horror that he and his command are "being wiped out." With the arrival of television there have been more attempts to tell the story with the 2007 the BBC one hour drama-documentary titled *Custer's Last Stand* being probably the historically most accurate. However, the all-time classic released in 1941 must be *They Died with Their Boots On,*[26] which gave a highly fiction-alized account of the battle with Custer portrayed by Errol Flynn. It tells the life of Custer, from the time he enters West Point, his wooing of Elizabeth "Libby" Bacon (Olivia de Havilland[27]) who becomes his loving wife, through the American Civil War, and finally to his heroic death at Little Big Horn. Classic, confident, un-self-conscious Hollywood of the golden era, Custer is portrayed as a fun-loving, dashing figure who chooses honour and glory over money and corruption, and is finally downed by a gunshot from Crazy Horse, having followed through on his promise to teach his men "to endure and die with their boots on." Three men were killed during the filming, one falling from a horse and breaking his neck and another stuntman having a heart attack. The third insisted on using a real sabre to lead a cavalry charge under artillery fire.[28] When an explosive charge sent him flying off his horse, he landed on his sword, impaling himself. Despite its historical inaccuracies, the film was one of the top-grossing films of the year, making $2.55 million for Warner Bros, the studio's second biggest hit in 1941.

Much as it may be pleasant to think of Custer as portrayed by Errol Flynn, in reality he was not a pleasant character. It is not necessary to be pleasant to be an effective military leader but Custer seemed to lack the redeeming moral quality of recognising that war is a means to an end rather than the end in itself. Great men find war repug-nant but Custer enjoyed "Glorious War" as young, gung-ho and uninjured men some-time do.[29] He had held the Brevet rank of Brigadier General in the Civil War, and never grew up, remaining the bad boy, cock-sure cadet of his West Point days where he passed out 34th out of 34.[30] Ostentatiously brave and always to be found at the front of a charge, he loved flamboyant uniforms and would sport velvet, braided jackets, sailor shirts, scarlet cravats and long black boots with gilt spurs. His long blond locks were suggestive of a narcissistic intention to draw attention to himself, a less than morally attractive trait. After the war he was Court Martialled for insubordination and made a habit of making allegations against officials. Looking at Custer's life and

24   Born 8 August 1937.
25   Played by Richard Mulligan 13 November 1932–26 September 2000.
26   Produced by Hal B. Robert and Fellows Wallis and directed by Raoul Walsh. Written by Æneas MacKenzie and Wally Kline,
27   It was the eighth and final film collaboration between Errol Flynn and Olivia de Havilland.
28   Actor Jack Budlong.
29   Keegan, *War Paths*, p.295.
30   Keegan, *War Paths*, p.285.

exploits in the 11 years between Appomattox and the Little Big Horn, one gets a sense of frustration, depression and decline, insufferable for a man of ego and past glories.[31]

The cavalry strength on the Western Plains throughout the period was always ten regiments of 500-600 men and therefore there were never more than 6,000 men policing the 2.5 million square miles of the plains against 1000,000 hostiles (including 20,000 warriors).[32] However, the Indians could never organise themselves as a unified force against their opponent. Typical of post-Civil War cavalry regiments, the Seventh was organized as a 12-company regiment, with four Companies to a Battalion. However, like other regiments, they were seldom stationed together but garrisoned small forts at single company strength or a battalion of three to four companies. The equipment was adapted from the US Civil War and throughout this period, the cavalryman was armed with Colt Single Action Army .45 calibre "Peacemaker" revolver, the single-shot Springfield carbine, calibre .45–55 and, from 1873, the accurate Spencer Repeating Carbine.[33] The cavalryman used one of the many variants of the McClellan saddle, including a newer lighter version in 1874, and although sabres were issued they were not carried on campaign. From 1866 the Army had up to 1,000 Indians employed as scouts to track hostiles, provide military intelligence, interrogate prisoners and provide an understanding of the Indian culture and the operating terrain.[34] One thing that was accurate from *They Died with Their Boots On* was that the Seventh Cavalry's band adopted the Irish air *Garryowen* as their favourite tune and thus gave the Seventh their nickname among the rest of the Army.

When Tom Custer returned with the remounts, Captain Myles Walter Keogh liked the look of Comanche and bought him for his personal mount. Keogh had been born in County Carlow, Ireland on 25 March 1840 and in 1860 had volunteered, along with over 1,000 of his countrymen, to rally to the defence of Pope Pius IX[35] against the Piedmontese, following a call to arms by the Catholic clergy in Ireland. Keogh was appointed second lieutenant in the Battalion of St. Patrick, within the Papal Army and was posted to Ancona, a central port city of Italy. When the Papal forces were defeated in September at the Battle of Castelfidardo.[36] and Ancona was surrounded, Keogh was forced to surrender and was imprisoned. After his release, Keogh went to Rome and was invited to wear the green uniform of the Company of St. Patrick as a member of the Vatican Guard. During his service, the Pope awarded him the Medaglia for gallantry[37] and also the Cross of the Order of St. Gregory.[38]

31   Keegan, *War Paths,* pp.292-299.
32   DiMarco, *War Horse,* p.281.
33   DiMarco, *War Horse,* p.282.
34   DiMarco, *War Horse,* p.282.
35   Pope Pius IX (13 May 1792–7 February 1878), born Giovanni Maria Mastai-Ferretti, reigned from 16 June 1846 to 1878.
36   18 September 1860.
37   The Pro Petri Sede Medal.
38   Ordine di San Gregorio.

However, Vatican Guard duties were dull and with civil war raging in America and the Union seeking experienced European officers, Keogh was soon itching to leave Rome. Thus in March 1862 he resigned his commission and boarded a steamer bound from Liverpool to New York, arriving on 2 April. He was given the rank of Captain and his performance caught the attention of George B. McClellan,[39] the commander of the Potomac Army, who appointed him to his personal staff during the Battle of Antietam[40] and then to General John Buford's staff,[41] notably at the enormous cavalry battle of Brandy Station on 9 June 1862.

On 30 June, Buford, with Keogh by his side, rode his white horse Grey Eagle[42] into the soon to be famous town of Gettysburg to find that they were facing a large force of rebels. Burford realised the importance of holding the high ground around the town and in so doing established the battle lines for one of the most iconic battle in American history. The bravery and tenacity of his dismounted men allowed time for the Union Army to gain possession of the all-important heights. Despite Lee's barrage of 140 cannons and Pickett's Charge on the third day of the battle, the Union army won a highly decisive victory and Myles Keogh received his first brevet promotion to the rank of Major for *"gallant and meritorious services"*.

In July 1864, Keogh was part of a risky raid behind Confederate lines to destroy railroads and industrial works, and to free prisoners held at Macon, Georgia and at Andersonville prison. The Union cavalry did destroy the railroads but the attack on Macon failed and on 31 July, 1864, Keogh and his comrades were surrounded and captured after his horse was shot out from under him. Keogh was held for 2½ months before being released through Union general William Tecumseh Sherman's efforts.[43] Although he held the brevet rank of Lieutenant Colonel in the union army, at the end of the war, like many others he dropped in rank to accept a commission as a Captain in the 7th Cavalry. On 28 July 1866 he was assigned to Fort Riley in Northeast Kansas to become the Captain of Company I under the command of Custer who was spoiling for a fight.

For the US cavalry, the tactical problem was finding and fixing the enemy across tremendous distances. The US Army had learned the concept of Total War in the Civil War and now applied it to the Plains Indians. Sherman realised that pursuing mobile Indians was playing to their strengths so instead he decided to hit the whole tribe and not just the warriors and to counteract Indian mobility they hit their static

39   3 December 1826–29 October 1885.
40   17 September 1862.
41   4 March 1826–16 December 1863.
42   Buford died in 1863, possibly from contracting typhoid. At his funeral, General Stoneman commanded the escort in a procession that included Grey Eagle. President Lincoln was among the mourners. <http://agreenhorse.blogspot.co.uk/2009/12/horses-of-military-war.html> (Accessed 4 January 2015).
43   8 February 1820–14 February 1891.

winter camps.[44] The temperature extremes ranged from arctic conditions to 100 degree Fahrenheit and soldiers often discarded their issued uniform for more effective items of civilian kit. However, their issued winter equipment was excellent with ankle length Buffalo coats, muskrat hats, face masks, fur mittens and boots and therefore they could undertake missions in the dead of winter.[45] The focus was on attacking their families and pony herds and them moving the families under guard to the reservations, thus removing the warriors support and mobility. They could attack a village via mounted charge or by dismounted skirmish line with every fourth man holding the horses. The Springfields and their discipline were usually enough to win the day. Employing these tactics at the Battle of the Washita on 17 November 1868, Custer attacked Chief Black Kettle's camp in Washita Valley killing the chief and an estimated 100 Cheyenne,[46] including women and children. However, the regiment sustained 21 losses, including 17 who died when they chased after the Cheyenne and were surrounded.[47] Custer did not go to their rescue which caused some ill-feeling in the regiment.

Although absent from the Washita battle, Custer's encounter of substance with hostile Indians prior to the Great Sioux War, Keogh did have sole responsibility for defending the Smoky Hill route against Indian raids from late 1866 to the summer of 1867. While the 7th were fighting the Comanche in Kansas, Keogh was fighting Indians almost every day. His as yet unnamed horse was wounded in the hindquarters by a Comanche arrow, but continued to carry him in the fight. As the story goes, Keogh named the horse "Comanche" to honour his bravery. During this period he showed himself to be a noble warhorse and quickly gained a reputation as a fearless and powerful steed. Comanche participated in frequent actions with the Regiment and sustained some 12 wounds as a result of these skirmishes, but always exhibited the same toughness and never gave in. In 1873 the 7th Cavalry moved its garrison post to Fort Abraham Lincoln, in the Dakota Territory. It was from here in 1874 that the regiment carried out their historic reconnaissance of the Black Hills. The expedition had been designed to demonstrate that rumours of gold in the black hills were a myth but instead led to the discovery of gold and started the subsequent rush that precipitated the Great Sioux War of 1876–77.[48]

In that summer of 1874, Keogh was on 7 months leave in Ireland, while Custer was leading the controversial expedition through the Black Hills and returned to Fort Abraham Lincoln in October to find tension between the natives of the Great Plains and the encroaching settlers was rising. Whilst many natives agreed to relocate to ever-shrinking reservations, others resisted, and in 1875, Sitting Bull created an alliance between the Lakota and the Cheyenne and a large number of "Agency Indians"

44   DiMarco, *War Horse,* p. 285.
45   DiMarco, *War Horse,* p.282.
46   Keegan, *War Paths,* p.278.
47   Keegan, *War Paths,* pp. 292-299.
48   Keegan, *War Paths,* p. 280.

who had slipped away from their reservations to join them. During a Sun Dance on 5 June 1876 on the Rosebud Creek in Montana, Sitting Bull had a vision of "soldiers falling into his camp like grasshoppers from the sky."

At the same time, a summer campaign to force the Lakota and Cheyenne back to their reservations was underway. In a three-pronged approach, Colonel John Gibbon's[49] column marched east from Fort Ellis in western Montana on 30 March 1876, to patrol the Yellowstone River whilst Brigadier General George Crook's[50] column moved north from Fort Fetterman in the Wyoming Territory on 29 May 1876, marching toward the Powder River area. The third column under Brigadier General Alfred Terry,[51] included 12 companies of the 7th Cavalry under Custer's immediate command, Companies C and G of the 17th U.S. Infantry, and the Gatling gun detachment of the 20th Infantry. They departed westward from Fort Abraham Lincoln in the Dakota Territory on 17 May 1876. All army elements were to converge on around 26 or 27 June 1876, attempting to engulf the hostiles.

The coordination and planning began to go wrong on 17 June 1876 when Crook's column was surprised at the Battle of the Rosebud. Despite holding the field at the end of the engagement, Crook was astonished by the large numbers of hostile natives, and decided to pull back, regroup and wait for reinforcements. Unaware of Crook's battle, Gibbon and Terry continued and joined forces in early June near the mouth of the Rosebud River. Terry and Gibbon's united forces then moved in a westerly direction toward the Bighorn and Little Bighorn rivers, the likely location of native encampments. On 22 June 1876, Terry ordered the 7th Cavalry, composed of 31 officers, including Captain Keogh riding his much loved Comanche, and a total of around 600 enlisted men, scouts and civilians to begin a reconnaissance and pursuit along the Rosebud,[52] with the prerogative to "depart" from orders upon seeing "suffi-cient reason." Custer had been offered some Gatling guns, but declined, believing they would slow his march. Each of the heavy, hand-cranked weapons could fire up to 350 rounds a minute, but they were known to jam frequently and had to be hauled by four horses with soldiers often having to drag them by hand over obstacles. His rapid march to the Little Big Horn averaged nearly 30 miles a day, so his assessment was accurate, even if in hindsight they would have come in handy when he finally caught up with Sitting Bull.

Many men of 7th Cavalry were veterans of the American Civil War, including most of the leading officers. A significant portion of the regiment had previously served four-and-a-half years at Fort Riley, Kansas, during which time they had fought one major engagement and numerous skirmishes. About 20 percent of the troopers had

---

49   20 April 1827–6 February 1896.
50   8 September 1830–21 March 1890.
51   10 November 1827–16 December 1890.
52   Nathaniel Philbrick, *The Last Stand: Custer, Sitting Bull and the Battle of the Little Big Horn* (London: Vintage Books, 2010), pp.314-316.

been enlisted in the prior seven months,[53] were only marginally trained, and had no combat or frontier experience. On entering the cavalry, recruits trained at Jefferson Barracks, Missouri where horsemanship was important but exceptional skill was not required. Workmanlike riders were produced but the emphasis was on horse care since it was obvious that when 100 miles from anywhere, a trooper's life depended on the health of his horse and they took pride in the health and stamina of their mounts.[54] A sizable number of these troopers were immigrants from Ireland, England and Germany and many were malnourished and in poor physical condition, despite being the best-equipped and supplied regiment in the army. All men were volunteers for a five years period[55] but they were far from a pristine force of highly professional, experienced fighting men and the desertion rate was high.

The US Army carefully studied march technique for travelling long distances without destroying their horses. They could average 25 miles a day for six days a week by following a well-planned regime. They rose at "reveille" and at the bugle call "stables" they groomed and fed their horses. "Breakfast" followed and on the call "General" the troopers packed their kit. This was followed by "Boots and Saddles" and on the command "mount" they were ready to move out in columns of four on the command "Forward".[56] They would walk for one hour and then halt for 10 to 15 minutes to adjust tack and check the horses over. Then they would only stop for five minutes every hour. At the second halt they would dismount and walk for the first 20 minutes rather than ride, then mount and trot for 20 minutes before walking the horses for the remainder of the hour, when they would dismount for another five minute rest. This routine of lead, trot and walk would be maintained for three hours with short canters and gallops to allow the horse to stretch. In the first hour they would cover four miles and for the next four hours they would cover 20 miles or more with the goal of 25 miles in less than six hours. In this way they could cover 150 miles a week or 600 a month.[57] They could push this out to 50 miles a day for three days in an emergency and in 1879 a squadron of the 5th Cavalry covered 170 miles in 65.5 hours to relieve a besieged garrison.[58] No horses were lost and they were fit for service when they arrived.

Custer had a reputation for pushing both men and horses hard and they had been riding for a week prior to the battle, covering 60 miles in the 33 hours leading up to the action. By the time of the Little Big Horn, Comanche was, at the age of 14 years with eight years' service, a veteran and used to the rigours of campaigning but many of the other horses were new and unaccustomed to such distances and they

53 139 of an enlisted roll of 718.
54 DiMarco, *War Horse*, p.288.
55 DiMarco, *War Horse*, p.282.
56 DiMarco, *War Horse,*.p.282.
57 DiMarco, *War Horse*, p.282.
58 DiMarco, *War Horse*, p.282.

entered the battle tired.[59] It is hardly surprising that on the day of the battle, at least four troopers dropped out because their horses were exhausted. On the evening of 24 June Custer's scouts arrived at view point known as the Crow's Nest, 14 miles east of the Little Bighorn River and at sunrise on 25 June 1876, reported they could see a massive pony herd and signs of the Native American village roughly 15 miles away. The Army assumed on the basis of information provided by the Indian Agents that no more than 800 hostile Lakota led by Sitting Bull were in the area. This would have been true had it not been for the "reservation Indians" who had joined Sitting Bull for the summer buffalo hunt. Thus, Custer unknowingly faced 1,000s of Indians. After the battle, Custer would be severely criticized for not having accepted reinforcements and for dividing his forces, but he, along with Terry and Gibbon, had worked off their available intelligence. Custer had wanted to take a day to scout the village before a surprise attack against the encampment, but he then received a report informing him that several hostiles had discovered the trail left by his troops. Assuming his presence had been given away, he knew the warriors in the village would soon be aware of his approach.[60] Therefore Custer, with inadequate reconnaissance but wanting to prevent any escape by the hostiles to the south, launched an immediate attack on the south end of the camp. On the morning of 25 June, Custer divided his 12 companies into three groups. Three companies were placed under the command of Major Marcus Reno[61] and three under Captain Frederick Benteen.[62] Five companies remained under Custer's immediate command,[63] including Keogh's. B Company had been assigned to escort the slower pack train carrying provisions and additional ammunition. They approached the village at noon and prepared to attack in full daylight.

After parting with Reno's command, from 2.5 miles away Custer could observe only women preparing for the day, and young boys taking 1,000s of horses out to graze south of the village. Custer's Crow scouts told him it was the largest native village they had ever seen but he thought most of the warriors were still asleep in their tepees. Contrary to modern ethics of combat, Custer's battalions intended to ride into the camp, secure non-combatants hostages and force the warriors to surrender before widespread resistance could develop.

The first group to attack was Major Reno's. After receiving orders from Custer to charge and "bring them to battle", Reno's force crossed the Little Bighorn at the mouth of what is today Reno Creek at around 3:00 p.m. Reno advanced rapidly across the open field towards the northwest, with all three 40 man companies charging

59   DiMarco, *War Horse*, p.288.
60   Unknown to Custer, the group of Native Americans seen on his trail were actually leaving the encampment on the Big Horn and did not alert the village.
61   Marcus Albert Reno (15 November 1834–30 March 1889) commanded A, G, and M companies.
62   Frederick William Benteen (24 August 1834–22 June 1898) commanded H, D, and K companies.
63   C, E, F, I, and L

together. His movements were masked by the thick trees that ran along the southern banks of the Little Bighorn river, but these trees also obscured his view of the village until his force had passed the bend on his right. Suddenly they were within arrow shot and for the first time realised the size of the encampment they were attacking. Reno stopped a few 100 yards short of the village and sent his Indian scouts forward on his exposed left flank whilst he ordered his troopers to dismount and deploy in a standard skirmish line, with every fourth trooper holding the horses for the troopers in firing position, thus reducing his firepower by a quarter. With five to ten yards separating each trooper, Reno's men fired into the village as mounted warriors began streaming out to meet the attack. With Reno's men anchored on their right by the impassable tree line, the Indians rode hard against the exposed left of Reno's line. After about 20 minutes of long-distance firing, Reno had taken only one casualty, but the odds against him had risen with the Indians massing in the open area shielded by a small hill to the left of Reno's line. From this position the Indians turned Reno's exposed flank, mounting an overwhelming attack against the left and rear of his line, and forcing a hasty withdrawal into the woods along the bend in the river. Here the Indians pinned Reno and his men down and set fire to the brush to try to drive the soldiers out of their position.

After giving orders to mount, dismount and mount again, Reno finally told his men, "All those who wish to make their escape follow me," and led a disorderly rout across the river toward the bluffs on the other side, disrupted all the way by Cheyenne attacks at close quarters. Reno's hasty retreat may have been precipitated by the death of his Arikara scout, Bloody Knife, who had been shot in the head as he sat on his horse next to Reno, his blood and brains splattering the side of Reno's face. Most of these men were left behind in the woods, although many eventually re-joined the detachment so that by 4:10 p.m. about 80 survivors of Reno's original 130 men were left standing with him.[64] On top of the bluffs, known today as Reno Hill, Reno's shaken troops were joined by Captain Benteen's column, arriving from the south thus saving Reno's men from annihilation. Benteen had been summoned by Custer's hand-written message "Come on … big village, be quick … bring pacs"[65]. They were reinforced by Company B with the pack train and the 14 officers and 340 troopers on the bluffs organized an all-around defence, digging rifle pits with whatever implements they had to hand.

The route taken by Custer to his "Last Stand" remains a subject of debate. One possibility is that after ordering Reno to charge, Custer, riding his horse Vic,[66]

64   Philbrick, *The Last Stand*, p.199.
65   The "pacs" were in reference to ammunition resupply.
66   "Vic", the Kentucky thoroughbred, was his battle horse, because of his speed in charges
       and manoeuvrings for battle. Dandy was acquired during the Wichita campaign of 1868
       and 1869. He was called Dandy because of his spirited "proud little peacock airs" and
       endured the harsh cold and lack of forage of the snowy plains winters by digging for grass
       and eating the bark of the cottonwood trees, and the dehydrating heat and lack of water

continued down Reno Creek to within about half a mile of the Little Bighorn, but then turned north, and climbed up the bluffs, reaching the same spot to which Reno would soon retreat. From this point on the other side of the river, he could see Reno charging the village. Riding north along the bluffs with E and F Troops, Custer could have descended into Medicine Tail Coulee, which led to a crossing of the river from which he might launch an attack against the north end of the enormous encampment. Some historians believe that part of Custer's force, including Yates' troops, descended the coulee, going west to the Little Bighorn River and attempted unsuccessfully to cross into the village even as 100s of warriors were massing around Keogh's wing on the bluffs. According to some accounts, a small contingent of Indian sharpshooters opposed this crossing so it is possible to speculate that Custer may have got within striking distance of the camp before being repulsed by Indian defenders and forced back to Custer Ridge.[67] As the scenario seemed compatible with Custer's aggressive style of warfare and with evidence found on the ground, it has become the basis of most accounts of the battle. Other historians claim that Custer never approached the river, but rather continued north across the coulee and up the other side, where he gradually came under attack.

Despite the speculations of historians, archaeologists and Custer enthusiasts, it remains a mystery whether he made a river crossing and attacked or whether he was just caught on the hill. Whatever happened, the Indians had now discovered him. They were soon joined by a large force of Sioux who, freed from their engagement with Reno, rushed down the valley. Custer was forced to turn and head for the hill where he would make his famous 'last stand'. Clearly, by the time Custer realized he was badly outnumbered, it was too late to break out southwards back towards Reno and Benteen. The precise details of Custer's fight remain a mystery since none of his men survived the battle and Indian accounts are conflicting and unclear. Fire from the southeast made it impossible for Custer's men to secure a defensive position all around Last Stand Hill where the soldiers put up their most dogged defence. According to native accounts, far more native casualties occurred in the attack on Last Stand Hill than anywhere else. Custer's remaining companies (E, F, and half of C,) were by almost all accounts annihilated within an hour. Recent battlefield archaeology indicates that some organized resistance in the form of skirmish lines probably took place. The remainder of the battle degenerated into a running fight. Fighting dismounted the soldiers' skirmish lines were overwhelmed as individual troopers were wounded or killed and initial defensive positions were abandoned as untenable.

during the dry season. This ability to survive separated the sturdier Indian ponies from the grain fed army horses. Dandy could trot along for mile after mile showing great endurance and never exhibiting erratic behaviour. On the day of the battle Dandy was with the extra mounts kept with the pack train.

67   Curley, Custer's Crow scout who had left Custer near Medicine Tail Coulee, reported that Custer had attacked the village after attempting to cross the river but was driven back, retreating toward the hill where his body was found.

Thus, the desperate last stand around Custer may not have been a "Last Stand", as traditionally portrayed in popular culture. This is a shame because the versions displayed by Errol Flynn in *They Died With their Boots On* and Robert Shaw in *Custer of the West*, are two vivid childhood memories from Sunday afternoon Westerns on the TV. Instead, archaeologists suggest that, in the end, Custer's troops were not surrounded but rather overwhelmed by a single charge led by Crazy Horse,[68] with the surviving soldiers fleeing in panic. Many of these troopers may have ended up in a deep ravine 300–400 yards away from what is known today as Custer Hill. At least 28 bodies[69] were discovered in or near that gulch, their deaths possibly the battle's final actions.

Despite hearing heavy gunfire from the north, including distinct volleys at 4:20 p.m., Benteen concentrated on reinforcing Reno rather than continuing on toward Custer. Benteen's apparent reluctance to reach Custer prompted later criticism that he had failed to follow orders. Around 5:00 p.m., Captain Thomas Weir[70] and Company D moved out, against orders, to make contact with Custer. They advanced a mile, to what is today known as Weir Ridge or Weir Point, and could see in the distance native warriors on horseback shooting at objects on the ground. By this time, roughly 5:25 p.m., Custer's battle may have been over and what Weir witnessed was probably warriors killing the wounded soldiers and shooting at dead bodies on "Last Stand Hill". Equally, he might have witnessed the destruction of Keogh's battalion which began with the collapse of L, I and C Company. The other entrenched companies eventually followed Weir, first Benteen, then Reno, but growing native attacks around Weir Ridge forced all seven companies to return to the bluff before the pack train, with the ammunition, had moved even a quarter mile. There, they remained pinned down as the Lakota and Northern Cheyenne regrouped to attack the remnants of the 7th Cavalry. The fight continued until dark and for much of the next day, with the outcome in doubt until on 26 June, as the column under General Terry approached from the north, and the Indians drew off in the opposite direction.

The soldiers on Reno Hill were unaware of what had happened to Custer until Terry's arrival on 27 June, and were stunned by the news that, about three and a half miles to the north, every soldier in the five companies under Custer's direct command, roughly 210 men, had been killed.[71] By the time troops came to recover the bodies three days later, they found most of the dead stripped of their clothing, ritually mutilated, and in an advanced state of decomposition. Still under threat of attack the first American soldiers on the battlefield identified the 7th Cavalry's dead

---

68   The Lakota asserted that Crazy Horse personally led one of the large groups of warriors who overwhelmed the cavalrymen in a surprise charge from the northeast, causing panic among the troops.

69   The most common number associated with burial witness testimony.

70   1838–76.

71   Among the dead were Custer's brothers Boston and Thomas, his brother-in-law James Calhoun, and his nephew Henry Reed.

as best as possible and hurriedly buried the troopers in shallow graves, more or less where they had fallen. Custer's body was found near the top of *Last Stand Hill*, with shots to the left chest and left temple,[72] although it is not clear whether Custer's mount, Vic, was killed or taken as a prize.[73] After two days of fighting on the bluffs, Reno and Benteen had suffered 18 dead along with one officer and 51 troopers wounded in addition to the men Reno had lost during his charge. There were 350 men still alive but all of Custers 215 men had been wiped out and in total the 7th Cavalry had suffered over 50 percent casualties.[74] The number of Sioux casualties is not known with any certainty.[75]

Keogh's body was found at the centre of a group of troopers, stripped but not mutilated, perhaps because of the "medicine" the Indians saw in the Agnus Dei ("Lamb of God") he wore on a chain about his neck. Keogh's left knee had been shattered by a bullet that corresponded to a wound through the chest and flank of Comanche, indicating that horse and rider may have fallen together prior to the last rally. The Sioux were not interested in the severely wounded Comanche, leaving him for the burial party to find, very weak and barely able to stand, but he was the sole military survivor discovered on the battlefield.[76] By this time Comanche was a well-known veteran of the 7th Cavalry and was recognised by a Sergeant in a ravine where he had sought sanctuary to die. His wounds were serious, but not necessarily fatal if properly looked after. He carried seven scars from as many wounds, four back of the fore shoulder, one through a hoof, and one on either hind leg. Captain Nowlan ordered the men to get water for the horse from the river, and other troopers coaxed Comanche onto his feet and led him away to be tenderly cared for as the farrier field dressed the wounds. Despite his wounds, Comanche marched with the command the 20 miles to the junction of the Little Bighorn and Bighorn Rivers. What a painful march that must have been for the poor injured but trusting warhorse. He was then loaded aboard a steamer with the battle casualties, heading home to Fort Lincoln, 950 miles away. Comanche spent the next year recuperating there and was nursed back to health by the soldiers

---

72   He appeared to have bled from only the chest wound, meaning his head wound may have been delivered *post-mortem*. He also suffered a wound to the arm. Some Lakota oral histories assert that Custer committed suicide to avoid capture and subsequent torture, though this is inconsistent with his known right-handedness.

73   Dandy survived with the pack train animals on Reno Hill although he was slightly injured. After the battle, Dandy was sent to Mrs. Custer in Monroe, Michigan, and she in turn gave the horse to Custer's father. It became a custom for Dandy and his new rider to appear in the local parades, including the grand procession at the Michigan State Fair. Father Custer would allow no one else to feed or groom his horse, until at 26 years of age Dandy died and was buried in an orchard on the farm.

74   Philbrick, *The Last Stand*, p.251.

75   Native American casualty estimates vary from as few as 36 dead to as many as 300.

76   Other horses are believed to have been taken by the Indians and several other badly wounded animals were destroyed at the scene.

as a regimental mascot. Three bullets were extracted from his body at Fort Abraham Lincoln but the last one was not taken out until April 1877.

News of the defeat arrived in the East as the United States was celebrating its centennial, and shocked an American people accustomed to victories and convinced of their manifest destiny. The US Army wanted to avoid bad press and their investigations were hampered by a concern for survivors and the reputations of the officers involved. Custer's widow wrote three popular books in which she fiercely protected her husband's reputation and Captain Frederick Whittaker's 1876 book, which celebrated Custer as an ideal leader, was a best seller. Thus the familiar image of Custer as a heroic officer fighting valiantly against savage forces was popularized in the *Wild West* shows of "Buffalo Bill" Cody,[77] and others. As we have seen, later, many films would retell the story of Custer's last stand which must be one of the most celebrated military actions in cinema history. Perhaps the Custer myths have been more influential than his actual actions since, despite his defeat and massacre, the inevitability of the eventual defeat of the Plains Indians and destruction of their way of life is very apparent when the events are observed from an historical distance. The romance of the cavalry in the West must, however, be contrasted with a read of *Bury My Heart at Wounded Knee*[78] to get a native perspective on what can be seen as, at best, a very clumsy housing policy and, at worst, a 19th century genocide.

Within 48 hours of the battle, the large encampment on the Little Bighorn broke up into smaller groups as the resources of grass for the horses and game could not sustain a large population. The scattered Sioux and Cheyenne feasted and celebrated during July with no threat from soldiers but soon many slipped back to the reservation and the number of hostile warriors shrank significantly. The 7th Cavalry were assigned new officers and new recruits began to fill their depleted ranks as the US Congress expanded the Army to avenge the defeat. Reorganized into eight companies, they remained in the field as part of the Terry Expedition, now based on the Yellowstone River at the mouth of the Big Horn and reinforced by Gibbon's column. The 7th Cavalry returned to Fort Abraham Lincoln and General Nelson A. Miles[79] took command in October 1876. In May 1877, Sitting Bull escaped to Canada and within days, Crazy Horse surrendered at Fort Robinson and the Great Sioux War ended on 7 May with Miles' defeat of the remaining band of Sioux. Threatened with starvation, the Sioux ceded the Black Hills to United States but they never accepted the legitimacy of the transaction.[80]

77   26 February 1846–10 January 1917.
78   Dee Brown, *Bury My Heart at Wounded Knee* (London: Vintage Books, 1991).
79   8 August 1839–15 May 1925.
80   In the 1980 the United States Supreme Court finally acknowledged the United States had taken the Black Hills without just compensation although the Sioux refused the money offered, and continue to insist on their right to occupy the land.

On 10 April 1878, Colonel Samuel D. Sturgis,[81] the Colonel of the 7th Cavalry, who had not been present at the battle issued General Orders No. 7, stating that,

> The horse known as 'Comanche,' being the only living representative of the bloody tragedy of the Little Big Horn, 25 June 1876, his kind treatment and comfort shall be a matter of special pride and solicitude on the part of every member of the Seventh Cavalry to the end that his life be preserved to the utmost limit. Wounded and scarred as he is, his very existence speaks in terms more eloquent than words, of the desperate struggle against overwhelming numbers of the hopeless conflict and the heroic manner in which all went down on that fatal day.[82]

Comanche's initial keeper at Fort Lincoln was a farrier with Keogh's troop named John Rivers, who loved Comanche and cared for his wounds. He also became the spokesperson for the famous horse whenever a newspaper wanted an interview.

Keogh's successors as the commanding officer of I Company ensured that Comanche had a comfortable stable and that he was not ridden by any one whatsoever, under any circumstances. Nor would he be put to any kind of work apart from all ceremonial occasions when Comanche was saddled, bridled, draped in mourning, with stirrups and boots reversed, and led by a mounted trooper of Company I at the head of the Regiment. Once Comanche was declared retired, he was cared for by farrier, Gustave Korn.[83] They became inseparable and Comanche would follow Korn everywhere. He was allowed the freedom of the post, the only living thing that wandered at will over the parade grounds at the fort without a reprimand from a commanding officer or regimental sergeant major. He would be given sugar cubes on demand at the door of the officers' quarters and then saunter on down to the enlisted men's canteen where a specially placed bucket of beer awaited him, but when the bugle sounded "formation," Comanche would trot out to his place in front of the line of Troop I.

Comanche moved with the 7th Cavalry to Fort Meade in June 1879. Again he was kept at Meade like royalty. When orders came for the cavalry to relocate to Fort Riley, Kansas in 1888, Comanche, aging but still in good health, accompanied them and continued to receive full honours as a symbol of the tragedy at Little Bighorn. He was made "Second Commanding Officer" of the 7th Cavalry and spent some time touring in parades and patriotic gatherings. Whilst at Fort Riley, it is stated that Korn was visiting a lady friend in the nearby town of Junction City. When Korn did not return to the base to feed and groom Comanche for the evening, the horse looked all over the base for him, finally going directly to the house of the girlfriend to escort Korn back to the post. When Korn was killed at Wounded Knee in 1890, Comanche's health

81   11 June 1822–28 September 1889
82   DiMarco, *War Horse*, p.288.
83   1852-90.

began to slowly deteriorate and shortly after that he died of colic on 7 November 1891. He was about 29 years old and it is widely believed that he died of a broken heart. He is one of only two horses in United States history to be buried with full military honours.[84]

However, death was not the end of the Comanche story. The officers of the 7th Cavalry, wanting to preserve the horse, summoned Lewis Lindsay Dyche,[85] a professor at the University of Kansas Museum of Natural History to mount the remains. For a fee of $400, but on condition that Dyche be permitted to show the horse in the Chicago Exposition of 1893, the 7th Cavalry agreed to Dyche completing the taxidermy. Later, when for reasons still not clear, the bill was not paid Dyche agreed to keep Comanche in lieu of payment. Comanche still stands today for all to see having been donated to the university's museum by Dyche.[86]

Perhaps being stuffed and mounted is a way of preserving a legacy but to my mind it is not a very edifying one. A more fitting tribute to this brave survivor is the ongoing survival and preservation of his genetic lineage in the form of the Mustang breed. By 1900 North America had an estimated 2,000,000 free-roaming horses, but since 1900, the Mustang population has been reduced drastically. Mustangs were viewed as a resource that could be captured and used or sold, especially for military use, or slaughtered for pet food. Today the Mustang of the modern west has several different breeding populations which are genetically isolated from one another and thus have distinct traits traceable to particular herds. In some modern mustang herds there is clear evidence of other domesticated horse breeds having become intermixed with feral herds. Other, more isolated herds, retain a strong influence of original Spanish stock. Today, free-roaming horses are protected under United States law, but have disappeared from several states.[87] More than half of all Mustangs in North America are found in Nevada,[88] with other significant populations in Montana, Wyoming and Oregon and a few 100 free-roaming horses survive in Alberta and British Columbia. Perhaps their preservation is the best and most constructive way in which to celebrate the remarkable horse, Comanche.

---

84 The other being Black Jack, General Pershing's, the commander of American Force's in WWI, horse.
85 20 March 1857-20 January 1915.
86 Comanche is currently on display in a humidity-controlled glass case at the University of Kansas Museum of Natural History, Dyche Hall, Lawrence, Kansas complete with what is assumed to be the original saddle, blanket and bridle.
87 The feral Mustang population in February 2010 was 33,700 horses and 4,700 burros with another 34,000 horses are in holding facilities.
88 Which features the horses on its state quarter in commemoration of this fact.

5

Appaloosas: The Heroic Breed

In the course of this book the author has focused on individual heroic horses whose stories are impressive, inspirational and extraordinary. However, in this chapter he must single out not one horse, but a breed of horse, the Appaloosa. This distinctive, spotted breed was key in enabling the Nez Perce tribe to outsmart and outrun the US Army over 1,700 miles of mountainous terrain, fighting off or evading troops at every turn.[1]

To understand their amazing contribution to the campaign of 1877 we must first consider the origin of the Appaloosa. Traditional wisdom on the origin of the breed is that the Spanish Conquistadors first introduced horses to North America in the 16th century and when in 1680 the Pueblo Indian slaves revolted and drove the Spanish from northern New Mexico, they traded off the horses to the Plains tribes. Through trade and theft, horses made their way east and north. The Shoshones from southern Idaho were the most important distributors of horses and by the early 1700s the Nez Perce had acquired horses and quickly became adept at breeding them. An alternative story of their origin has arisen from recent genetic research which has found a strong DNA link between free roaming herds in remote valleys of Kyrkestan and the Appaloosas in the United States. This suggests indigenous herds of Appaloosas from Asia roamed pre-Columbian America and became the foundation stock of the Appaloosa. Whatever their origin, the land occupied by the Nez Perce was even better-suited to raising horses than that of the Shoshones, and was better protected from enemy raids, so their herds increased rapidly.

The name Appaloosa first appears around the late 1800s to describe the spotted horses of the region of Washington and Idaho drained by the Palouse River and early white settlers referred to the spotted horse of the area as a Palouse horse. Over time the French "a" and Palouse merged together to form the name Apalousey and later Appaloosa.The Nez Perce became excellent horsemen and, unlike other tribes, they practiced selective breeding by gelding the inferior stallions, keeping the best and

---

1   Robert Forczyk, *Nez Perce 1877: The Last Fight* (Oxford: Osprey, 2011), p.89.

trading off the poorer stock. In an economy where horses were the measure of wealth, the Nez Perce became known as an affluent tribe and their mounts were prized and envied by other tribes. Their horses were often distinguished by their coat pattern, varying from sprinkles of white or large dark spots on lighter bodies, to complete leopard like appearance.

Horses gave the Nez Perce greater mobility and power, altering their culture forever. With their superior horses they had little difficulty killing what buffalo they needed and soon they began to use the Plains-type tipi in place of their old community houses. The Appaloosa was used to catch a running buffalo by putting the rider alongside for the kill, so the Nez Perce tribes bred the Appaloosas for intelligence and to be able to run at speed over any kind of terrain for long periods. Appaloosas were also bred for the best short-legged stock that could endure long trips up and down the mountainous terrain of their traditional homeland, rather than for the genetic marker of their spotted colour. Thus they became the ideal horse for steep mountain trails and passes such as those connecting Idaho with Montana. As a result of all this focused breeding they were able to produce better horses than other tribes which they reflected in their name for the breed, "the Horse of the Iron Heart", and soon their herds multiplied into the thousands.

The Nez Perce loved their Appaloosa and a culture of horse decoration evolved with patterns painted on the animal, and its mane and tail tied, woven, feathered, and laden with other art. When the tribes battled each other the warrior fresh from battle would slap the horse on its rump with his fingers up to congratulate him so later the hand was painted there with red paint if the warrior and horse combination were of the highest valour. Once an Indian was trapped and ambushed by a warring tribe, his last act was to slap the horses front right shoulder with his bloody hand. The horse ran all the way back to its encampment where its tribe was warned of the coming battle by the red hand with the fingers pointing down. Eventually, if a warrior was going into battle that red hand would be painted there whilst a circle would be painted around the horse's eye to help him see danger.

Unfortunately, the equine idyll of the Nez Pearce was not to last forever. Ever since the Nez Perce provided food, shelter, and horses to the Lewis and Clark Expedition in 1805,[2] they were well known among fur traders for their willingness to allow whites to pass freely through their country. During the 1830s, only a handful of missionaries and fur traders settled on their lands, but by the mid-1840s, 100s of emigrants passed through every year on the way to Oregon and California. A Presbyterian mission and school was established in the 1830s, but most Nez Perce stayed away and very few

2   Elliott West, *The Last Indian War: The Nez Perce Story* (Oxford, University Press, 2009), p.20. The famous explorer Meriwether Lewis (18 August 1774–11 October, 1809) best known for his role as the leader of the Lewis and Clark Expedition, who happened to be a skilled horseman, was impressed with the breeding accomplishments of the Nez Perce, when he passed through the territory in 1805. As noted in his diary entry from 15 February 1806.

converted to Christianity. From a legal perspective, the United States had no right to allow missionaries into Indian country, but many groups including churches, fur traders, farmers, and prospectors felt they had the right to enter the territory without permission of the tribes. Despite this no settler was ever killed even though they caused disruption to many hunting and fishing areas.

In 1853, Congress, without asking the Indians, created the Washington Territory, carving the Nez Perce homeland into two "American" political areas. Then, seeing the need for a federal right of-way for emigrants heading to Oregon and California and for a Pacific transcontinental railroad, in 1855, Congress sent Governor Isaac I. Stevens[3] to gather the region's chiefs together at Walla Walla for a treaty council. Here the Nez Perce were coerced into giving up their ancestral lands and moving to the Umatilla Reservation in Oregon Territory. The Nez Perce leaders present, agreed to relinquish Over 5,000,000 acres of their homeland to the US government for a nominal sum, and the right to remain in a large portion of their own lands in Idaho, Washington and Oregon territories, with the caveat that they be able to hunt, fish and graze their horses on unoccupied areas of their former land. The Reservation consisted of 7,500,000 acres and seemed a reasonable middle-ground for Indians and whites to coexist in a region gaining popularity among miners and settlers. What began as a potentially workable solution to white demands for fertile farm lands and native need to preserve sacred sites and resource habitat soon turned violent. The Yakima and other Columbia river tribes rose in revolt, feeling betrayed by Stevens, whose treaty had not even been ratified before the U. S. Senate opened up Indian lands for white settlement. However, the Nez Perce remained non-combatants in the Yakima War, which lasted from September 1855 to November 1856, and resulted in several dozen deaths on both sides.

By 1860, there were 60,000 American settlers bordering 12,000 square miles of territory held by only 3,000 Nez Perce,[4] and soon they experienced trespass on their reserved territory when gold was discovered at Orifino Creek on their land near the Clearwater River in October 1860.[5] In contravention of the treaty, gold-seekers rushed onto the Nez Perce Reservation and a town of two thousand people was illegally established at Lewiston. Ranchers and farmers followed the miners, and the Nez Perce became incensed at the failure of the U.S. government to uphold the treaties, as settlers squatted on their land and ploughed up their camas prairies, which they depended on for subsistence.

Fearing violence, federal Indian commissioners arrived in 1863, determined to reduce the size of the original 1855 Nez Perce Reservation. A group of Nez Perce were coerced by the government into signing away a further 7,000,000 acres, approximately 90 percent of their reservation, to the US, leaving only 750,000 acres in Idaho

3   25 March 1818–1 September 1862.
4   Forczyk, *Nez Perce 1877*, p.7.
5   Forczyk, *Nez Perce 1877*, p. 7.

Territory.[6] The cooperative Nez Perce headmen who, as the designated signatories for the entire "Tribe", approved the treaty were mostly Christian and welcomed the reservation's protection. This Lapwai Treaty is often called the "Thieves Treaty" by the Nez Percé and others and under its terms all Nez Perce were to move onto the new and much smaller reservation east of Lewiston. A large number of Nez Perce, however, did not accept the treaty and remained on their traditional lands. From this point on, the tribe was split between the Lower Nez Perce or "non-treaty" group and the Upper Nez Perce or "treaty" group. The "non-treaty" Nez Perce followed the "Dreamer" religion and included the 200 or so members Lamátta band of Chief Joseph,[7] still living in the Wallowa Valley on their ancestral lands,[8] outside the "official" boundaries of the 1863 reservation. As Dreamers, they believed that one day the white man would be driven away forever, and all Indians, both living and dead, would reside together in a utopian world.

The United States Senate finally ratified the Treaty of 1863 in 1867, but promises made were not being met. The situation with white ranchers and farmers grew tense and led to the murders of several Nez Perce which were never prosecuted by the US officials. An 1873 executive order from the President gave the title to the Wallowa Lake region to Joseph's descendants, but white homesteaders demanded that these fertile lands be renegotiated and in 1875, the Wallowa country was reopened to non-Indian settlement. A commission met with Nez Perce leaders in 1876 and recommended to the Indian Bureau that all non-treaty bands be persuaded to move into the formal 1863 reservation boundaries by 1 April 1877. Brigadier General Howard[9] was head of the U. Army's Department of the Columbia, and was placed in charge of the relocation. He called a council at Fort Lapwai on 4 May 1877 and gave the Nez Perce an impossible deadline of thirty days to bring the People,[10] their belongings, and their vast herd of horses back to the reservation by 15 June 1877. Joseph and the other Nez Perce leaders considered military resistance to be futile and agreed to report as ordered to Fort Lapwai. They knew noncompliance would only bring the US cavalry down on them, and that they stood little chance in prolonged combat. So in good faith, Joseph and his brother, Ollokot,[11] a warrior and leader of buffalo hunters, agreed to move the entire Wallowa Band of Nez Perce to Idaho.

In leaving Oregon, Joseph's people had to cross the Snake River, which was running high and fast with spring rains. They rounded up their horses, packed camp

6   West, *The Last Indian War;* p.94.
7   Forczyk, *Nez Perce 1877,* p.7.
8   Born in 1836 near present-day Lewiston, Idaho, and baptised a Christian with the biblical name, "Ephraim." His father, Old Chief Joseph, was a leader of the Wallowa Band of the Nez Perce, was one of the first to show interest in Christianity and was married by the minister.
9   1830-1909.
10   Forczyk, *Nez Perce 1877,* p. 8.
11   1841-77.

and crossed the river, losing some horses and cattle, and joined other non-treaty bands to continue toward the reservation in Idaho. About 590 Nez Perce from Joseph's and White Bird's[12] bands gathered six miles west of present-day Grangeville.[13] Joseph's Wallowa band of 55 warriors and White Bird's Bands of 50 mustered at the traditional camping ground on the Camas Prairie at Tolo Lake,[14] only two days' ride from the agency at Lapwai, to rest and enjoy the last days of their traditional lifestyle. White observers at the lake estimated that a third to a half of all the Nez Perce horses there were Appaloosas. Since the non-descript coloured were used largely as pack animals, this would indicate that well over half the war horses were of the spotted breed.

Tolo Lake was not far from locations where whites had committed the unpunished murders against Nez Perce and not all the Nez Perce agreed with the course of peace and compliance. Throughout the early summer of 1877, White Bird, arrayed in his war paint, rode through the country, defying the whites and proclaiming that they would not go to the reservation and that they would fight anyone who tried to take their land. Shortly before the deadline for moving onto the reservation, White Bird's band held a tel-lik-leen ceremony, in which the warriors paraded on horseback in a circular movement around the Tolo Lake camp while individually boasting of their battle prowess in war and drinking heavily.

While Joseph and his brother Ollokot were away from the camp, an aged warrior challenged the young participants over the fact that their relatives' had died, unavenged, at the hands of whites. One named Shore Crossing whose father had been shot dead by a white miner three years earlier rose to the bait. Humiliated and fortified with liquor, he and two of his cousins rode to the Salmon River settlements in search of revenge. On the evening of 14 June 1877, they returned to announce that they had killed four white men and wounded another.[15] This aroused a desire for vengeance among other warriors and resulted in more attacks on settlers in the area the next day, in which at least 14 more settlers were killed avenging the recent deaths of at least 40 Nez Perce at the hands of white ranchers and miners.[16] The settlers immediately sent messengers to Fort Lapwai demanding assistance from the military. The Nez Perce War had begun!

General Howard mobilized a force to punish the Nez Perce, anticipating that his soldiers would "make short work of it." By this time most of the Nez Perce were aware that Howard was preparing to send his soldiers against them and sought refuge ten miles south at the southern end of White Bird Canyon, which was about five miles long, one mile wide, and bounded by steep mountain ridges. After much deliberation, the Nez Perce had decided that they would make an effort to avoid war, but fight if they were forced to do so.

12   18??-1892.
13   Forczyk, *Nez Perce 1877*, p. 9.
14   Forczyk, *Nez Perce 1877*, p. 27.
15   Forczyk, *Nez Perce 1877*, p.9.
16   Forczyk, *Nez Perce 1877*, p.9.

On the night of 16 June 1877, Captain David Perry commanding Company F and Captain Joel Graham Trimble commanding Company H of the US 1st Cavalry Regiment prepared to fight the Nez Percé. The officers and men of the two companies totalled 106, and together with 11 civilian volunteers and three friendly Nez Perce scouts they advanced on White Bird Canyon.[17] Nearly half the soldiers were foreign-born and most were inexperienced horsemen and poor marksmen. Their horses were untrained for battle and arrived exhausted at the canyon after a two-day ride of more than 67 miles.[18] The Nez Perce had over 100 warriors, but they had stolen a large quantity of whiskey in their raids and, on the morning of 17 June, many were too drunk to fight. Furthermore, they had only 45 to 50 firearms,[19] including shotguns, pistols, and ancient muskets, while some warriors fought with bows and arrows. Thus there were somewhere between 45 and 70 men available for Ollokot and White Bird to lead into battle.[20] However, their knowledge of the terrain and their horsemanship in partnership with their well-trained Appaloosa were major advantages. Accustomed to economic use of bullets when hunting, the Nez Perce were also good marksman who usually dismounted to fire while their Appaloosas would stand and eat grass. By contrast, many US Cavalry horses would panic in the battle.

That night look outs reported the approach of the soldiers from the north. Awaiting them, 50 warriors under Ollokot deployed to a butte on the western side of White Bird Canyon and 15 warriors to the east, covering the cavalry's descent along a wagon road from the north east.[21] To show their good intentions, six braves had been chosen to carry a white flag and wait behind a knoll. An advance party, consisting of Lieutenant Edward Theller, Trumpeter John Jones, a few Nez Perce scouts, seven soldiers from Company F and a civilian volunteer Arthur "Ad" Chapman made first contact with the truce party of six warriors. As the six rode out from behind the knoll, inexplicably, Chapman, fired at the them. The Nez Perce returned fire and Theller dismounted to deploy his men as skirmishers on top of a low ridge. He ordered Jones to signal all troops forward to join him but before Jones could finish his trumpet call, he was shot from his horse. Perry also dismounted his company and formed a skirmish line on the east side of Theller's advance party, while Trimble's Company H deployed in a mounted line on the west side. The civilian volunteers attempted to position them-selves on the low ridge line at the eastern end of the cavalry line. Unfortunately, they encountered warriors hidden in the bushes below and the majority fled north out of harm's way, while the few remaining men found themselves between the attack on Perry's left flank led by Two Moons and the sniping fire from warriors protecting the White Bird camp.

17 West, *The Last Indian War*, p.131.
18 Forczyk, *Nez Perce 1877*, p.32.
19 Forczyk, *Nez Perce 1877*, p.36.
20 West, *The Last Indian War*, p.140.
21 Forczyk, *Nez Perce 1877*, p.33.

Perry tried to advance to join Theller against the warriors menacing his left flank, but his trumpeter had lost his trumpet and the charge never happened. Instead Perry made a stand on the ridge line, ordering a *Number fours* with every fourth man taking the reins of the horses and leading them out of the line of fire. Meanwhile, Trimble attempted to deploy Company H along the ridge while still mounted but the horses were too much to handle for inexperienced troops to be able to shoot from their saddles. Trimble also dispatched Sergeant Michael M. McCarthy and six men to the highest point above the battle to protect his right flank. Perry, riding back and forth between the two companies, saw the volunteers retreating up the canyon and, with his flank collapsing, tried to rally his men on McCarthy's position and make a stand on the high ground about 300 yards to the south. However, Company F, having suffered numerous casualties, misinterpreted Perry's order as a general retreat which Company H joined, leaving McCarthy and his men stranded.

Sensing victory, Ollokot's warriors, mounted on their Appaloosas, chased the retreating soldiers. McCarthy and his six men, now cut off, held off the Nez Perce briefly and then retreated, but were unable to catch up with the main body. McCarthy's horse was killed and he survived by hiding in the brush for two days and then walking to Grangeville.[22] Lieutenant Theller attempted to retrace his approach but became trapped in a steep rocky ravine and ran out of ammunition before he was killed with his seven men. Perry and Trimble fled to the northwest up steep ridges and as Nez Perce warriors continued the attack, the survivors retreated for several miles toward Mount Idaho, where they were rescued by fresh volunteers. In total 34 soldiers had been killed, whilst only three Nez Perce warriors had been wounded.[23] Furthermore, 63 carbines, many pistols, and 100s of rounds of ammunition were picked up off the battlefield by Nez Perce warriors. Outnumbered two to one and fighting uphill with inferior weapons, the Nez Perce had won the first battle of the Nez Perce war, in a US military blunder comparable to the Little Bighorn in proportion to the numbers engaged.

After the battle, the Nez Perce rounded up their herd and drove them to the Salmon River. To say they crossed the river sounds easy but such crossings were a major undertaking. Light and buoyant rafts made of tightly-rolled skins were lashed together and used to pull the women, children, old people, invalids, and all the belongings they needed, across the quarter mile stretch of swollen torrent to the west bank. Four good horses with their riders towed each raft, being swept 100 yards or more down the stream before they could gain the opposite shore and safety. It took many trips to get everyone across the river which at flood stage rages down its steep, rocky course. It takes a fantastically conditioned horse to carry the weight of his rider, and at the same time, pull a heavy object through the white water. The Appaloosa has that kind of strength! The rest of the band rode across on their sturdy, range-bred horses, with the

22   He received a Congressional Medal of Honor for his role in the battle.
23   Forczyk, *Nez Perce 1877*, p. 41.

very young children strapped to their mothers' backs. The spare horses were brought down to the shore at a gallop and were all well on their way across at the first plunge. In an hour the whole band could be safely across, the pack animals re-loaded, and the column on its way.

When General Howard arrived several days later with around 500 men the Nez Perce taunted him and his soldiers from their side of the river.[24] The Nez Perce, then numbered about 750 men, women, and children,[25] along with 3,000 horses and other livestock.[26] With difficulty, Howard managed to cross the Salmon with his men, but rather than fight Howard's superior force, they quickly re-crossed the river several miles downstream, leaving Howard stranded on the opposite bank, thus gaining a head start in their flight to elude the US Army.

Joseph and other chiefs, now led their people, on the start of their legendry trek across 1,700 miles of the most rugged terrain possible, in an attempt to reach Canada, where they hoped to join Sitting Bull and his people. Leaving Howard behind, the Nez Perce headed east across the Camas Prairie, having made the decision to flee into the Bitterroot Mountains. In their path, stationed at Norton's Ranch[27] was Captain Stephen Whipple with 66 soldiers and several civilian volunteers.[28] Whipple sent out Lieutenant Sevier Rains with ten soldiers and two civilians to investigate but the Nez Perce ambushed and killed them all. Whipple dug in around Norton's ranch with his remaining soldiers and was reinforced on 4 July by Captain David Perry with survivors from White Bird Canyon. Perry took command of the combined force who stayed in their rifle pits while the Nez Perce sniped at them all day from long distance and bypassed a mile away heading eastward. A group of 17 civilian volunteers now appeared and tried to reach the soldiers,[29] but had to take up a defensive position on a hilltop about one and a half miles to the west. Although Perry could see them from his fortifications he declined to send help until the Nez Perce had withdrawn and thus three of the volunteers were killed and two wounded, ensuring them a place in Idaho history as the "Brave Seventeen."

The Nez Perce continued their journey east for 25 miles, burning ranches and farms, which they considered to be illegal, before pausing to establish a camp in the steep-walled valley of the South Fork of the Clearwater River. There, on 7 July 1877 they were joined by Looking Glass[30] and other Nez Perce bringing their total strength

24 West, *The Last Indian War*, p.140.
25 West, *The Last Indian War*, p.152. Wikipedia states about 600, of whom 150 were warriors
     whilst other figures state 250 warriors and 500 women and children. Figures vary
     depending upon when a young man is considered a warrior.
26 Forczyk, *Nez Perce 1877*, p.42, and West, *The Last Indian War*, p.140.
27 Today it is Cottonwood.
28 Forczyk, *Nez Perce 1877*, p.44.
29 Forczyk, *Nez Perce 1877*, p.45.
30 1832-77

up to about 740 people and 200 fighting men.[31] The next day 75 civilian volunteers under Edward McConville,[32] found the camp and reported its location to General Howard but the Nez Perce discovered them and attacked, forcing them to take refuge on a hilltop. Out of water and with their horses stolen by the Indians, the volunteers dubbed their hilltop "Fort Misery." About noon on 11 July 1877 the volunteers withdrew from their hill to Mount Idaho without opposition.

The Nez Perce thought that Howard's force would arrive from the northeast, the same direction as the volunteers, but instead he approached from the south following the east bank of the South Fork of the Clearwater downstream through rugged country and at midday on 11 July 1877, saw the Nez Perce village, spread along both banks of the river. The Nez Perce were surprised at the sudden appearance of Howard's force who opened fire with his howitzers and Gatling guns from the ridge above. Horsemen scampered over the hills in every direction while old Indians, squaws and children herded their stock into the hills in the rear. The old warrior Toohoolhoolzote and some Nez Perce, rode to the top of the ridge where they built a stone fort and began firing at the soldiers, thus stalling Howard's cavalry. Soon, they were nearly surrounded and had to retreat back to the village but this action gave others time to set up defensive positions around three sides of a prairie about a mile and a half wide and two miles long above the east side of the Clearwater River. About 100 Nez Perce opposed Howard's advance and after fighting all afternoon, the day ended in a stalemate with both sides in their fortified lines. The soldiers spent the night hungry and thirsty whilst the Nez Perce were supplied by women from the village in their rear.

The next morning Howard was preparing to attack the Nez Perce left flank when, out of the blue, a pack train bearing supplies for Howard appeared on the battlefield. Captain Miller moved forward to protect the train and, taking advantage of his advanced position, ordered a charge. The Nez Perce retreated and soon were in full flight as Howard's men advanced into the village. The Nez Perce men crossed the Clearwater River with their women and children and as many of their possessions as they could gather. However, Howard failed to pursue them beyond the river and the battle ended with 15 US dead and 25 wounded and four dead Nez Perce with six wounded warriors.[33] The next day Howard pursued the Nez Perce 12 miles northward to the village of Kamiah but was too late and he saw them cross the Clearwater River. On 15 July Howard received a message that Joseph and his band wished to surrender, while Looking Glass, White Bird, and Toohoolhoolzote planned to continue eastward. The next day Joseph failed to appear, but 35 Nez Perce did which reaffirmed Howard's view that the Nez Perce were disintegrating as a fighting force. Joseph apparently argued against leaving Idaho and their traditional lands, but Looking Glass had many friends in Montana and argued that once there they would be safe, not under-

---

31   Forczyk, *Nez Perce 1877*, p.45.
32   Forczyk, *Nez Perce 1877*, p.45.
33   Forczyk, *Nez Perce 1877*, p.53.

standing perhaps that Idaho and Montana were states in the same nation. White Bird, Looking Glass, and Toohoolhoolzote prevailed and the Nez Perce decided to follow the rugged Lolo trail to Lolo Pass and Montana.

Howard learned that the Nez Perce had moved to Weippe Prairie, about 15 miles away and he set off in search of them, sending out a strong reconnaissance force on 17 July who were ambushed with two killed and one wounded. However, Howard now knew that the Nez Perce were travelling on the arduous Lolo Trail through miles of brutally rugged, densely forested, uninhabited mountains. A switchback trail went over the 7,200 foot Lolo pass which was so narrow that one stumble could plunge both horse and rider to death. Fallen trees blocked the way in many places, and cold torrential rain, typical of that altitude, kept the trail oozing with mud. From 16 to 22 July they travelled 90 miles at 15 miles a day on mountain passes to the summit of the pass, with the Appaloosas carrying the warriors, the wounded, the Nez Perce belongings and their families. Howard, with 730 men,[34] would not set off after the Nez Perce on the Lolo Trail until 30 July 1877 but he telegraphed ahead and soldiers awaited the Nez Perce just over the Montana border. By this time the Nez Perce had given Howard the nick-name *General-Day-After-Tomorrow* because of his slow, careful movements.

White settlers and US army soldiers in the Bitterroot valley, knew that the Nez Perce were coming their way and on 23 July 1877, Captain Charles Rawn received a message that the Nez Perce were camped at Lolo Hot Springs, on the Montana side of the pass, only a few miles from the settlements in the Bitterroot Valley, and that they wished to pass peacefully through the valley. Rawn, however, had orders to stop them and on 25 July 1877, his 35 men and 50 civilian volunteers constructed a fort of logs and earth two or three miles below where the Nez Perce were camped and about five miles west of Lolo, Montana.[35] The next day Rawn met with Looking Glass who asked to pass unmolested, but Rawn demanded that they surrender their arms and ammunition and the meeting terminated without any agreement.

By this time there were about 200 armed men gathered at the improvised fort as Rawn and Looking Glass met again and each repeated their demands.[36] When Rawn informed the volunteers that he expected a battle most of them left, so that by the next morning barely 60 men were left to man the fort which was constructed in a constriction in the canyon enclosed on both sides by precipitous ridges.[37] Nevertheless, on 28 July 1877 the Nez Perce, men, women, children, and livestock, climbed the ridges and bypassed the fort, leaving the defenders in their rear. Rawn and his soldiers exchanged a few shots with the Nez Perce on the ridge and then abandoned the fort and followed the Indians down into the Bitterroot Valley. Of the civilian volunteers, 50 stumbled

34   Forczyk, *Nez Perce 1877*, p.56.
35   West, *The Last Indian War*, p171.
36   Forczyk, *Nez Perce 1877*, p57.
37   Forczyk, *Nez Perce 1877*, p57.

into the Nez Perce camp and were captured, but were released after Looking Glass promised no violence against anybody. The soldiers retired to Missoula, Montana, the civilian volunteers disbanded, and the Nez Perce continued on their way south through the valley, buying fresh horses, food, and supplies from local ranchers and farmers. Thus, the makeshift fort acquired its name, *Fort Fizzle* and the fiasco prompted charges and counter-charges of cowardice and ineptitude between and among the government and citizens of Montana and the US government and its army.

Looking Glass now persuaded the Nez Perce that General Howard was far behind and that the citizens of Montana did not want war with them. Thus, their progress became leisurely with few precautions for defence as they left the Bitterroot Valley and camped in the Big Hole Basin. They had gone without shelter for about 30 days and Chief Joseph let his weary people rest and replenish their tipi poles from the surrounding forest.[38] He did not know that Colonel John Gibbon[39] had left Fort Shaw 200 miles to the north east with 161 officers and men of the United State 7th Infantry and a howitzer.[40] Following the trail of the Nez Perce he collected 38 civilian volunteers and on 8 August 1877, located the Nez Perce in the Big Hole encampment.[41] He marched to reach it at dawn, leaving his 12-pound howitzer and a pack train to follow behind. With orders for no prisoners and no negotiations, he had come to fight the Nez Perce.

White Bird had neglected to post sentries around the V-shaped camp of 89 tipis,[42] so between Gibbon's position and the encampment, the only protection was the waist-deep, willow-lined Big Hole River. Approaching on foot at dawn on 9 August, Gibbon's men crossed the river, rushed into the village and began firing into the tipis where most of the Nez Perce were still sleeping. They fled in all directions whilst the soldiers fired indiscriminately at men, women, and children. However, Lieutenant James H. Bradley leading Gibbon's left wing was killed early in the battle and his leaderless men failed to advance, leaving the northern end of the village unoccupied and this became a rallying point to the Nez Perce.

Gibbon ordered his men to burn the tipis which proved to be more difficult than expected and gave White Bird and Looking Glass time to organise and return fire from the opposite end of the village. Gibbon's horse was hit and he was wounded in the leg whilst several other soldiers were killed and 20 minutes into the action, he ordered a retreat back across the river to a wood. Here the soldiers dug rifle pits and constructed rock and log barriers as Gibbon's howitzer arrived and fired two or three ineffectual rounds before the Nez Perce killed or wounded most of the crew. They abandoned the gun after dismantling it and the battle settled down into a sniping duel between the Nez Perce under Ollokot and the soldiers. During the afternoon the

38   The Nez Perce still numbered about 750 persons in all with about 200 warriors.
39   1827-96.
40   Forczyk, *Nez Perce 1877*, p.60.
41   Forczyk, *Nez Perce 1877*, p.60.
42   Forczyk, *Nez Perce 1877*, p.59.

women packed up, gathered the horse herd, and moved out south-east, going about 18 miles to Lake Creek where they made camp, this time with defensive works. That night Gibbon's men had no food or water and many seriously wounded men to tend to and he sent out messengers to request immediate relief from Howard. The next day 20 or 30 Nez Perce sharpshooters kept the soldiers holed up in their fortifications all day, leaving Gibbon and his soldiers alone but immobile on the battlefield. General Howard and an advance party of cavalrymen found Gibbon the next morning after a 71 mile ride in a day and a night.

The Battle of the Big Hole had lasted fewer than 36 hours, yet casualties were high. Of the 17 officers with Gibbon, 14 lay dead or were wounded, and his force was unfit to pursue the Nez Perce having suffered 31 dead and 38 wounded.[43] Around 60 to 90 Nez Perce died and every Nez Perce family suffered at least one loss,[44] mostly women, children and old men slaughtered during the initial attack on the sleeping camp. Chief Joseph and his brother Ollokot's wives were wounded and the proud leaders were infuriated. Gibbon's success in surprising the Nez Perce caused Looking Glass's prestige as a leader to plummet since he had promised them they would be safe in Montana and Chief Joseph seems to have resumed his role as the principal leader. The Nez Perce now realised that all white men were their enemies and they could expect no quarter in future battles. Howard's force took up the pursuit and followed Joseph toward Yellowstone National Park.

Thinking that the Crow Tribe, would help them out, the survivors proceeded south-ward towards Idaho via the Bannock Pass. Along the way, more Nez Perce warriors, as well as several women and children who had been wounded at the Big Hole, died, adding to the grief and fuelling the thirst for revenge among the young warriors. Chief Joseph and other leaders attempted to restrain them, but on 12 August, they killed five ranchers on Horse Prairie,[45] precipitating a siege mentality among the whites throughout the region who took up arms in stockades. After their losses at Big Hole, the Nez Perce decided to confound the army by taking a circuitous route rather than their usual direct route to the Montana Great Plains.

General Howard was now coming under severe criticism for his failure to defeat the Nez Perce after two months in the field. He and his 310 soldiers, several dozen civilian volunteers, and Indian scouts,[46] did not follow directly, but instead took a shorter route across southern Montana hoping to intercept the Nez Perce near Yellowstone National Park. Howard's plan was to cross into Idaho via the Monida Pass and catch the Nez Perce at Camas Creek near Dubois, Idaho. On 18 August, the Nez Perce camped at a place they called *Kamisnim Takin*, meaning "camas meadows", 15 miles to Howard's east. Howard arrived at Camas Meadows the next day but the Nez Perce had left,

---

43   Forczyk, *Nez Perce 1877*, p. 65.
44   Forczyk, *Nez Perce 1877*, p. 65, estimates 30 warriors, 30 non-combatants and 18 women.
45   Forczyk, *Nez Perce 1877*, p. 66.
46   Primarily Bannocks, but also some Nez Perce friendly to the US.

continuing eastward. He set up camp there that night, placing pickets in all directions but these precautions were observed by the Nez Perce who decided to carry out a raid with the aim of putting Howard's cavalry on foot. At about 4:00 a.m., several Nez Perce crept among the picketed horses to cut them loose but as the mounted warriors approached a sentry challenged them and a gun went off alerting the whole camp before many horses had been released from their picket lines. Despite this, 200 mules and about 20 horses were free and the Indians stampeded them northward.

The cavalrymen quickly dressed and mounted and by dawn three companies of cavalry were galloping northward in pursuit of the raiders,[47] who had several miles' head start. The rear guard of the Nez Perce detected them and set up an ambush, while several warriors continued driving the mules onwards. A few Nez Perce deployed in a thin skirmish line in a grassy meadow about half a mile wide, bordered by a high lava ridge. The soldiers dismounted to return long-distance fire but the distance between the lines was too great for effective marksmanship. Soon the soldiers discovered that the Indians in the meadow were serving as a decoy, while others had been creeping forward on both flanks. A retreat was ordered and two companies got away but 50 men were left in a strong defensive position in the lava rock where they were forced to halt by the encircling Nez Perce. For the next two to four hours the two sides sniped at each other. Meanwhile, Howard received word that the cavalry companies were in trouble and came with reinforcements to find the two retreating cavalry companies. By mid-afternoon, one man had died and two were mortally wounded, but the Indians suffered six dead and melted away as the battle ended.[48] The Nez Perce were disappointed only to have captured mules, but the loss crippled Howard's mobility who had failed to defeat the Nez Perce and again failed to pursue.

The Nez Perce now entered the 3,000 square mile wilderness of Yellowstone National Park and began moving up the Madison and Firehole rivers.[49] Newspapermen throughout the country were now reporting the saga of the fleeing Nez Perce, especially since they had entered the nation's only "national park" where tourists were at risk.[50] Howard's troops were tired, having marched for 26 days averaging 20 miles a day, and he called a halt to the chase and rested for several days at Henrys Lake. However, the Nez Perce, burdened with wounded, women, children, and elderly had travelled 100s of miles and fought several battles in which they defeated or held off the US army forces. Now the US nation was angry in the wake of the earlier defeat of General Custer the year before at the Little Big Horn and demanded revenge. Howard's superior General Philip Sheridan,[51] was collecting more than a thousand

---

47   Forczyk, *Nez Perce 1877*, p.67.
48   Forczyk, *Nez Perce 1877*, p.67.
49   Forczyk, *Nez Perce 1877*, p.67.
50   There were eight or nine tourists parties (at least 35 people) in the park, plus several groups of prospectors. Two of these experienced hostile encounters during which 3 were killed and several wounded.
51   6 March 1831–5 August 1888.

Wellington on Copenhagen, painted by Thomas Lawrence.

Artist's impression of Wellington and staff at Waterloo.

Lord Cardigan leads
the Light Brigade on
Ronald, Balaclava,
25 October 1854.

Old Baldy.

Comanche as pictured in a contemporary postcard.

Author on his Appaloosa 'Sylvanner'.

Two Basuto ponies on trek in
South Africa.

Lord Roberts on Vonolel.

9th Lancers charge during the Second Afghan War of 1878-80.

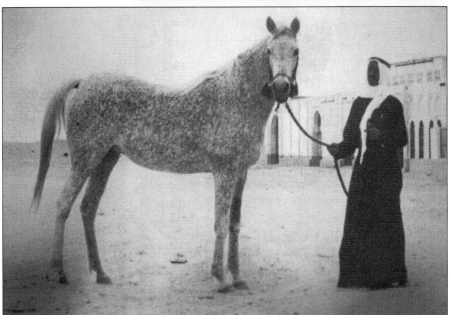

Desert Arabian.

Bolton astride favourite mount 'Monty'. (Family collection)

Australian mounted infantry, Palestine 1917.

'Warrior' in 1934 by Sir Alfred Munnings.

Brigadier-General Jack Seely and staff, c. 1917.

Amedeo riding Sandor photographed with his Spahy orderly photographed on 26 December 1935, the day after the cavalry actions at Selaclaca. (The dedication of the photograph is to his Uncle Rodolfo, the father of his future wife Beatrice. Oddly, the original photograph was mistakenly reversed when it was printed, making it appear that his right hand was wounded.)

Reckless and her combat trainer, Sgt. Joseph Latham and after the Korean conflict.

viii

experienced soldiers and Indian scouts from many tribes to defeat the Nez Perce when they emerged from Yellowstone. The Army was aware that the Nez Perce would emerge from the mountains near the Clark's Fork or the Shoshone Rivers so Howard continued on down the Clark's Fork River hoping to trap the Nez Perce between his force and that of Colonel Samuel D. Sturgis[52] on the plains below. Sturgis had set up his base where he had an expansive view and could move quickly toward either Clark's Fork or to the Shoshone River. He discounted the Clark's Fork exit, thinking that no trail could possibly lead through it. The Nez Perce, suspecting the Army would be waiting for them at all the usual exits, selected an unknown and most difficult route over the Absaroka Mountains reaching an elevation of nearly 10,000 feet and to prevent any news of their location getting to the army during their difficult passage down to the Plains they hunted down and killed white prospectors and hunters in the area.[53] It was the roughest country possible, obstructed with dead and fallen timber and huge boulders.

They reached the divide on the evening of 5 September 1877, and the next morning, they continued northeast down Crandall Creek and into the canyon of the Clark's Fork of the Yellowstone. On 8 September, when the Nez Perce reached a point on top of a ridge six miles from Sturgis's force, their advance scouts observed the soldiers far below and knew that if they took the open and easy route to reach the Plains, their 2,000 horses and 700 people would be easily visible. Instead they took a route going south toward the Shoshone River, and then, invisible to army scouts, milled their horses in a big circle to conceal their trail and convince the army that they were heading south. They then sneaked back north, concealed by heavy timber, and traversed Dead Indian Gulch, a narrow, steep-sided slit in the rock, dropping almost vertically for 1,000 feet and barely wide enough for two horses to go side-by-side. Sturgis took the bait and led his soldiers away from the Clark's Fork and headed south to the Shoshone. Thus the Nez Perce passed out onto the plains unopposed before Sturgis realized his error. Although General Howard's forces had never really been very far from the Nez Perce, they never engaged the Indians while in the park and chose an easier more northerly route, reaching the northeast corner of the Park on Clark's Fork on 11 September. By the time Howard and Sturgis met, their forces were two days and 50 miles behind the Nez Perce.

The Nez Perce, having now travelled nearly one thousand miles and fought several battles next headed north out of Wyoming into Montana. The Nez Perce believed that they would find safety among their friends, the Crow who lived near the Yellowstone River but the Crow now realized that helping the Nez Perce would lead to retaliation by the US Army and rejected the Nez Perce appeal for help. Moreover, a few Crow warriors joined the Army as scouts with an eye on capturing the large Nez Perce

---

52   11 June 1822–28 September 1889.
53   Ten men were killed by the Indians and additional bodies were discovered over the
      ensuing months.

Appaloosa herd. At this point, the Nez Perce realized that their only hope was to join the Sioux leader Sitting Bull in Canada, 250 miles to their north. General Howard, who had been chasing them unsuccessfully for three months, now ordered Sturgis to continue the pursuit with his 360 men of the 7th Cavalry companies,[54] divided into two battalions, one of which was commanded by our old friend Captain Frederick Benteen who we last met at the Little Bighorn. Howard reinforced Sturgis with 50 additional cavalrymen, two mountain howitzers, 25 white scouts, and a few Bannock and Crow scouts. Howard and his soldiers, whose horses were worn out, would rest and follow a couple of days behind Sturgis.

The Nez Perce camped on 12 September 1877 near the entrance to Canyon Creek and the next morning, they suddenly became aware that Sturgis was nearby. Driven by ambition and military imperative, Sturgis had advanced the 7th Cavalry 60 miles in 18 hours.[55] This feat of equine endurance had left his horses spent and his men exhausted. They anticipated a rest after crossing the Yellowstone River but seeing an opportunity, Sturgis decided to attack. He sent one battalion along a ridge to head off the Nez Perce traversing the shallow canyon below and sent Captain Benteen and his men on a swing to the left to plug the exits from the canyon and trap the women, children, and Appaloosas. The first battalion advanced into the canyon to threaten the column, but was halted by a scattering of Nez Perce rifle shots, the caution of the soldiers perhaps due to the now formidable reputation of the tribe for military prowess and marksmanship. Benteen also ran into opposition and was unable to head off the Appaloosa herd. The Nez Perce rear-guard held the soldiers off until nightfall and most of their horse herd, women and children reached the plains and continued north.

The next day Sturgis' men were joined by a large number of Crow,[56] riding fresh horses, who were sent ahead with Bannock scouts and stole many of the Nez Perce Appaloosa. Sturgis and the cavalry followed behind and journeyed 37 miles that day, but at the cost of wearing down their already tired horses and putting themselves on foot.[57] Sturgis was forced to halt on the banks of the Musselshell River to await supplies from General Howard and his men who arrived two days later. The Nez Perce had escaped from a cavalry force outnumbering them at least two to one, but the loss of horses placed an additional burden on their remaining and increasingly worn-out Appaloosas. They had also expended much of their scarce ammunition and the betrayal of the Crow was a psychological blow. After three months of a fighting retreat they were physically exhausted.

The Nez Perce believed that they had shaken off Howard. However, they were unaware that the recently promoted Brigadier Nelson A. Miles,[58] having received a

---

54   Forczyk, *Nez Perce 1877*, p.70.
55   Forczyk, *Nez Perce 1877*, p.73.
56   Estimated at between 50 and 200.
57   Forczyk, *Nez Perce 1877*, p.75. The Crow and Bannock declined to share their captured horses with the soldiers.
58   8 August 1839–15 May 1925.

message from Howard on 17 September 1877 requesting his assistance, was on his way diagonally north from the Tongue River Cantonment to intercept them and prevent an alliance between the Nez Perce and the Lakota Sioux of Sitting Bull.[59] Miles left the next morning, leading units of the 5th Infantry, 2nd Cavalry and George Armstrong Custer's former command, the 7th Cavalry, a total force of 520 soldiers, civilian employees, along with about thirty Indian scouts, mostly Cheyenne with a few Lakota.[60] To give Miles the time he needed to get into position between the Nez Perce and the Canadian border, Howard slowed down his pursuit and the exhausted Nez Perce, unaware of Miles' advance, also slowed down, believing themselves a safe distance ahead of Howard's forces. By now, the flight of the Nez Perce was celebrated and admired by large segments of the American public, although both Sherman and Sheridan were determined to punish them severely to discourage other Indians considering rebellion.

On 23 September 1877, the Nez Perce arrived at at Cow Creek on the Missouri where an army garrison of 12 men and four civilian clerks manned Cow Island Landing where 50 tons of freight, offloaded from steamboats, lay under tarpaulins awaiting shipment.[61] The garrison retreated into an earthen entrenchment a few 100 yards from the ford, which had been built around their tents to divert rain water, whilst the tribe crossed to the north bank and camped about two miles up the creek. However, a small group rode to the entrenchment and asked for some of the stock-piled food and the sergeant gave them a bag of hardtack and a side of bacon. Despite this generosity, at sundown the Indians fired into the entrenchment and two civilians were wounded. The soldiers were pinned down and the supplies outside the entrenchment were pillaged by the Indians who took what they fancied and set the rest on fire. The large stockpile of bacon burned brightly for most of the night, lighting up the area and preventing a concerted attack. After sporadic exchanges of gunfire throughout the night, the Nez Perce moved off up Cow Creek at 10:00 a.m. the next morning having gained plenty of supplies, but having lost a vital day of travel. The soldiers sent a message downriver to Colonel Miles who knew the Nez Perce were only 90 miles from the Canadian border. Two days later, while still in Cow Island Canyon, a wagon train from the landing, heading for Fort Benton, was attacked by the Nez Perce as a small army relief force of soldiers and civilian volunteers who had come from the fort, approached the rear of the Nez Perce column. Some warriors went down the canyon to take up positions on the heights to meet this new threat and opened fire. After two hours the engagement ended as the troopers broke off and began a slow and cautious withdrawal to Cow Island Landing as couriers reported the Nez Perce location to Miles who was advancing cross country from Fort Keogh with fresh troops. Having

59   Later to be called Fort Keogh after Comanche's owner.
60   Forczyk, *Nez Perce 1877*, p.57. Some of the Indian scouts had fought against Custer at the Little Big Horn only 15 months earlier, but had subsequently surrendered to Miles.
61   Forczyk, *Nez Perce 1877*, p.79.

received the dispatch, Miles crossed the Missouri, and headed toward the northern side of the Bear Paw Mountains.

Now only 80 miles from Canada, the Nez Perce who had travelled more than one thousand miles and fought several battles and the leadership was split between those who wanted to press on and those, including Looking Glass, who wanted to slow and rest the tired and weakened people and their horses. Since they believed the soldiers were now far behind them, those who wanted to go slower won the debate. It was to be the deciding factor in determining their fate. As they moved slowly toward Canada over the next four days, looking to the south for Howard and his soldiers, they were unaware that Miles was coming upon them from the southeast, driving his troopers and horses 93 miles in four days.[62] On 29 September, several inches of snow fell and Miles' Cheyenne scouts found the trail of the Nez Perce. A few soldiers and civilian scouts had a skirmish with Nez Perce warriors, who reported to their leaders the presence of a large number of people to their east. Most wanted to continue quickly on toward Canada, but Looking Glass prevailed, suggesting that the people seen must have been other Indians. The next morning the Cheyenne found the Nez Perce encampment on Snake Creek north-east of the Bear Paw mountains, just 40 miles from Canada.

At 9:15 a.m. on 30 September while still about six miles from the camp, Miles deployed his cavalry at a trot, with 30 Cheyenne and Lakota scouts leading the way, followed by the 2nd Cavalry consisting of about 160 soldiers who were ordered to attacked the Nez Perce camp immediately. Miles, riding with the 115 soldiers of the 7th Cavalry followed the 2nd's charge with 155 soldiers of the 5th Infantry mounted on horses as a reserve along with a Hotchkiss gun and the pack train.[63] However, the Nez Perce were warned by scouts a few minutes in advance and they scattered, some gathering up the Appaloosa herd, some packed to leave, whilst others gathered to defend the encampment. In all, 50 to 60 warriors and many women and children attempted an escape to the north and Canada.

Miles' plan fell apart quickly. The Cheyenne scouts veered to the left to snatch the horse herd and the 2nd Cavalry, followed them. They captured most of the Nez Perce horses and cut off about 70 men from the village, including Chief Joseph, plus many women and children. Joseph told his 14 year-old daughter to catch a horse and join the others in a flight toward Canada whilst he, unarmed, mounted a horse and rode through a ring of soldiers back into the camp, several bullets cutting his clothing and wounding his horse. One company chased the Nez Perce heading toward Canada, pursuing them about five miles before retreating when they organized a counter-attack. Once the women and children were safely out of reach of the soldiers, some of the Nez Perce warriors came back to join their main force.

62 Forczyk, *Nez Perce 1877*, p.82.
63 Forczyk, *Nez Perce 1877*, p.85.

Meanwhile the 7th Cavalry attacked the village and were welcomed by a group of Nez Perce who rose up from a coulee and opened fire, killing and wounding several soldiers. They fell back and Miles ordered two of the three companies in the 7th Cavalry to dismount, and quickly brought up the mounted infantry of the 5th, to join them in the firing line. By 3:00 p.m., Miles had occupied the higher ground and the Nez Perce were surrounded having lost all their horses. Miles ordered another charge on the Nez Perce positions with the 7th Cavalry and one company of the infantry, but it was beaten back, and by nightfall he had lost 23 dead and 39 wounded.[64] As if they had not suffered enough at the Little Bighorn, the 7th Cavalry took the heaviest losses with 16 dead and 29 wounded two of them mortally.[65]

During the snowy night both sides fortified their positions, while some Nez Perce crept out between the lines to collect ammunition from wounded and dead soldiers. The Nez Perce dug large, deep shelter pits for the women and children and rifle pits for the 100 or so warriors covering all approaches to their camp which was a square about 250 yards on each side. Miles greatest fear, and the Nez Perce's greatest hope, was that Sitting Bull might send Lakota warriors south from Canada. Looking Glass was killed when he thought he saw an approaching Lakota and raised his head above a rock to see and was hit by a sniper's bullet. Three Cheyenne scouts rode into the Nez Perce fortifications to propose talks but when Chief Joseph and five other Nez Perce entered negotiations with Miles they were taken prisoner. Miles' violation of the truce was countered when a young inept Lieutenant wandered into the Nez Perce camp during the truce and was taken hostage. The next day Joseph was exchanged for the hapless officer and on 3 October, the soldiers opened fire with a 12-pounder gun which did little damage to the dug-in Nez Perce although a woman and a small girl were killed. On the evening of 4 October General Howard arrived at the battlefield but allowed Miles to retain tactical control of the siege.

The Nez Perce were now divided, with Joseph in favour of surrender while White Bird, the one other surviving leader, favoured a break-out through the army's lines and a dash toward Canada. The next morning at 8:00 a.m. all firing ceased and Howard sent a message into the camp promising that none of the Nez Perce would be executed, that they would be given blankets and food, and that they would be taken back to the Lapwai reservation in Idaho. With these new assurances, White Bird now agreed to surrender and two Nez Perce returned to Mile's lines with the now famous message from Joseph:

> Tell General Howard I know his Heart. What He told me before I have in my heart. I am tired of fighting. Our chiefs are killed. Looking Glass is dead. Toohoolhoolzote is dead. The old men are all dead. It is the young men who

64   Forczyk, *Nez Perce 1877*, p.86.
65   The Nez Perce had 22 men killed. Several Nez Perce women and children had also been killed.

say yes or no. He who led on the young men is dead. It is cold and we have no blankets. The little children are freezing to death. My people, some of them have run away to the hills, and have no blankets, no food; no one knows where they are – perhaps freezing to death. I want to have time to look for my children and see how many of them I can find. Maybe I shall find them among the dead. Hear me, my chiefs! I am tired; my heart is sick and sad. From where the sun now stands, I will fight no more forever.[66]

Thus, after six days of fighting, with men, women and children suffering and dying from wounds and exposure to freezing weather, Chief Joseph surrendered the Nez Perce to the US Army commanders. That afternoon Joseph appeared for the formal surrender, mounted on a black pony with a Mexican saddle in a grey woollen shawl showing the marks of four or five bullets, with his forehead and wrist clearly scratched. Joseph dismounted and offered Howard, who he knew personally, his Winchester rifle. Howard motioned for him to give it to Miles. The total number of Nez Perce who surrendered on 5 October or were captured was 418 of which 87 were men, 184 women and 147 children.[67] The soldiers captured 1,531 horses in the battle and the Cheyenne and Lakota scouts took 300 as payment for their services.[68] About 700 horses were, by order of General Miles, to be returned to the Nez Perce the next spring, but that return of the horses never occurred.

Meanwhile, White Bird and about 50 followers had slipped through the army lines on the night of 5 October and continued on to Canada,[69] joining other Nez Perce who had escaped earlier during the battle. Estimates of the number of Nez Perce who escaped across the border vary,[70] but in total, about 105 Nez Perce warriors and 70 to 100 non-combatants led by White Bird arrived with some 300 head of horses at Sitting Bull's camp in Saskatchewan. The Canadian authorities reported that they were in a pitiful condition, but they were hospitably received by Sitting Bull and White Bird and his family settled in Pincher Creek, Alberta, to live out their lives. Perhaps it is victor's history which has focused on the heroic failure of Joseph's Nez Perce rather than viewing it as an incredible success for White Bird and his warriors.

After 113 days The Nez Percé had carried out an epic fighting retreat of 18 engagements, including four major battles, successfully evading the cavalry for over 3.5

66   West, *The Last Indian War*, p.283-4.
67   Forczyk, *Nez Perce 1877*, p.87. Other estimates put the figures at 431 including 79 men, 178 women and 174 children; some 30 refugees were rounded up a few days later.
68   See <www.nezperce.org/ Nez Perce Tribe of Idaho> (Accessed 11 May 2016).
69   Forczyk, *Nez Perce 1877*, p.87.
70   Forczyk, *Nez Perce 1877*, p.87. Wikipedia states 105 warriors and 70 to 100 non-combatants. Another source states 103 men, 60 women and eight children. Yet another estimate is 233, including 140 men and boys and 93 women and girls (including Joseph's daughter). Forty-five Nez Perce were reported to have been captured en-route to Canada and at least five (possibly as many as 34) were killed by the Cree who were encouraged by Miles to "fight" any escapees.

months and 1,700 miles across four states, only to be halted 40 miles from safety in Canada. The US Army of up to 1,500 soldiers, plus as many as 500 civilian volunteers and Indian scouts had been outrun and outsmarted by 250 Nez Perce warriors and about 500 non-combatant women and children of whom about 150 escaped to Canada. Many people, including Howard and Miles, praised the Nez Perce for their exemplary conduct and skilled fighting ability and even General Sherman applauded their military prowess and the relative lack of atrocities they committed. Joseph's Nez Perce and their Appaloosa horses had impressed the entire nation.

Miles marched his captives 265 miles to the Tongue River Cantonment in southeast Montana Territory, where they arrived on 23 October 1877, and were held until 31 October. Chief Joseph surrendered himself with a pledge from U S officials that his people could spend the winter on Tongue River and return to Idaho in the spring to live on their reservation in peace. However, despite the protests of Howard and Miles, this promise was overruled by Sherman, and on 1 November the able-bodied warriors were marched out to Fort Buford at the confluence of the Yellowstone and Missouri rivers, whilst the ill, wounded, and women and children travelled in 14 Mackinaw boats. They left Fort Buford for Custer's old post of Fort Abraham Lincoln across the Missouri River at Bismarck in the Dakota Territory, some in boats, whilst the rest travelled on horseback escorted by troops of the 7th Cavalry en-route to their winter quarters. A majority of Bismarck's citizens turned out to welcome the Nez Perce prisoners, providing a lavish buffet for them and their troop escort, before on 23 November, they were loaded into freight cars and eleven rail coaches for a trip to Fort Leavenworth in Kansas, where they were forced to live in a swampy malarial bottomland. Chief Joseph went to Washington in January 1879 to plead that his people be allowed to return to Idaho.

He met with the President and Congress and was greeted with acclaim, but opposition in Idaho prevented the US government from granting his petition. Instead, Joseph and the Nez Perce were sent to Oklahoma and eventually located on a small reservation near Tonkawa where conditions were hardly better than those at Leavenworth. Many died of disease and despondency and the place is still remembered to this day as "The Hot Place". Joseph made several trips back to Washington, D.C. and dictated his own account of the war hoping to draw sympathy and support from those in power. He met Indian reform groups, befriended Buffalo Bill Cody and even became friends with General Gibbon, his foe during the Nez Perce War, until finally, in 1885, Joseph and 268 surviving Nez Perce were permitted to return to the Northwest. Those who had converted to Christianity were allowed to return to Idaho, but those who continued to practice the old ways were refused permission to live in their homeland in the Wallowa River Valley. Joseph and 150 of his non-Christian band were exiled to the Colville Reservation in central Washington State, where he lived out the rest of his life. He had a log cabin, but he preferred the old way of living in tipis and mat lodges. On 21 September 1904, aged 64, he died; his doctor said of a broken heart.

Chief Joseph and his large tribe had been able to lead four armies on a chase over 1,700 miles, criss-crossing the terrain, caring heavy loads, because their Appaloosa were so superior to the horses of the US Army. Throughout the campaign the horses' misery was worsened by meagre rations, minimal rest, and each day saw a few abandoned horses because of sprained or broken legs, tender feet, or sore backs. And yet, the Appaloosas still averaged 16 miles a day and the Nez Perce still had over 1,000 head at the time of their surrender. Only the toughest, hardiest horses had survived the war and they included the survivors of the spotted-horse herds of the Chief Joseph band. The government ordered the confiscation of the tribe's beloved Appaloosas as it became illegal for an Indian to own a spotted horse. Thus the spots became a mark of death for the Appaloosas and they were often shot on sight. Appaloosas were also sold at auction where the bidding was brisk. Ironically it is the buyers of these horses who were the downfall of the Appaloosa breed because they bred them to anything "to throw a little colour on them". Soon, those spotted horses that were swifter, savvier, tougher and more sure-footed than the mounts of the cavalry, were near extinction as the Appaloosa was crossbred into near oblivion.

The breed remained in pitiful obscurity until the early 1920s by which time there were only few pure Appaloosas still alive. However, because the outbreak of the war had caught the Nez Perce leaders by surprise, many of their horses were still on the open range when they started their flight and a large number escaped the hasty round-up. They were claimed later by the first white men who could corral them and then sold to cattlemen throughout the West. In the late 1800s and early 1900s, interest in the breed gradually began to grow as Appaloosas began appearing in Western roundups and rodeos. The Appaloosa's flashy coat patterns caught the eye, and in 1937 an article in Western Horseman entitled "The Appaloosa, or Palouse Horse" revealed a widespread interest in the breed. The Appaloosa Horse Club was formed and has since grown into one of the leading equine breed registries in the world. On 25 March 1975 Idaho named the Appaloosa as the state horse, a deserving tribute for the breed. Today, the beautiful spotted horse is one of the most beloved of American horse breeds and can be found throughout the world, including the author's own paddock. They excel in many disciplines including endurance and reliability as family horses. They are also prized for their easy-going dispositions and distinctive beauty. I am biased but I believe them to be the most wonderful breed with the most remarkable history.

6

Warrior: The Jumper

Colonel Henry Evelyn Wood, VC[1] had expected little trouble as his cavalry ascended Hlobane Mountain. What he met was a massive Zulu army and as a consequence we can now hear the tale of the massacre of Weatherley's Horse and the dramatic jump to freedom of Trooper George 'Chops' Mossop and his Basuto pony *Warrior*. Mossop was a 17-year-old new recruit to the Frontier Light Horse,[2] who had run away from home at the age of fourteen to become a hunter in the Transvaal. As a member of the Frontier Light Horse Mossop had no uniform, aside from the distinguishing strip of red cloth tied around his hat, but what made the Frontier Light Horse stand out was that they were mounted, in the main, on Basuto horses and his was aptly called *Warrior*.

The Basuto is a pony breed from South Africa, who can be up to 14.2 hands high,[3] but rarely taller. Due to its size the Basuto might normally be called a pony, but it is considered a small horse since it possesses many horse-like characteristics, such as an exceptionally long stride. Basutos are not the prettiest member of the equine species and have a rather heavy head, long neck, long straight back, straight shoulder, and muscular, sloping croup. They can be chestnut, brown, bay, grey or black, and have white markings but the one important feature of the breed is that they are very sure-footed, with very tough legs and sound, very hard hooves. Fast, fearless and known for their stamina, they have the great quality of rugged durability and hardiness.

The origin of the Basuto Pony can be traced to the development and subsequent decline of what was known as the "Cape Horse", which formed the foundation stock on which the Basuto breed was founded. Horses had first reached the Cape thanks to the Dutch East India Company in 1653, when four cross Berber-Arabian ponies imported from Java were landed after an extremely dangerous voyage. Although breeding was initially slow, by 1665 sufficient numbers were available to sell. Inbreeding was avoided

---

1   Of the 90th (Perthshire Volunteers), Light Infantry. 9 February 1838–2 December 1919.
2   Born near Durban on 10 October 1861.
3   56.8 inches/142cm.

by the fortuitous stranding of a ship en-route from Java to Persia, which carried four-teen Arabian horses, among the best in Shah of Persia's stud. These swam ashore and were caught. These Persian Arabs and the original horses from Java, formed the basis of what eventually developed into a recognized breed, known at the time as the Cape Horse. It was to become well-known for its sound temperament, bravery, intelligence, endurance, extreme sure-footedness and hardiness.

Natural selection also played a crucial role in shaping the breed. In 1719, and again in 1763, many thousands of horses died from the dreaded African Horse Sickness, which, on the positive side, can be seen as a process that removed animals suscep-tible to disease from the population. By 1769 horse-breeding had developed into a thriving industry, leading to the exportation of war horses to the British army in India. Around 1778 several horses of Andalusian origin,[4] were imported from South America in effect providing another infusion of oriental blood from a different source. The first eight stallions imported from England arrived in 1782 and they were what was then known as "English Blood Horses", descendants of three great oriental sires.[5] Subsequent importations to the Cape from England prior to 1810 also included many of the sons and daughters from the oriental sires and from 1795-1803 several excel-lent English stallions were imported bringing further improvement. The blood of the Cape Horse reached its zenith under the patronage of Lord Charles Somerset, the then Governor of the Cape, who stimulated horse breeding by importing 40 stallions from England to the Cape, each with lengthy Thoroughbred pedigrees during the years 1811-1820.[6] The colonists were so pleased with the Governor's excellent scheme of using the Thoroughbred to ennoble the Cape country-bred that the importation of good stallions continued and the decade 1820-1830 saw many notable sires reach the shores of South Africa. Thus 1811 may be said to mark the beginning of the reign of the English Thoroughbred at the Cape which lasted for half a century.

For many decades the tract of land now known as Basutoland in the Drakensberg mountains and the adjoining country of the Orange Free State, was sparsely inhabited by bushmen, and later more thickly populated by Bantu tribes from the north, east and west of Southern Africa. The comparative peace which these tribes had enjoyed for a couple of centuries came to an end when the Zulu invasions began early in 1822. It was during this period of invasions that the tribes saw horses for the first time, and it was the remnants of these tribes which were later welded into the Basuto Nation by Moshoeshoe who was presented with his first horse in 1829. It had been captured

---

4   A Barb and Arabian cross.
5   Herod (1758) best descendant of Byerly Turk (1689), Matcham (1748) best descendant of Godolphin Barb (1728) and Eclipse (1764) best descendant of Darley Arabian (1706) who readers will remember from the chapter on Copenhagen. In the same year five stud horses were imported from Boston, USA; they were derived from the Barb through the Andalusian horses of Spain, the English Blood Horse, Utrecht and early Dutch horses.
6   See < http://www.saboerperd.com/a3/general/the-origin-of-the-sa-boerperd.html>, *The Origin of the SA Boerperd,* (accessed 3 January 2018).

from a nearby farm and the great Chief, after many struggles, learned to ride and then lost no time in securing further horses.[7] The majority of the horses, acquired by the tribes living in what is now Basutoland and the Free State up to the year 1835, were obtained by raids and thefts from the Cape Farmers on the borders of the Orange River and there is little doubt that the blood of these great progenitors of the Thoroughbred was at least a small component of the horses that entered Basutoland in 1830-50. However, the foundation Basuto stock was, predominantly of the earlier gene pool, as it must have taken many years after Governor Somerset imported his Thoroughbreds for their genes to have reached the horses of Transvaal taken by the Basuto. It may, therefore, be fairly safely assumed that predominantly oriental blood flowed in the veins of the Basuto Pony. So, whilst the Cape Horse and the Basuto Pony were created contemporaneously and from the same foundation stock, with the continual infusions of Thoroughbred and Arabian blood, the Cape Horse became a larger, better-quality animal, whilst the Basuto remained smaller and stockier as a result of harsh conditions and interbreeding with local ponies.

The local tribes, many of whom were vassals of Moshoeshoe, had for some years been invaded and attacked by the Zulus and in 1835, to add to their difficulties, Boer farmers began to arrive amongst these harassed people. The Boers were descendants of the original Dutch colonists of the Cape but during the Napoleonic Wars, a British military expedition had landed in the Cape Colony and defeated the Dutch. Having acquired the colony in 1814 the British encouraged immigration by British settlers and many Dutch Boers who hated the British administration, in particular Britain's abolition of slavery on 1 December 1834, elected to migrate away from British rule in what became known as the Great Trek. The Trekkers initially followed the eastern coast towards Natal and then, after Britain annexed the Natal in 1843, journeyed northwards towards the interior. At first these farmers came for short periods, but later their visits became prolonged. They brought with them their horses and these newcomers, unlike the Zulu raiders had come to stay. There they established two independent Boer republics: the South African Republic in 1852, also known as the Transvaal Republic, and the Orange Free State in 1854.

This occupation resulted in further wars, raids and counter raids, in which much stock, including horses, changed hands. Once the Orange Free State had been occupied, and particularly once the wars between the Europeans and Basuto ceased, the local people were largely employed by the Boers as farm labourers and were paid for their labour in stock. In this way many horses were acquired by the Basuto and European livestock speculators, realising that they were prepared to pay handsomely for good horses, obtained droves of horses which they took to Basutoland and exchanged for cattle. Thus large numbers of horses found their way into the Territory.

7   By 1830 he apparently went to see an old friend accompanied by 23 young men on horseback and in 1833 Moshoeshoe's eldest son received his first horse from his father.

Hence the horses which entered Basutoland from 1835 to 1840 were mostly of excellent oriental blood with possibly an infusion of Thoroughbred from the earlier importations to the Cape. From 1840 to 1870, horses continued to find their way into Basutoland, and these later importations had a greater proportion of Thoroughbred blood than the earlier importations. Basutoland is the most mountainous and coldest part of South Africa and the Basuto were fast and fearless riders but poor horse masters: shelter and food, other than that supplied by nature, were seldom considered. Furthermore, a Basuto pony was and is galloped up and down precipitous mountains where any other horse and rider would fear to proceed at a walk. This treatment, together with the climatic and topographical conditions, tended to increase and accentuate the inherited characteristics of endurance, fearlessness and surefootedness. There is no doubt that the Basuto Pony became a definite and well-established type due to its origin, conformation, character, paces, action and high powers of endurance. Thus they developed into tough, surefooted animals with great stamina and courage.

In 1868, the British annexed Basutoland following an appeal from Moshesh,[8] for British protection from the Zulus and Boers. This created the pre-conditions for the Anglo-Zulu War a decade later. The British governor of Cape Colony and high commissioner for native affairs in South Africa, Sir Henry Edward Bartle Frere,[9] and his military commander, Lieutenant General Frederic Augustus Thesiger, the second Baron Chelmsford,[10] had a plan for the invasion of Zululand. Chelmsford knew that the country was vast, and occupation was out of the question. Therefore, the British advanced on the Zulu capital of Ulundi to capture their king, Cetshwayo,[11] smashing any Zulu izimpi (armies) as they went. Lord Chelmsford divided his army into five columns. Nos. 1, 3 and 4 columns, and advanced on Ulundi from three different directions supported by Columns No.'s 2 and 5 who were held in reserve to protect Natal from any Zulu surprise attack. Chelmsford went with the centre column and on 11 January 1879, British troops crossed the Buffalo River at Rorke's Drift and entered the land of the Zulu. No. 4 Column, under Colonel Wood, was to engage the Zulus dwelling on the flat-topped mountains rising out of the plains of north-west Zululand. Chelmsford required these Zulus to be distracted so that they would not interfere with the operations of No. 3 Column during its advance to Isandlwana and onto Ulundi.

Informed by his scouts of the three-pronged British offensive, King Cetshwayo had committed some of his available regiments to deal with each of the British forces, but kept most of them concentrated in a single, highly mobile 23,000 – 25,000 man impi,[12] with which he intended to engage each of the slow-moving enemy prongs in

8   c. 1786–11 March 1870.
9   29 March 1815–29 May 1884.
10   31 May 1827–9 April 1905.
11   c. 1826–8 February 1884.
12   Rattray, David and Greaves, Adrian, *Guidebook to the Anglo-Zulu War Battlefields* (Johannesberg & Capetown: Jonathan Ball Publishing, 2003), p. 48.

turn. On 22 January, 1879, a sizable part of Chelmsford's central column and part of Colonel Anthony Durnford's[13] No. 3 Column ran into Cetshwayo's main impi at Isandlwana and were famously annihilated with 858 British and 471 native troops wiped out.[14] Equal numbers of Zulus gave their lives in defence of their homeland, but with his entire offensive thrown off balance, Chelmsford had to beat a hasty retreat to Natal.

Scarcely 11 days after the commencement of the invasion of Zululand, the British plans were in ruins on the blood-soaked battlefield of Isandlwana. This part of the Zulu War is very familiar to film goers thanks to the two great movies, *Zulu*[15] and *Zulu Dawn*,[16] but the wider history of the war may be less familiar to the average reader. On the same day as the Isandlwana debacle, No.3 Column, under the command of Colonel Charles Knight Pearson,[17] repulsed a poorly coordinated attack by a Zulu impi at Nyezane on the Indian Ocean coast of Zululand, and advanced to the abandoned mission station at Eshowe, which they fortified. On 28 January, they received a despatch from Chelmsford informing them of the Isandlwana massacre and instructing them to act on their own ingenuity. They decided to defend the mission station and thus the siege of Eshowe began.

With two columns destroyed and another besieged, Chelmsford looked to Wood's No.4 Column and No.5 Column, commanded by Colonel Hugh Rowlands, VC.[18] Chelmsford directed that most of Rowland's command be absorbed into Wood's which was further reinforced by the arrival of the Edendale Troop of the Natal Native Horse and the 1st Squadron, Mounted Infantry, transferred from the shattered remains of No.'s 2 and 3 Columns respectively. On 17 January 1879, Wood had advanced his column north-eastwards and three days later he established a defensive wagon circle, or *laager*, at Tinta's Kraal, ten miles south of a chain of three flat-topped mountains, Zunguin, Hlobane and Ityentika, connected by a nek, and running for 15 miles in a north-easterly direction. After falling back to Tinta's Kraal, Wood decided to move his column north-westwards to Khambula, about 14 miles due west of Zunguin to take up a good defensive position on the crest of a hill. Their arrival on the 31 January was met with a message from Lord Chelmsford informing Wood that all orders were cancelled, and that he was now on his own with no expectation of reinforcements and should be prepared to face the whole Zulu Army.

13   1830–1879.
14   Rattray and Greaves, *Anglo-Zulu War Battlefields*, p. 52.
15   *Zulu* is a 1964 epic (directed by Cy Endfield, produced by Stanley Baker, with Joseph E. Levine as executive producer) depicting the Battle of Rorke's Drift. The film stars Stanley Baker and introduces Michael Caine, in his first major role.
16   *Zulu Dawn* is a 1979 war film about the Battle of Isandlwana (screenplay by Cy Endfield, directed by Douglas Hickox) and is a prequel to Zulu, staring amongst others, Peter O'Toole, Burt Lancaster, John Mills, Simon Ward, Denholm Elliott and Bob Hoskins.
17   July 1834–2 October 1909.
18   Formerly of the 34th (Cumberlandshire) Regiment of Foot. 6 May 1828–1 August 1909.

February saw Wood receive much needed reinforcements in the form of Transvaal Rangers, mounted troops, a troop of German settlers and five companies of the 80th Regiment of Foot. His Column, operating from its encampment of Khambula, became a thorn in the side of the Zulu forces in north-west Zululand. Wood had hoped to capitalise on the near-autonomy of the Zulus surrounding him, by trying to break their allegiance to Cetshwayo. He centred his hopes on Cetshwayo's half-brother Uhamu, who had always been friendly towards the British and on 13 March, Uhamu entered the camp with some 700 of his people, requesting escorts to bring the rest of his people out of hiding. They were hiding in caves 50 miles to the east and only 40 miles from Ulundi. It would be risky to escort large numbers to safety over this area, but Wood judged the risks to be worth it and an escort of British mounted men, with some of Uhamu's warriors were able to return to Kambula with around 900 further refugees.

On 20 March 1879, with the Anglo-Zulu War well into its third month, Lord Chelmsford desperately needed a victory to silence his critics back in Britain. Reinforcements arrived in the wake of the Isandlwana reverse, and with these troops he decided to the relieve Eshowe. On 20 March Wood received an order from Chelmsford to 'demonstrate' against the abaQulusi, in order to draw Zulu forces away from southern Zululand and enable Chelmsford's relief column to lift the siege of Eshowe. Wood saw the logic of the order which provided him and his cavalry commander, Brevet Lieutenant Colonel Redvers Henry Buller,[19] an excuse to carry out an operation that they had been considering ever since they established their camp at Khambula. Wood's goal was the destruction of the stronghold of the abaQulusi, located on a mountain 20 miles to the southeast, known as Hlobane,[20] the refuge of the abaQulusi people, a clan allied with the Zulus.[21] Although he is now largely remembered for his blunders during the Boer War, of which we will hear more in forthcoming chapters, Buller had, at this stage of his career, had an exemplary military career. Schooled at Eton, Buller was commissioned into the 60th Rifles in May 1858 and took part in the Second Opium War,[22] the Canadian Red River Expedition of 1870, and was the intelligence officer during the Ashanti campaign of 1873-74, during which he was slightly wounded. He was promoted to major and then served in South Africa during the 9th Cape Frontier War in 1878.

Wood was aware that the abaQulusi were not his only opponents in the area since they had been reinforced by a contingent of renegade amaSwazi, led by Khosa (prince) Mbilini kaMswati. Most amaSwazi were loyal to the British, but Mbilini, a

---

19   7 December 1839–2 June 1908.
20   Pronounced "shlo-BAH-nyeh".
21   The abaQulusi were not a chiefdom in the usual sense of the word but were regarded as followers of the Royal House and ruled over by *izinduna* appointed directly by the kings. As such, they were particularly loyal to the Zulu crown, and from the first had played a prominent part in resisting the British invasion of northern Zululand.
22   King's Royal Rifle Corps.

pretender to the Swazi chiefdom, had broken with them and had allied himself with Cetshwayo. Prince Mbilini's greatest success in the region was the surprise attack on 12 March 1879 by his followers, on a wagon convoy being escorted by a company of the 80th (Staffordshire Volunteers) Regiment of Foot under Captain David Moriarty, encamped on the Ntombe River. Moriarty and 64 soldiers along with 15 black levies perished, 20 presumed drowned in the river, as Mbilini pillaged the convoy's supplies and ammunition, and then joined the abaQulusi at Hlobane.[23]

Thus the forces which ranged against Wood on Hlobane were a mix of Zulus, abaQulusi and the amaSwazi followers of Prince Mbilini, totalling an estimated 1,500 warriors. This was insufficient to threaten Wood's camp, but they began counter-raiding, stealing cattle and striking terror into the civilian population along the Zulu/Transvaal border and Wood realized that there could be no peace to the northwest of Zululand until the abaQulusi were subdued.

Meanwhile, at his royal *kraal* (village) at Ulundi, King Cetshwayo had received a message from Prince Mbilini, boasting of his success at the Ntombe River and requesting that Zulu reinforcements be sent to Hlobane. Some 20,000 Zulu warriors of his main *impi* had taken some time to ceremoniously cleanse themselves after 'washing their spears' at Isandlwana, replacing their losses and allowing their wounds to heal. By 24 March 1879 they were ready to move and Cetshwayo answered Mbilini's pleas, by dispatching them to Hlobane.

Knowing that an impi was preparing to leave Ulundi and attack either Khambula or another British fort, Utrecht, Wood thought that by attacking Hlobane he could drive cattle off the mountain, and thus wrong-foot the abaQulusi as well as depriving any approaching Zulu army of essential food supplies. This he hoped would prompt the impi to attack him in his well-prepared position at Kambula. On 26 March, Wood heard reports that the main *impi* had left Ulundi taking the road that led directly along the southern flank of Hlobane, and Wood decided to gamble with the safety of his camp by marching on Hlobane. Having reconnoitred the approaches to Hlobane and worked out his plan, he proposed to mount a night attack against the stronghold with two independent columns of mounted troops. Preparations were made, and long before daylight on 27 March 1879, a long column of about 700 mounted men rode out of the camp at Khambula towards Hlobane, carrying extra rations and twice the amount of ammunition normally issued on such a raid.

The summit of Hlobane forms a great, irregular, flat-topped plateau measuring approximately four miles long and 1.5 miles wide, rising to nearly 1,000 feet above the surrounding plain and, apart from two or three precipitous pathways, a skirt of vertical cliffs, and great impenetrable jutting buttresses of rock protects the virtually inaccessible mountain from below. The natural fortress, described by the abaQulusi as the *Painted Mountain*, was in fact two adjoining plateaus with a steep linking ridge

---

23   Rattray and Greaves, *Anglo-Zulu War Battlefields*, p. 89. Along with a civilian surgeon, three European wagon conductors and 14 African voorloopers.

that would thereafter be known as the Devil's Pass. The lower and smaller of the two plateaux rose to a height of about 850 feet at the eastern end of the 4-mile-long Nek connecting it to Zunguin to the south-west. At the eastern end of this lower plateau rose the narrow, very steep, boulder-strewn 'Devil's Pass' in a series of steps to another higher plateau 200 feet up. This knife-edge link between the upper level of Hlobane and its lower level, Ntendeka, had never been visited by a European and its precipitous descent would severely test Buller and his men. There were two possible routes to the top and Wood thought that a dismounted cavalry force might be able to lead their horses up the western slopes of Zunguin Nek, over the lower plateau, then move on to the upper plateau. At the eastern end of the mountain lay Ityenka Nek, a high saddle of ground that gave way to steep cliffs and a high rocky terrace, notched and honey-combed with caves. There, a path twisting its way up and across the jumbled rocks was another possible route to the top.

Wood's plan was for mounted troops led by Buller to scale the eastern track to the higher plateau of Hlobane, supported by rocket artillery and friendly Zulus and once on top he was to drive off the cattle. Buller divided his force into two sections, intent on attacking the abaQulusi simultaneously from both ends. He took 400 Colonial horsemen and 280-foot auxiliaries to strike Hlobane from the eastern end. Buller's mounted men were all local volunteer horsemen except for a few Imperial officers. They consisted of the Frontier Light Horse, under the command of Captain Robert Barton of the Coldstream Guards, Transvaal Rangers, the Border Lancers and the Cape Colony volunteers of Baker's Horse. The Border Horse were commanded by an experienced ex-cavalry officer, Lieutenant Colonel Frederic Augustus Weatherley,[24] who had fought in both the Crimean War and the Indian Mutiny. Also accompanying the eastern assault force were the 2nd Battalion of Wood's Irregulars, part of the Natal Native Contingent, Africans officered by whites. They were mostly local recruits from the Transvaal, supplemented by loyal Swazi warriors–under the command of Major William Knox Leet. In addition, Petrus Lafrus (Piet) Uys, a Boer farmer who had lost his father and a brother to the Zulus many years earlier, commanded about 40 scouts, including two of his sons.

Meanwhile Brevet Lieutenant Colonel John Cecil Russell, 12th (The Prince of Wales's Royal) Lancers, commanding 200 Colonial cavalry with 440 native auxilia-ries, including 200 Zulu defectors,[25] and rocket batteries, would assault from the lower plateau at the western end and so trap the abaQulusi in a pincer movement. Wood believed the final stage of the plan was equally easy to execute with Russell meeting up with Buller and their combined force driving the captured cattle back to Khambula. Russell's force comprised of a Royal Artillery rocket party, and his mounted troops made up of the 1st Squadron, Mounted Infantry and some the Edendale Troop of the Natal Native Horse, which had been present at the debacle at Isandlwana. There were

24   1830–79.
25   Rattray and Greaves, *Anglo-Zulu War Battlefields*, p96.

also the Kaffrarian Rifles of 40 officers and men. The bulk of his force were the 440 black auxiliaries which included the 1st Battalion of Wood's Irregulars, numbering some 240 officers and other ranks, accompanied by the disaffected Zulus who were the followers of King Cetshwayo's step-brother, Prince Hamu kaNzibe.

On the top of Hlobane plateau were over a thousand Zulu of the abaQulusi, who, unknown to Buller, were about to be joined by a major Zulu force numbering some 10,000 warriors heading for Sir Evelyn Wood's column at nearby Kambula. Even though the defeat at Isandlwana was still fresh in his mind, Wood had not subjected Hlobane to any form of reconnaissance other than a cursory appraisal some two weeks earlier. The routes up and down the mountain were based on Wood's view from a distance, and his worst and most costly assumption was that the connecting ridge between the two levels of Hlobane and Ntendeka presented an easy passage; it would prove to be a graveyard for many men.

At midday, the column halted and unsaddled their horses for an hour to take lunch and then moved off to the south of Hlobane. They were clearly seen by the abaQulusi on the mountain who lit a row of signal fires, although the significance of the fires was not realized by Buller who proceeded for several miles beyond Hlobane before making camp, the intention being to give the abaQulusi the impression that his target was the Zulu Army on its way from Ulundi. The next leg of their journey was up to the foot of the mountain at the western end of Hlobane. Once there, the troops off-saddled near a deserted Zulu kraal, and when the sunset they gathered timber and made large fires, as though they were camping for the night. When it got dark, at about 8;00 p.m. Buller led his men back towards Hlobane where they began climbing a cattle track that led up to the plateau. Meanwhile Russell rode toward the lower plateau in the west and bivouacked at the foot of the mountain for the night.

Colonel Wood had left Khambula two hours after the main column, accompanied by his personal staff of 20-year-old, Second-Lieutenant Henry Lysons[26] of the 90th Light Infantry, Captain the Honourable Ronald Campbell,[27] Coldstream Guards, and his political agent and interpreter, Llewellyn Lloyd. The party also included a number of friendly mounted Zulus, among them Prince Mthonga kaMpande, a younger brother of King Cetshwayo, who had sought refuge in the British Colony of Natal in 1865 fearing that his own brother might order his death. He also had eight mounted men from the 90th (Perthshire Volunteers) Light Infantry. Wood received intelligence that the main Zulu army were heading in his direction from Ulundi, and therefore placed scouts to watch the possible approaches. Before resting that night, Wood held lengthy discussions with Petrus Lafrus Uys, the veteran Boer commando leader of the Burgher Force, and Captain Charles Potter, of the 2nd Battalion of Wood's Irregulars, who had traded in the region before the war.

26   30 July 1858–24 July 1907.
27   1848-79.

At 3:00 a.m. on 28 March 1879, Buller's force commenced their ascent of the steepest part of the slope up to the plateau. A heavy storm broke over them and as flashes of lightning lit up the ascending force, the rain turned their route into a sodden path. The storm stopped as suddenly as it had started and the clambering troops and their horses picked their way up through the boulder-strewn track. Dawn revealed that Hlobane's abaQulusi defenders had erected barricades among the boulders and caves, from which they now opened fire. Two officers of the Frontier Light Horse, were cut down, as were two troopers. At this point Buller still had no idea of the fast approaching Zulu Army.

Having left Khambula later than intended, Lieutenant-Colonel Frederick Augustus Weatherley and his Border Horse became mixed with Russell's force and in the confusion, spent most of the night unsuccessfully trying to find Buller. During the storm they had become separated and now lagged behind, wet and cold, and not in a good frame of mind. However, by searching for Buller, Weatherley's scouts inadvertently discovered the encamped Zulu Army and reported the fact to Weatherley. Colonel Wood and his staff had spent the night with Russell's force and at dawn rode out five miles along the southern foot of Hlobane following the route taken by Buller, also unaware of the fast approaching Zulu Army. Wood and his escort rode to the sound of the firing and early that morning, just below the summit of the mountain plateau they came upon Weatherley and his Border Lancers who reported the Zulus' location to Wood, only to have his report dismissed out of hand. Wood could just about see Buller's column high on the trail, so he ordered the Border Horse to follow it up and they then began the climb intending to join Buller's main force.

Weatherley again lost the trail to the summit, and the abaQulusi riflemen, concealed behind boulders and in caves on a rocky terrace, began sniping at them. As Wood came up he expressed his contempt of the Zulu marksmanship at the same moment that a Zulu rifleman took aim at Lloyd, who had been casually chatting to a friend about his days at Oxford University. He fell back, exclaiming, "I'm hit badly! My back is broken." Wood attempted to lift the mortally wounded man but stumbled under the weight. According to Wood, Campbell, came to his aid, impetuously ran forward and carried the dying Lloyd out of the line of fire back to a stone cattle kraal where Wood's staff were sheltering. Again, a Zulu fired at Wood, killing his led mount which fell against him and caused him to stumble. A gasp went up from his men, fearing for their commander, but Wood shouted reassurance and picked himself up to make his way downhill to the troops' position.

Angered at being pinned-down, Wood directed Weatherley to dislodge the abaQulusi defenders but only two of the Border Horse responded. The rest refused to advance and Captain Campbell, who was only 30 years old and the second son of the Earl Cawdor was horrified. This was tantamount to mutiny, if not cowardice and such behaviour was unheard of within the class to which he belonged. Uttering his contempt of the fainthearted volunteers, he sprang forward supported by Lysons and four mounted infantrymen of Wood's escort. They advanced, clambering over boulders and through crevices, which led to the Zulu position. Leading the charge into a cave, Campbell peered into the darkness and was promptly shot in the head at point blank range. With Lysons covering the cave mouth, Campbell's body was brought down and placed alongside Lloyd, who had succumbed to his wound. Undeterred, Lysons and Private Edmund Fowler, following the captain's footsteps, rushed into the mouth of the cave and killed the sniper who had just killed Campbell, forcing the Zulus to withdraw into a series of subterranean passages. For this courageous act, Lysons and Fowler were both awarded the Victoria Cross.

Wood had been extremely fond of Campbell and Lloyd and was stunned by their deaths. Fearful of bodies being mutilated, he lost all interest in the ongoing fight while he concentrated on giving his friends a proper burial. Since the abaQulusi were still sniping from the rocks, he decided to move the bodies three hundred yards further downhill, where the soil was less rocky. Wood ordered his Zulu retainers to dig a shallow grave with their assegais, under the watchful eye of Prince Mthonga. Only when he was certain that his friends could rest without their legs doubled up would he permit the bodies to be lowered into the grave and interred. Being the son of a clergyman, he wished to conduct a proper burial service, only to realise that his service book was still in his saddle on his dead mount. He ordered his trusty bugler, Private Alexander Walkinshaw, to go forward under fire and recover the prayer book. Walkinshaw calmly strode up, under heavy fire and dragged the saddle off the dead horse, placed it on his head, and ran back to the relative safety of Wood and his remaining escort. Wood committed the two bodies to the ground, reading an abridged version of the burial service from the prayer book which belonged to Captain Campbell's wife, who was the daughter of the Bishop of Rochester. Meanwhile skirmishing carried on as Weatherley's Border Horse found their courage and recommenced their ascent on search of Buller.

Finally, at 10.30 a.m. Wood and his remaining escort rode off along the southern flank towards the Western side of Hlobane. It was now that one of his native retainers pointed south-east to the plain below where Wood had the shock of seeing five large columns of a 20,000 strong Zulu impi assuming it's Buffalo formation. Sweeping round the southern flank of the mountain a day earlier than Wood expected, they would effectively trap Buller's and Russell's commands on the summit leaving the scattered British units no choice but to find an alternative way down as quickly as possible. Even if Wood could withdraw both groups, a rapid retreat to Kambula would be required before the Zulus could reach it so he hurriedly sent a message to Russell, ordering him to move up to the nek. Wood headed for Khambula, narrowly escaping the advancing Zulu Army and could only hope that Buller too had seen the massive Impi.

Throughout the morning the abaQulusi on Hlobane had seen Russell's column heading to the western end of the mountain and correctly anticipated that their stronghold was to be attacked from both ends. They had prepared for the attack by building stone barriers at each end of Hlobane, knowing that the approaching Zulu army was now camped less than five miles away. Buller's advance had been virtually unopposed and once on top, Buller left A Company at the top of the path as a rear-guard. The morning appeared to have gone well for Buller's mounted troops who had reached the summit by 6:00 a.m. The abaQulusi on the plateau declined to close with Buller's force disappearing into a number of underground caves, enabling the native infantry to loot their cattle as they headed to the far end of the plateau to meet up with Russell. It seemed probable that Buller would have no great difficulty in joining with Russell on the lower plateau to the west, after which they could drive the captured cattle back to Khambula via the lower plain. Unbeknown to Buller, Russell had ascended the lower Ntendeka plateau but found that the only way up to the summit of Hlobane was via the steep, narrow and largely impassable staircase of rock. So, Russell remained on the lower plateau. At this point at the far eastern end Buller began to come under pressure from the abaQulusi who rallied against him and cut off the paths by which he had ascended. Russell and his staff officer were on the edge of the lower plateau, when Russell observed, "Look at that black cloud shadow moving slowly towards us". His staff officer replied, "How strange, there isn't a cloud in the sky!" Their supposed cloud shadow was the Zulu impi, on their way from Ulundi to engage Wood's column at Kambula, some 10 miles distant.

Buller still thought he was about to meet Russel's column on the lower plateau, until he came to the steep drop of The Devil's Pass at least 130 feet down, studded with rocks and boulders. On the plateau, Buller met with Captain Edward Browne, of the 1st Battalion, 24th (2nd Warwickshire) Regiment of Foot, who had with him some 20 men of the mounted infantry from Russell's column who had scaled the Devil's Pass to inform him that Russell had concluded that it was impossible to climb up with his entire command. Buller rapidly decided that men might be able to scramble down on foot, but to get the horses or cattle down was impossible. It seemed that they would have to turn back and take the long route back down the trail they had followed that morning. Therefore, he dispatched Captain Barton, Coldstream Guards, commanding the Frontier Light Horse, and 30 troopers with instructions to descend the terrace on the south-eastern trail and find and bury the men who had been killed in the earlier skirmishes there. Barton was then to locate Weatherley and tell him to make his way back to Khambula. Barton had just left when Buller saw the great *impi* below, approaching from the south-east and realized that retreat for Barton or himself by reversing the previous day's march was now impossible with the fast-moving Zulu warriors upon them and immediately sent a trooper after Barton to tell him to retire to the north of the plateau.

The abaQulusi warriors now left Hlobane's caves to join some 2,000 reinforcements that had climbed onto Hlobane from the east. Together they attacked Buller's men and quickly routed A Troop who had been left defending the original ascent route. They fled towards Buller's men now being driven towards the Devil's Pass at the western end of Hlobane. Before attempting the descent with his troopers, Buller ordered his African levies in the Natal Native Contingent to abandon the livestock they had taken and make their way down first. However, they forced the looted cattle down the steep face with the intention of driving them back to Khambula, gingerly scrambling down through the boulders before taking to their heels. During their subsequent flight from

Hlobane about one hundred of them were outpaced by the fleet-footed young Zulu warriors and killed.

Barton was still unaware of the encircling Zulu army when, several hundred yards ahead of him, he saw Weatherley and his force reach the summit rim of Hlobane. At that very moment the two troopers arrived with Buller's message which read 'return by the right of the mountain', meaning he should withdraw in the direction of Khambula. The message was sadly misconstrued, and Barton unwittingly led the pitifully small force straight into trouble. Having concentrated their attention on the steep climb in front of them, no one in Weatherley's force had noticed the rapidly closing Zulu army now only one mile away. Barton presumed he should continue as previously ordered by Buller and so Weatherley's combined force of the Border Horse with the Frontier Light Horse behind, headed back down the original ascent route to the base of the cliff and directly into the path of the approaching Zulus. Once off Hlobane they realized that they had inadvertently ridden towards the main Zulu army who were now less than a quarter of a mile away and rapidly closing around them. Weatherley had two sons accompanying his column, and 15-year-old Rupert, who had joined up as a sub-lieutenant, was riding at his side, exuberant with the enthusiasm of youth and looking forward to his first campaign. Weatherley, however, was alarmed by the developing situation. The terrain was not good for mounted men, even on Basuto ponies, to be caught in by marauding bands of Zulus and the lower slopes of Hlobane seemed to have turned into a seething mass of black fury.

Weatherley and Barton turned back and tried to cross to the west in the mistaken belief that they could ride across the saddle and descend to safety down the far side. The Zulus knew that the saddle ended abruptly at a 400-foot precipice to the valley below. Colonel Weatherley and his eighty horsemen of the Border Horse and Frontier Light Horse had no option but to charge the abaQulusi. The top of the mountain was a relatively level, undulating, plateau whose surface was covered in slabs of weathered rock and boulders. Just how the Colonial cavalry managed to ride across this rock-strewn surface on their Basuto ponies on the 28 March 1879, and survive, is a tribute to the Basuto breed. Dressing their line, they charged, desperately trying to cut their way out to the north. But the abaQulusi stood fast, and the horsemen crumbled before the forest of assegais. The Zulus rushed at Weatherley's trapped force and drove them to the very edge of the cliff that ran along the whole of the northern side of Hlobane. Some of the Border Horse were squeezed and herded against these precipitous cliffs and, still mounted, horses and riders were unceremoniously tossed over the edge, to plunge hundreds of feet onto the boulder strewn valley below.

Weatherley had lost contact with his son Rupert and refused to leave the boy. Turning back, he found Rupert on some open ground. He dismounted, heaved the badly wounded boy up onto his horse and turned to face the onrushing abaQulusi. With his arm tightly clasped around his son, he charged into the swirling mass of plumed warriors, who cut the pair to pieces with their deadly blades. Only a handful evaded the slaughter, and in the fierce fighting that ensued, in addition to Weatherley and his son, 66 men were killed.

Meanwhile, Captain Barton and twenty others had managed to make their way to the valley, only to encounter the advance party of the Zulu impi who promptly attacked and quickly killed three-quarters of them. Barton somehow managed to climb down the cliff and having found a loose horse, made off towards the camp at Khambula. He was wounded, his horse had been speared, and he now faced a 20-mile ride as other survivors stumbled away from the carnage on foot. Barton knew that these men without mounts were as good as dead. Moments later he recognised one of his officers, Lieutenant Poole of the Border Horse, who had also climbed down the cliff and was running for his life having been unhorsed. He reined in his horse and picked Poole up as he fought his way clear of the melee, pursued by a number of Zulus. With the exhausted Poole behind him the pair set off but were quickly spotted by a group of fleet footed Zulus who gave chase for the next eight miles. The heavily-laden and weakening horse stumbled along for several miles but eventually, and inevitably, floundered under the weight of the two men and the Zulus closed in on their prey on the bank of the Manzana River. Finally, when the wounded animal could struggle on no further they tried to escape on foot, but Poole was overtaken and killed and then when Barton's pistol failed to fire, he was shot and finished off with an assegai.

By now Buller realised the seriousness of his predicament. The only option was to make for the lower plateau, where he hoped to be supported by Russell's force. It was now Russell's turn to receive an ambiguous message, this time from Wood who you will recall had sent a message at 10:30 a.m. Unsure whether Buller and Russell had seen the approaching Zulus, Wood tried to warn his two commanders but his dispatch to Russell mistakenly ordering him to move immediately to Zunguin Nek five miles from the scene in the direction of Khambula. The message read:

> Below the Inhlobane. 10.30 A.M. 28/3/79
> There is a large army coming this way from the south. Get into position on Zunguin Nek.
>   E.W.

Wood intended that Russell should remain on Ntendeka and support Buller, but he did not hesitate and departed as fast as he and his men could ride, controversially abandoning Buller and his men to the encircling Zulus.

Meanwhile, on the summit, eighteen-year-old George 'Chops' Mossop, was galloping west to try to re-join the rest of his unit.

> Suddenly the ground dipped into a hollow, and scattered about were some three or four hundred Zulus, who sighting me, began shouting and pointing their spears while they formed a half moon, which covered a considerable distance cutting me off ... I think my horse realised the predicament ... he was pulling hard to get away in the direction of the running Zulus who had almost completed their formation ... cut off on all sides, it did not matter where I galloped, and I gave the horse its head ... he became a wild animal, all his instincts urging him

to break away from the enemies who surrounded him. When about fifteen paces from the enemy, a few on our right rushed in to support those immediately in our front, leaving a narrow gap in their line. Like a hare with a pack of dogs behind it, the horse swerved and darted into the breach.[28]

For the moment George 'Chops' Mossop, thanks to Warrior, was alive to tell the tale but their ordeal was far from over, even though they had made it to the top of Devil's Pass and joined up with what remained of A troop.

Colonel Buller and his men were also huddled at the top of the Devil's Pass. Surrounded by sheer cliffs, Buller had expected to receive some support from Russell, but due to the dispatch from Wood, it was now a case of scrambling down the treacherous traverse or being slaughtered. At this point Mossop rode up on Warrior to join Brown and Buller as they peered over the cliff edge into Devil's Pass. Looking down, Mossop could see that even if he and his pony could make it down the 130 feet to the ridge, they would still have to descend 700 feet more to reach the valley below and then somehow make the 20 mile trek to Khambula. The cavalrymen now tried to fight their way down the incline, causing much confusion among nervous troopers with their frenzied horses. Meanwhile, in the turmoil, Buller banded together a small rear-guard of the Frontier Light Horse, including Captain Brown's mounted infantry, who did their best to hold off the overwhelming Zulu numbers and permit the escape of a great number of his men. As the mounted men slowly picked their path down the steep slope, leading their horses and threatened on all sides by Zulus, the weight of Zulu pressing the rear-guard forced Buller to abandon his position, and fight gave way to flight.

Men and horses were rolling down into the pass as the abaQulusi crawled over the rocks, jabbing at the horses with their assegais. Several troopers were captured and hurled from the mountain to their deaths. Mossop asked a man standing next to him, 'Can we get down?' 'Not a hope,' replied the trooper who then placed the muzzle of his carbine in his mouth and pulled the trigger. "A lot of his brain's soft stuff splashed on my neck. I gave one yell, let go the bridle of my pony, and bounded down the pass…. my only thought was to get away from all these horrors." With that yell Mossop left Warrior to his fate and headed towards the bottom of the pass for relative safety. Suddenly, an arm gripped him, and he looked up into the enraged face of Colonel Redvers Buller. He later related;

Suddenly a grip of steel was on my shoulder and I received such a clout on my ear that had the grip not been there to hold me up I would have shot yards away". "Where is your horse boy?" it was Major Buller. "Up there I said", pointing back

28   McAdam, John, 'Hlobane Plateau on horseback – Retracing the route of Lieutenant Colonel Redvers Buller VC', *Journal of the Anglo Zulu War Society No. 20* (December 2006).

up the pass. "Then go back and get him" shouted Buller, "and don't leave him again."[29]

Clearly more terrified of Buller than the abaQulusi, Mossop climbed back up to the pass to get Warrior:

> Scrambling and slipping, clutching at anything I could find, I crawled back up the pass. As my head appeared on top of the pass, a loud whinny of joy met me from my pony. I was immediately struck with remorse at having left him to be stabbed by the Zulu, which was already happening to the horses on my left.

By now, most of the men still on the cliff top were dead and as the abaQulusi came ever closer, Mossop ran to the horse, only to find himself being encircled by Zulus; he later described the scene:

> Zulus, crawling over the huge rocks on either side, were jabbing at the men and horses. Some of the men were shooting, and some were using clubbed rifles and fighting their way down. Owing to the rocks on either side the Zulus could not charge. The intervening space was almost filled with dead horses and dead men, white and black.[30]

Mossop and *Warrior* moved towards the sheer cliff edge facing certain death at the hands of the Zulus and with seconds to spare he jumped off the cliff with his horse. Both bounced down the cliff face and finally fell into a clump of trees. Miraculously both Mossop and Warrior survived the fall and he scrambled down again, dragging his Basuto pony behind him. Warrior seemed to be all right but on closer inspection Mossop saw that he was bleeding profusely from injuries sustained in the fall. Thankfully the area was free of Zulus, so Mossop adjusted the saddle and girth to staunch the horse's bleeding before mounting up. Evading the Zulus, who were intent on dealing with Buller's men higher up, Mossop was able to escape on *Warrior* in the direction of Khambula.

Many of Buller's men and horses fell to their deaths on the steep descent down the Devil's Pass as the Zulus fired at point-blank range into the desperate soldiers. Others stabbed and speared them to death or hurled them off the mountain and rather than share this fate some turned their own weapons on themselves. However, Buller worked desperately to save as many as he could as they had fought their way down the deep rocky pass. So long as there was one man left, Buller would not flee as time and again he plunged into the melee to rescue more of his men to the safety of the lower plateau and send them on their way to Khambula. His fearless example was

29   McAdam, *Hlobane.*
30   McAdam *Hlobane.*

followed by Browne, and by Major William Knox Leet, of the 1st Battalion, 13th (Prince Albert's Own Somersetshire) Light Infantry, who repeatedly rode back into the fighting to rescue the isolated men. Captain Cecil D'Arcy had turned to face his attackers when Buller rode up, took him up behind him, and carried him to the lower plateau and relative safety, earning Buller one of the six Victoria Crosses awarded in the battle.[31]

Most of the Boers had reached the lower plains and only Piet Uys and his two sons stood with Buller as the men below managed to make their escape. Commandant Uys now at the bottom of the Pass, looked back and saw his elder son, Petrus unmounted and struggling to calm his frightened horse unaware that a number of Zulus were closing in on him. He immediately rode back into the mêlée and extricated his son, but a Zulu raced up behind him, and plunged his assegai deep into Uys's back, killing him instantly. However, the Uys boys escaped and a marker was later placed at the foot of Devil's Pass to mark the spot where Piet Uys fell and part of it still remains today.

For the survivors, the ordeal grew even more serious as the Zulus from the main force now reached the lower reaches of the pass and began closing in on both sides of Buller's desperate men. There was little that Buller or his surviving officers could do other than hold their men together and pour rapid fire into the attacking Zulus. With hundreds of Zulus converging on the Devil's Pass the fighting was soon over and only those who had reached the lower plateau with their horses had any chance of getting away. Buller finally made his way over the plateau on to the plains, back to Khambula. What had started as a promising raid against the abaQulusi that morning had turned into a bloody massacre.

At the bottom of the Devil's pass Mossop had mounted Warrior once more, just as the abaQulusi rushed him, and bounded down the steep slopes that led to the valley below. Once on the plain, Mossop came to a stream. Dismounting, he plunged his face into the cold water. Although somewhat revived, he now saw the exhausted *Warrior* was in a bad way. Feeling weak himself, the boy lay down beside his faithful mount, but no sooner had he done so than he was roused by the sharp cry '*uSuthu!*' The Zulus had seen him and were running toward him. Mossop frantically

---

31   These included Lieutenant Colonel Redvers Buller, Major Knox-Leet and Lieutenant Edward Browne. Three years of lobbying by Major General Sir Daniel Lysons, (Quartermaster General at the War Office) and Lady Lysons on behalf of their son, Lieutenant Henry Lysons, resulted in the young officer and Private Edmund Fowler, both being awarded the VC. Lieutenant D'Arcy of the Frontier Light Horse was recommended for the VC but denied on the grounds of being a colonial. This was later rectified. Several DCM's were also awarded to Colonial troopers including one to Wood's Bugler Walkinshaw. Veterinary Surgeon 1st Class Francis Duck, was recommended for the VC by Buller, only to have his name struck out by the Commander-in-Chief on the grounds "that he had no right to be there."

sprang onto Warrior's back once again, and, heroically, the injured pony managed to outpace his Zulu pursuers.

Despite the catastrophe, many of the British and Colonial forces were able to get off the plateau, onto the plains, and make for Kambula, abandoning the field, broken and disorganised, at about noon. The Zulu impi reached the plain shortly after the British had departed and wanting revenge, they followed them for 12 miles, skirmishing from all sides. With many horses lost, a lot of the men were forced to ride pillion to make Kambula and the harrowing flight for their lives continued for several miles. Any horse unable to maintain the pace was overhauled and its rider slain by the jubilant Zulus. Buller arrived back at Khambula after sunset and learned that several of his men whom he had seen escaping were still missing. He then took a fresh horse and went in search of his men and they all returned safely just before midnight.

Having been pursued by the Zulus, stopping only to drink water and to bandage the wounded Warrior where the saddletree had pierced his withers, Mossop and *Warrior* arrived safely at Kambula camp late in the evening. He took *Warrior* to the horse lines, washed and bandaged his wounds and gave him his feed, which he only nibbled. Mossop nursed his dying horse through the night but the following morning, he went straight to the horse lines and in his own words:

> Such is youth! I awoke in the morning stiff and bruised, with a black eye and numerous bumps on my head, but otherwise quite well, and the stiffness soon wore off. The first thing I did was to run to the horse lines to see *Warrior*. I found him lying down, and thought he was dead, but he was alive, although very far gone. I lifted his head on my knee. He knew at once, and gave a pitiful whinny, shuddered twice, and died. I laid his head down, and taking his small silken ears in my hand, caressed it gently, with such a big lump in my throat that, had I not jumped up and run away, I would have blubbered.[32]

Warrior was far from being the only fatality of the action. Fifteen officers and 79 white troops were dead, as were some 140 African levies, the highest British casualty list of the war after iSandlwana.[33] Of the 750 native volunteers of Wood's Irregulars, only 50 remained after the battle; of the rest, those who had not been killed had deserted. Precise Zulu statistics for the battle are unknown, but they described their own losses as 'negligible.' Russell's unit had fared better than others although some of the survivors of the debacle later regarded his actions as bordering on cowardice, but Russell's friendship with the Prince of Wales, averted any possibility of a court-martial. Wood and his escort had made their way west, and once clear of Hlobane, scaled some high ground and remained there until dusk, watching the retreat before he then made his way back to Khambula.

32   McAdam, *Hlobane*.
33   Rattray and Greaves, *Anglo-Zulu War Battlefields*, p. 100.

The Battle of Hlobane had been a British defeat and the loss in horses gravely weakened Wood's mounted capability. Following the battles of Isandlwana and the Ntombe River, Hlobane was the third and last major Zulu victory of the war and never again would a British force be caught while on the move and in the open. Wood was certain that the Zulu impi would now attack Kambula as he hoped, and he was confident of victory and to saving his reputation from the sort of savaging inflicted upon Lord Chelmsford. At Kambula, a hexagonal laager was formed with wagons tightly locked together, and a separate kraal for the cattle was constructed on the edge of the southern face of the ridge. Trenches and earth parapets surrounded both, and a stone-built redoubt was constructed on a rise just north of the kraal. A palisade blocked the hundred yards between the kraal and redoubt, while four 7-pounders were positioned to cover the northern approaches, with two more guns in the redoubt covered the north-east. On 29 March 1879, when the Zulu army attacked the camp they were beaten off and Buller led the ruthless pursuit by the mounted troops of the Frontier Light Horse who were merciless in their revenge, paying the fleeing Zulus back in kind as they would do several more times in the war.

By attacking Hlobane, Wood and Buller had together embarked upon an incautious expedition, disregarding all the lessons from Isandlwana. The reconnaissance was scant and even when Weatherley informed Wood of the proximity of the Zulus, Wood scornfully dismissed his warning. Collectively, they precipitated the second greatest disaster of the war, yet the news of the defeat at Hlobane was forgotten after the British defence of Khambula the following day, just as the successful defence at Rorke's Drift screened Isandlwana.

On 4 July 1879, Buller again commanded mounted troops at the Battle of Ulundi, the decisive British victory which effectively ended the war. Young George Mossop survived Khambula and also went on to fight at Ulundi, surviving the war to become a frontiersman and big-game hunter until his death on the 22 May 1938 at the age of 77. Today, Hlobane is an open-cast coal mine known to the Zulu since 1879 as the "Stabbing Mountain." Buller would go on to be Sir Evelyn Wood's chief of staff in the First Anglo-Boer War of 1881 and the following year was sent to the Sudan in command of an infantry brigade and fought during the expedition to relieve General Gordon in 1885. Promoted to major-general, he was sent to Ireland in 1886 and as a full General, became head of the troops stationed at Aldershot in 1898. Then on the outbreak of the Second Anglo-Boer War in 1899, he was dispatched as commander of the Natal Field Force and we will hear more of his story in the next chapter. After the Zulu War the fame of the Basuto Pony steadily rose and would rise to the zenith of its fame during the Anglo Boer War (1900) along with the related Boerperd. Many of the best Basuto horses were killed in action during that war and there is now a concerted effort to re-establish the Basuto breed who are used for endurance racing, hacking, trekking or polo. The breed, and *Warrior* in particular, deserve their place in this book as one of the toughest and most durable breeds ever to provide military service. Who would not want to ride a horse as brave and honest as *Warrior*?

7

Arabs of Empire: Vonolel, Maidan, and Maharajah

With its distinctive head shape and high tail carriage, the Arabian is one of the most easily recognizable horse breeds in the world and has probably inspired more myths and legends than any other. One origin tale claims that King Solomon was given a pure Arabian mare named Safanad ("the pure") by the Queen of Sheba, whilst another has the Angel Jibril (Gabriel) descending from Heaven and awakening Ishmael with a "wind-spout" that whirled toward him. The Angel then commanded the thunder-cloud to stop scattering dust and rain, and gather itself into a handsome horse that seemed to swallow up the ground. Hence, the Bedouins bestowed the title "Drinker of the Wind" to the first Arabian horse. Another story tells how Muhammad, after a long journey through the desert, turned his herd of thirsty horses loose to race to an oasis. Before they reached the water, Muhammad tested them by calling for them to return. The five mares that faithfully returned to their master became his favourites, called Al Khamsa, meaning, the five, and became the founders of the five "strains" of the Arabian horse, which some breeders claim the modern Bedouin Arabian is descended from. The Bedouin did not geld male horses, and mares were preferred over intractable stallions for riding and breeding, since they were quieter, and would not give away the position of the fighters on raids. Thus, they kept very few colts, and pedigrees were traced through the female line with the ancestry of each horse tracked through an oral tradition. Horses of the purest blood were known as *Asil* and crossbreeding with non-*Asil* horses was forbidden. Over time, the Bedouin developed several sub-types of Arabian horse, each with unique characteristics, the five primary strains being known as the Keheilan, Seglawi, Abeyan, Hamdani and Hadban.[1]

Following the Hijra[2] in 622, the Arabian horse spread across the Middle East and North Africa. Muslim warriors controlled most of the Iberian Peninsula by 720 and probably the earliest horses with Arabian bloodlines to enter Europe came indirectly, through Spain and France. Others would have arrived with returning Crusaders, and

---

1 The first written pedigrees in the Middle East that use the term "Arabian" date to 1330.
2 Occasionally spelled Hegira.

Arabs were used to develop faster, agile light cavalry horses and spread to the rest of the world via the Ottoman Empire. There was a major infusion into Europe when the Turks sent 300,000 horsemen mounted on pure-blooded Arabians into Hungary. Here they were stopped by the Polish and Hungarian armies, who captured these horses to provide foundation bloodstock for the major studs of eastern Europe. The Turkish empire encouraged private stud farms to supply Arab cavalry horses, and Arabian horses were often sold, traded, or given as diplomatic gifts. With the rise of light cavalry, the stamina and agility of horses with Arabian blood gave an enormous military advantage and many European monarchs began to support large breeding establishments that crossed Arabians on local stock.[3]

Just like the long dessert journey of Muhammad, it was a long dessert journey on an Arabian horse that would seal the legend of one of the British Empires most towering figures. Lord Frederick Sleigh Roberts was towering in terms of status rather than physical stature,[4] but would become one of the highest ranking and most respected officers in British Army history. As the Commander-in-Chief in India[5] he would become known as "Kipling's General" and would eventually go on to be Commander-in-Chief of the British Army.[6] However, had his Arab horse, Vonolel not carried him 300 miles to Kandahar things might have been very different for both Roberts and the British Empire. Among his many actions, Roberts fought with the 23rd Peshawar Mountain Battery in an expedition against the Lushais, a tribe on Assam's southern borders who in January 1871 attacked and burnt a village, killing 25 people and taking 37 prisoner including a six year old called Mary. Mary's rescue became a major *casus belli* in an expedition which resulted in the restoration of all captives and during the campaign Roberts defeated the son of a locally renowned chief, Vonolel. Five years after his return, in 1877, he would purchase a nimble, four year old, white Arabian horse from a horse dealer in Bombay, who he named after the chief. *Vonolel* was only 14.2 hands high, and would be categorized as a pony in any modern show ring.[7] However, the Arabian horse has a greater density of bone than other breeds, short cannons, sound feet, and a broad, short back, all of which gives them physical

---

3   The Prussians set up a royal stud in 1732, and others to breed for the Prussian army; by 1873 some English observers regarded Prussian mounts superior in endurance to British.

4   Field Marshall Earl Frederick Sleigh Roberts of Kandahar, KG, KP, GCB, OM, GCSI, GCIE, KStJ, VD, PC 30 September 1832–14 November 1914. Born at Cawnpore, India, the son of General Sir Abraham Roberts, after Eton, Sandhurst and Addiscombe Military Seminary, he entered the East India Company fighting in the Indian Mutiny of 1857 (siege and capture of Delhi and relief of Lucknow in March 1858). Awarded the VC on 2 January 1858 at Khudaganj and also served in the Umbeyla (1863) and Abyssinian campaigns (1867–8).

5   1885-93.

6   1901-04.

7   The breed standard states Arabians should be 14.1 to 15.1 hands but they are classified as "horses" even though 14.2 hands is the traditional cut off height between a horse and a pony.

strength comparable to many taller animals. Thus, even a small Arabian can carry a heavy rider and, with Roberts being only 5 feet 4 inches, the pair were a perfect match.

During the opening stages of the Second Anglo-Afghan War, Roberts distinguished himself enough at the Battle of Peiwar Kotal[8] to receive the thanks of Parliament and be promoted to the substantive rank of Major-General on 31 December 1878.[9] The following May the Treaty of Gandamak signed with Mohammad Yaqub Khan,[10] obliged the Afghans to admit Sir Louis Cavagnari[11] to Kabul, but on 3 September 1878, Cavagnari and the other European members of the mission were massacred in a sudden uprising. With the British Empire thus snubbed, Roberts was despatched to Kabul to seek retribution. Yakub Khan was dethroned and exiled for suspected collusion, but in May 1880, a new British Liberal government gave instructions to bring all troops out of Afghanistan.[12] These plans for the evacuation were disrupted by Ayub Khan, the Governor of Herat, who after stirring up anti-British feeling, sallied out in early June with 6,000-8,000 followers.[13] A force of British and Indian troops,[14] together with Afghan levies, was sent to intercept them and at Maiwand, on 27 July 1880, the 1,900 British Empire troops clashed with the 10,000-15,000 Afghans who had now joined Ayub's force. In addition to the imbalance of numbers, many of the Indian troops in British service were new, inadequately trained recruits, and crumpled under pressure. Despite a heroic last stand by the 66th (Berkshire) Regiment, the British losses were heavy and the bedraggled survivors began a 45 mile retreat to the city of Kandahar. Attacked along the way, exhaustion and thirst contributed to the breakdown of the column's discipline, and 971 succumbed in the battle or the retreat.[15] The remnants of the straggling column reached Kandahar on the 28 July and by the end of the month the bazaars of Kabul were buzzing with the news of a great British defeat in the south. The whole garrison withdrew behind the walls of the fortified city and within a few days, they were besieged. On 8 August, Ayub Khan, the victor at Maiwand, opened fire from north west of the city, and then from the villages on the east and south and it was now clear that a rescue mission was urgently needed.

Roberts would lead a division on a 300 mile forced march from Kabul to rectify the calamity and relieve Kandahar. Given the Arabian's inherent strength, endurance and ability to cope with the hot conditions, Roberts was fortunate and wise to be mounted

8   28–29 November 1878.
9   And to be advanced to Knight Commander of the Order of the Bath (KCB) on 25 July 1879.
10   1849–November 15, 1923.
11   4 July 1841–3 September 1879.
12   Disraeli's Conservative government was replaced after the debacle at Isandlwana.
13   Robson, Brian, *The Road to Kabul: The Second Afghan War, 1878-1881*. (Stroud: Spellmount' 2007), p. 223.
14   Robson, *The Road to Kabul*, p232.
15   Laffin, J., *Brassey's Battles; 3,500 Years of Conflict, Campaigns and War A-Z* (London: Brassey, 1986), p260. Only 161 of the wounded reached the citadel of Kandahar.

on Vonolel as he started his journey. With a relatively long, level croup,[16] and naturally high tail carriage, well-bred Arabians have a deep, well-angled hip and well laid-back shoulder and their unique skeletal structure allows for agility and impulsion.[17] This gives them an efficient gait and hence their endurance. In addition, Arabians usually have dense, strong bone, and good hoof walls, which improves their durability and contributes to the superiority of the breed in Endurance riding competitions. At modern international endurance events, including the World Equestrian Games, Arabians and half-Arabians are the dominant performers in races that can cover up to 100 miles in a day. Endurance riding first developed as a sport in the United States in the early 1900s, based on European cavalry tests requiring the ability to carry 300 lb over 100 miles in one day or even to go on a 5-day, 300 mile ride carrying at least 200 lbs.[18] The cavalry tests became a civilian sport in the early 1950s, and organized endurance riding became a more formal sport in 1955, when a group rode from the Lake Tahoe area across the Sierra Nevada Range to Auburn in under twenty-four hours. This ride soon became known as the Tevis Cup, and it remains one of the most difficult of any 100-mile rides in the world because of the severe terrain, high altitude, and 100-degree (~37°C) temperatures. Endurance riding was brought to Europe in the 1960s and is now a timed test against the clock of an individual horse and rider's ability to traverse a marked, measured cross-county course of 50 to 100 miles, usually in one day.[19]

For Roberts speed was of the essence as there was no telling whether the Kandahar garrison was holding out, and on 7 August 1880, his force of 10,000 soldiers and 8,000 followers set off on their march.[20] Because of the unforgiving terrain, all troops were ordered to travel light (20-30 lbs of kit per trooper) and controversially, no wheeled transport was taken, with mules, donkeys and ponies utilised to carry the main supplies. Only 6 and 9 pounder mountain guns were taken and some thought this madness since it was Ayub's guns that had been one of the deciding factors at Maiwand. Like Custer before the Little Bighorn when he had to decide whether to proceed without infantry and Maxim Guns, Roberts opted for speed and mobility.

The forced march would be out of communication, with no base of operations behind it, and an uncertain strength of enemy in front. The longer route through the fertile Logar Valley was chosen, rather than a more direct approach through Maidan,

16 Top of the hindquarters.
17 Some Arabians have 5 lumbar vertebrae instead of the usual 6, and 17 pairs of ribs rather than 18. Most have a compact body with a short back.
18 *What is Endurance Riding?* See <http://www.olddominionrides.org/EndurancePrimer/01.html> (accessed 12 May 16).
19 Reductions of distance and time increased the number of riders/rides. In 1978 the Federation Equestre Internationale (FEI), the governing body for World and Olympic equestrian events, recognized endurance riding.
20 Ewing, G. *Lord Roberts' famous march from Kabul to Kandahar August 1880* <http://www.garenewing.co.uk/angloafghanwar/articles/kandahar_march.php> (Accessed 13 December 2017). A little over 2800 were Europeans, the rest being Indians.

so that they could gather supplies on the way. The army paid for everything including grain, fresh animals and even firewood and, the local Afghans were more than pleased to barter with the troops. En route, the city of Ghazni, an excitable population, turned out to be no threat, largely thanks to the orders of the new Amir who wanted Ayub Khan dealt with as much as the British did. The column set off again very early in the cool of the morning of the 16 August, continuing onto the stony open plains, where the heat and sandstorms really started to tell. During the march from Kabul to Kandahar the troops would be woken up at one or two in the morning in freezing cold and pitch black, to set off by four, in order to avoid the full heat of the sun. They halted a few minutes every hour, but by the time they stopped at one or two in the afternoon, the temperatures had risen to 105 degrees Fahrenheit, with no shade and a scarcity of water. Sore feet were the main complaint, as the sick list slowly increased. For some the going was too much and followers would give up and lie down, 30 or so going missing throughout the journey, and the rear guard who often did not get in until six hours later, having to force them on.[21]

By the time Robert's relief column reached the garrison at Khelat-i-Ghilzai on the 24 August they had averaged 15 or 16 miles a day, sometimes going as high as 20, double what a regular campaigning army would sensibly march. Still some distance and days away from Kandahar, Roberts received a letter, informing him that the citadel was not in immediate danger, thanks to a sortie out into the village of Deh Koja on 16 August which, though not a military success, did cause Ayub Khan to withdraw further away from the city. On 25 August the column, with Roberts on Vonolel at its head, joined now by the garrison of Kelat-i-Ghilzai, resumed their march towards Kandahar. The following day Roberts learned that Ayub Khan had lifted the siege of Kandahar and retired north. It was now only 19 miles to Kandahar and Roberts could rest for a day and take shorter marches. A week later on the morning of the 31 August 1880, a very tired British General on a small white Arab horse, Vonolel, ahead of his relief force of British and Indian troops arrived at the gates of Kandahar after their 300 mile march across the harsh Afghan terrain from Kabul. It had taken 20 days at an average of just over 15 miles a day and was a remarkable feat of human and equine endurance and organisation. However, for the last part of the trek General Roberts was struck down with fever and had to be carried in a dhooly. For dignity's sake, the general had forced himself upon Vonolel when within sight of the city.

Roberts immediately drew up plans to attack Ayub Khan the next day and at a little after 9:00 a.m. on 1 September, the artillery began its bombardment of the Afghans at the Babawali pass. Roberts sent forward the 92nd Highlanders and 2nd Gurkhas who met determined resistance against a bayonet charge by the Highlanders. The 72nd Highlanders[22] under the Command of Lieutenant Colonel Francis Brownlow, and the 2nd Sikh Infantry also attacked the Afghans who held well-defended posi-

---

21   Three soldiers took their own lives, one of the 72nd Highlanders and two Indian Sepoys.
22   1st Battalion Seaforth Highlanders.

tions. That day, Brownlow was astride possibly the most the remarkable and gallant Arab horses in history, called Maidan, a chestnut stallion foaled in 1869 in the Nejd, today's Saudi Arabia.

Maidan was brought to Bombay in 1871 where he was sold him to a Captain Johnstone who immediately commenced racing him, winning the Punjab Cup as an untried two-year and continuing his winning career for three more years until no further matches could be made for him.[23] Then at five years of age in 1874, Maidan was trained for battle and sold as a charger to Brownlow.[24] The lot of Maidan was to be more challenging than that of Vonolel because, whilst General Roberts was a small man, Brownlow was a heavy-weight. Maidan had already carried him for six years in campaigns through the mountains of India and Afghanistan when Brownlow rode him on that famous forced march with Lord Roberts's army. At eleven years of age Maidan was probably near his peak as an endurance athlete and would need to be to carry the nineteen stones of Brownlow and his equipment 300 miles.

On the day of the battle, after hard fighting, the left wing of the 72nd finally took their objective, but unfortunately Brownlow was killed. Maidan survived to add more battle honours to his racing laurels. The 92nd Highlanders met with determined resistance south west of the Babawali Pass, but despite reinforcements from Ayub Khan's main camp at Mazra, stormed the position. Determined resistance caused many Highlander casualties, but the British dispersed some 8,000 Afghans at bayonet point. In a decisive victory Ayub Khan's army was routed and he lost all his artillery, enormous quantities of ammunition, and about 1,000 men killed. He became a fugitive along with the small remnants of his battered army and the British appointed Abdur Rahman as the emir of Afghanistan,[25] under a protectorate which gave Britain the frontier territories ceded by the Treaty of Gandamak and control of Afghanistan's foreign policy. The British went back to Maiwand to bury their dead, and finally left the city, and Afghanistan, about six months later. Roberts and Vonolel left Kandahar on 9 September and marched to Quetta with part of his division. On the 15 October, at Sibi, he resigned his command, and sailed from Bombay with Vonolel on the 30 for England to recover properly from his illness, and to find himself a national hero, with the title Lord Roberts of Kandahar.[26]

The 72nd Highlanders and Maidan also left Kandahar on 15 September and after six more years of military service, at seventeen years of age Maidan was bought by

---

23 White, Linda, *The Arabian Horse In History: Maidan Gallant Heart, Iron Will* (20 December 2010). See <https://issuu.com/arabian-horse-times/docs/ed-maidan> (accessed 19 December 2017), p4.

24 Brownlow had joined the 72nd Highlanders in 1854 and served in the Crimea, before he went with his Regiment to the Indian Mutiny.

25 Ayub Khan got back to Herat and a year later raised a fresh rebellion against Abdur Rahman, but was swiftly defeated and killed, ending the threat to the new regime.

26 Created Baron Roberts of Kandahar in Afghanistan and of the City of Waterford 23 February 1892.

Lord Airlie who, perhaps rather cruelly by today's standards, again put him to racing. In the three years between 1881-1884 Maidan won the Ganges Hog Hunt Cup, the Kadir Cup (the Blue Ribbon of Pig sticking in India), and a four mile steeplechase. He was then sold to Captain the Honourable Eustace Vesey,[27] who bought him to take to England. Leaving India on the troopship *Jumna*, Maidan got as far as Suez, where the ship met an expedition going to the relieve a harassed the garrison at Massowah, near the lower end of the Red Sea, and was pressed into service as a transport for troops. So the old racehorse and charger had his journey lengthened before he reached Marseilles. Remarkably, shortly afterwards he won a race for his owner at Pau and later was raced successfully in England.[28] Upon the death of Vesey in 1889, Maidan was purchased by the Honourable Miss Ethelred Dillon, and won yet another steeplechase at the age of 22. Even at such an advanced age he was described in the London Live Stock Journal as "fresh and well, with immense bone below the knee and as clean in the legs as a four year old, notwithstanding the fact that he was hunted in Suffolk last year."[29] Very sadly, he slipped and broke a leg whilst out at exercise in 1892, and had to be destroyed at the age of 25.[30]

After a brief interval in South Africa, Roberts served in India from 1881 until he was sent to Ireland as Commander-in-Chief from 1 October 1895. Throughout this time, Vonolel stayed with the general and he accompanied Roberts to Ireland where he was retired to the Curragh in Kildare. He had impressed the British public and Queen Victoria so much that she awarded him the Kabul medal, with four clasps, and the bronze Kandahar star, which Lord Roberts hung round Vonolel's neck. He was also given the honour of being in the procession for Queen Victoria's Diamond Jubilee in 1897. Vonolel, at 29 years of age, passed away while at the Royal Hospital in Kilmainham, in June 1899 and was buried in the rose gardens of hospital in a small grave, marked by a headstone.[31] Roberts was said to be heartbroken, and stated that "During the 22 years he was in my possession he travelled with me over 50,000 miles, and was never sick nor sorry." Whilst no such honours or statues came Maidan's way, his performance was just as impressive, if not more so. Had his rider been more famous he would surely be as well known today. They were two marvellous Arabs who served the Queen with their endurance and durability.

Whilst Roberts, Brownlow, Vonolel and Maidan were dealing with troubles in Afghanistan, the British found themselves engaged in the first of two wars with the Dutch Boers in South Africa. The origins of the Boer Wars went back to the original British occupation of the Cape and the subsequent Great Trek by the Boers. The British had recognised the two Boer republics of the Orange Free State and the Transvaal in

---

27   31 January 1851-18 November 1886.
28   White, *Maidan Gallant Heart, Iron Will*, p. 9.
29   White, *Maidan Gallant Heart, Iron Will*, p. 9.
30   White, *Maidan Gallant Heart, Iron Will*, p. 9.
31   In 1914, Roberts' march was commemorated by a statue of him on Vonolel in Glasgow's Kelvingrove Park, unveiled by Lady Roberts.

1852 and 1854, but attempted British annexation of the Transvaal in 1877 led to the First Boer War in 1880–81. Whilst Roberts was successful in Afghanistan, the British suffered defeats in southern Africa, particularly at the Battle of Majuba Hill,[32] after which a peace treaty was signed with the Transvaal President Paul Kruger,[33] recognising the independence of the two republics. However, diamonds were discovered at Kimberley, prompting a massive influx of foreigners to the Orange Free State and then in 1886 the world's largest deposit of gold-bearing ore was discovered at the Witwatersrand ridge,[34] some 60 kilometres south of the Boer capital, Pretoria. This made the Transvaal rich but the Boers had neither the manpower nor the industrial base to exploit the resource. As a result they reluctantly accepted the immigration of *uitlanders*,[35] mainly from Britain, who came in search of their fortune. However, it would not be long before they would outnumber the Boers who sought to contain their influence by restricting their voting rights, and imposing taxes and tariffs. The Boers were worried about losing their independent control of the Transvaal and being absorbed into the British Empire.

The Cape Prime Minister, Cecil Rhodes[36] was a man driven by a vision of a British controlled Africa extending from Cape to Cairo and in 1895 he hatched a plan. A column of 600 armed men,[37] led by Dr. Leander Starr Jameson[38] made a dash over the border from Bechuanaland towards Johannesburg, hoping to trigger an uprising by the uitlanders. However, the Transvaal authorities were pre-warned of the raid and four days later, the weary column was surrounded and surrendered.[39] The raid united the Transvaal Boers behind President Kruger, and drew them together with the Orange Free State, led by President Martinus Theunis Steyn,[40] in a military pact. President Kruger re-equipped the Transvaal army, by importing the latest magazine Mauser rifles and the best modern European artillery. Many in Britain now favoured annexation of the Boer republics, confident that they would be quickly defeated. Lord Salisbury, the Prime Minister, despised such jingoism but believed he had an obligation to British South Africans and feared that the Cape Boers aspired to a Dutch South Africa. He and British public opinion also hated the Boers' treatment of black South Africans. In September 1899, the British sent an ultimatum demanding full equality for British citizens resident in Transvaal, at which Kruger simultaneously issued his own ultimatum, giving the British 48 hours to withdraw all their troops

---

32   1881.
33   10 October 1825–14 July 1904.
34   Literally "white water ridge", a watershed.
35   "Foreigners" meaning non-Boer whites.
36   5 July 1853–26 March 1902.
37   Pakenham, Thomas, *The Boer War* (New York: Random House, 1979), p. 2. Rhodesian and Bechuanaland policemen with Maxim guns and artillery.
38   9 February 1853–26 November 1917. The Administrator in Rhodesia of the British South Africa Company (or "Chartered Company") – Cecil Rhodes was the Chairman.
39   After losing 65 killed and wounded. The Boers lost only one man.
40   2 October 1857–28 November 1916.

from the border or face war against the Transvaal and Orange Free State. When news of the ultimatum reached London it provoked outrage and laughter in equal measure. If Kruger wanted war he would have it!

Or so they thought! Soon British pride would be dealt a severe blow. By midnight on 15 December 1899, at the end of the so called 'Black Week' of disasters at Stormberg,[41] Magersfontein,[42] and Colenso,[43] the British Army had earned a very bloody nose and came to the realisation that their war against the amateur Boer farmers was going to be no walk over for their professional army. They also realised that they were going to have to match the mounted mobility of the Boers with their own mounted infantry.

The Boers hoped for a quick victory and launched a pre-emptive offensive into the British-held Natal and Cape Colony on 11 October 1899. They had no regular army units[44] but relied on a civilian militia, with all the *burghers* (citizens) in a district forming a military unit called a *commando* and electing their officers.[45] Each man wore his everyday farming clothes, a slouch hat and brought his own weapon, usually a hunting rifle, although those who could not afford a gun were given one by the authorities. Each man also bought his own Boer horse or pony, known as the Boerperd which is a calm, tough animal standing between 13.3 and 15.3 hands high.[46] Whether black, brown, bay, chestnut, grey, roan, dun or even palomino, South Africa's frontier environment and severe conditions made the Boer horses exceptionally hardy. The "Boerperd" is now a breed but in those days they were a mixture of types, and two varieties existed; the Boerperd, a general breed, and the more refined Cape Boerperd. As we saw in the chapter on Warrior, the Boer Pony has similar origins to the Basuto pony, both having developed from the Cape Horse in the nineteenth century. However, the Boer Pony did not have to survive such rough conditions as the Basuto pony, and consequently became a larger, better-developed animal. The more refined Cape Boerperd was predominantly a mix of English Thoroughbred and Arabians and the resulting Anglo-Arab proved to be fast, nimble and strong. It had good endurance and was used for riding, hunting, sport and light farm work. The Cape Boerperd and hardy Boerperd ponies, with their great mobility and toughness would help the Boers move around and hold out against the British Empire.

A lifetime spent in the saddle, both as farmers and hunters, made the Boers tough, independent and well prepared for the hardships that they would face on campaign. On long hunting trips by horse in all weather and terrain, they had learned to fire from cover and to make the first shot count. Thus they made brilliant mounted infantry, and soon it became clear that they presented the British with the challenge of a mobile and innovative approach to warfare. The Boers struck with speed and surprise, driving

41   10 December 1899.
42   11 December 1899.
43   15 December 1899.
44   Apart from the 'States Artillery'.
45   A full-time official (*Veldkornet)* maintained muster rolls, but had no disciplinary powers.
46   In Afrikaans, 'boerperd' means 'farmer's horse'.

towards the major British garrison at Ladysmith and surrounding it, while to the north-west at Mafeking, a railway junction on the border with Transvaal, Colonel Robert Baden-Powell[47] was forced to defend when the Boers assaulted the town on 13 October 1899, beginning a 217 day siege. Lastly, on the borders of the Orange Free State, lay the diamond mining city of Kimberley, where from early November the Boer tried to starve the town into submission.[48] In retrospect, the Boer decision to commit themselves to sieges displayed a lack of strategic vision and handed the initiative back to the British.

It was at this point that our hero of Hlobane, General Sir Redvers Henry Buller VC, arrived with major British reinforcements. He sent one division up the Western Railway to the north to relieve Kimberley and Mafeking winning several bloody skirmishes,[49] before suffering losses of seventy dead and 413 wounded at the Modder River on 28 November 1899.[50] A smaller force of about 3,000 pushed north toward the railway junction at Stormberg about 50 miles south of the Orange River,[51] where, on 10 December 1899, they were defeated, with 127 killed and fifty-seven wounded, and two guns and over 600 troops captured.[52] The next day 11,000 British troops of the northern force attacked,[53] at Magersfontein but the Highland Brigade became pinned down by accurate Boer fire from well positioned trenches. After suffering from intense heat and thirst for nine hours, they eventually broke in ill-disciplined retreat, losing 192 killed and 690 wounded.[54] However, the nadir of Black Week was the Battle of Colenso on 15 December 1899 where 15,000 British troops commanded by Buller himself,[55] attempted to cross the Tugela River to relieve Ladysmith. Awaiting them were the Transvaal Boers under General Botha.[56] His first attacks failed against well sited artillery and accurate rifle fire, and Buller ordered a retreat, abandoning many wounded men, and ten field guns to be captured by Botha's men.[57] They suffered almost 1,450 casualties[58] and these three defeats showed that the British commanders had gone to war with antiquated tactics, failing to comprehend the impact of destructive fire from trench positions and the mobility of cavalry raids. With the sieges still

---

47 1857-1941.
48 Garrison was commanded by Lt Col R Kekewich with Cecil Rhodes also a prominent figure.
49 At Belmont on 23 November 1899, at Graspan on 25 November 1899.
50 Von Der Heyde, N., *Field Guide to the Battlefields of South Africa* (Cape Town: Struick, 2013), p271.
51 Von Der Heyde, *Battlefields of South Africa*, p. 301
52 Von Der Heyde, *Battlefields of South Africa*, p. 304.
53 Von Der Heyde, *Battlefields of South Africa*, p. 261.
54 Von Der Heyde, *Battlefields of South Africa*, p. 265.
55 Von Der Heyde, *Battlefields of South Africa*, p. 70.
56 27 September 1862–27 August 1919.
57 Buller lost 145 men killed and 1,200 missing/wounded, the Boers 40 casualties (8 killed).
58 Von Der Heyde, *Battlefields of South Africa*, p. 73.

continuing, an angry British government was forced to send two more divisions plus large numbers of colonial volunteers.[59]

The Imperial Yeomanry were born out of these disasters, since it became obvious that large numbers of mounted infantry were needed to counter the fast moving Boers. The Yeomanry were a volunteer organization that had been in existence for over a hundred years, and would now have their chance to prove their courage, loyalty and worth. On 27 March 1794 the British government, under threat of invasion by the French, had raised volunteer troops of cavalry to be composed of gentlemen and yeomanry,[60] and by the end of 1794 there were 28 yeomanry corps or troops, each of around 60 men,[61] based at the main towns of the counties. The government withdrew financial support for the Yeomanry in 1827 and many units disbanded,[62] whilst others survived thanks to the patronage of rich colonels, until in the 1850s there was a renewed threat from France and the Yeomanry were re-invigorated. However, it would be fair to say that, for some it became an excuse for gentlemen to impress the ladies with their cavalry uniform without having to undergo arduous campaigning. The Yeomanry were not required to go abroad on active service, but at the start of the Boer War there were many offers from the Colonels of Yeomanry regiments to provide forces for South Africa. All were politely but firmly rejected until the Black Week convinced the government that they needed many more mounted troops and on the 13 December 1899 the War Office decided to form the new *Imperial Yeomanry*, based on the standing county yeomanry regiments, to serve overseas as mounted infantry.[63]

The standing Yeomanry regiments were asked to provide service companies consisting of 115 rank and file,[64] one captain and four subalterns, the core being the men of the existing regiments, supplemented by volunteers. Candidates had to be from 20 to 35 years of age, of 'good character' and had to satisfy the Colonel of the regiment that they were good riders and marksmen. Their well-nourished and nurtured physiques were better than those of the regular soldiers but some men arrived in South Africa with minimal horsemanship skills and even more were poor marksmen, a fact that some of them would not live to regret. Strict uniform was not insisted on but the

---

59 By January 1900 it was the largest force Britain had ever sent overseas, some 180,000 men, with further reinforcements sought.

60 Mileham, Patrick, *The Yeomanry Regiments; Over 200 Years of Tradition*. (Staplehurst: Spellmount, 2003), p10. Yeomanry were respectable country people who farmed land as freeholders or tenant farmers.

61 Mileham, *The Yeomanry Regiments*, p12.

62 The only unit to face the French were the Pembroke Yeomanry who, in February 1797, defeated the small invasion force at Fishguard in Pembrokeshire.

63 This was confirmed by a Royal Warrant on the 24th December 1899. The term of enlistment for officers and men would be for one year, or not less than the period of the war.

64 Imperial Yeomanry. See <http://www.angloboerwar.com/unit-information/imperial-yeomanry-by-company/1946-imperial-yeomanry> (accessed 2 January 2018). Yeomanry re-organised as platoons/companies/battalions instead of troops/squadrons/regiments.

men were to be dressed in woollen Norfolk jackets, of neutral colour, breeches and gaiters, lace boots, and felt hats. Arms, ammunition, camp equipment and transport was provided by the government, but, although paid at cavalry rates,[65] officers and men had to bring their own horses, clothing, saddle and tack. Hence the original contingents of the Imperial Yeomanry were from a higher social stratum than the men of the regular army, often members of the local hunt, seeking honour, adventure and to test themselves against the sporting challenge of combat. For example, there was also the 19th Battalion, 'Paget's Horse', raised by Mr George Paget from gentleman's clubs, a battalion of Sharpshooters raised by the Earl of Dunraven, and the 20th Battalion, 'Rough Riders', raised by Lord Latham. The Yeomanry companies were numbered but retained their county identities, for instance the 34th and 35th Companies were also known as the Middlesex Yeomanry.[66]

One socially elite member of the Imperial Yeomanry was Captain Jack Seeley from one of the most respected families on the Isle of Wight.[67] Seeley was the Conservative candidate for the forthcoming election to Parliament and to give some idea of his social standing, his farewell dinner prior to leaving for South Africa was held at Osborne House with Queen Victoria herself.[68] Applications had to be addressed to colonels commanding Yeomanry regiments, or to general officers commanding districts but in Seeley's case the Colonel of his Regiment, the 12th Bn (41st Hampshire Company), was his father-in-law. They moved to Christchurch where they eagerly trained and awaited a ship. Keen to get to the war, Seeley by-passed normal channels and chartered a ship, *The Goth*, from his uncle Sir Francis Evans who owned the Union Castle Line and sent the bill to the War Office. However, rules were rules and they would not let him board with his superb Arab horse, Maharajah, because it was a grey and the War Office did not accept light coloured horses in case they attracted sniper bullets. Although, like Vonolel and Maharajah, many Arabians appear to have a white hair coat, they are not genetically white, this colour being created by the natural action of the grey gene. Most commonly purebred Arabs are bay, grey, or chestnut, with black, and roans being less common, but no matter their coat colour, have black skin, except under white markings, because black skin provided protection from the intense desert sun.

Undeterred, Seeley went to the back of the docks and using gallons of dark brown dye called Condy's Fluid, managed to give his near white horse the appearance of a Strawberry Roan.[69] This was a bold and fortunate move because it would be in large measure due to the iron legs, strong constitution and exceptional endurance of this remarkable Arab that Seeley would return to Southampton 18 months later. Others who took their trusted Hunters from the lush fields of Britain to the dry, stony, arid

65   With a capitation grant for horses, clothing, etc.
66   In all, 174 companies in 38 battalions were to serve in South Africa.
67   31 May 1868–7 November 1947.
68   Scott, Brough, *Galloper Jack* (Newbury: Racing Post, 2012), p. 65.
69   Scott, *Galloper Jack*, p. 66.

lands of the veldt soon found they had the wrong horses as they were reduced to limping wrecks. Having had his photo taken on his roan Maharajah, he joined the ship as the Hampshire Yeomanry sailed to war in January 1900 and landed at Cape Town three weeks later[70] with the First Contingent of Imperial Yeomanry who arrived in South Africa between February and April, 1900.[71] Once in the Cape the men were sent five miles to Maitland Camp which had few facilities for the huge influx of men and horses but on the positive side, many of the companies were retained in the camps for long periods, awaiting transport to the front, giving time for much needed training and acclimatisation. For many the journey up country would be a welcome change from the cramped conditions and tedium of the camp.

Meanwhile, Buller made another bid to relieve Ladysmith. Having successfully crossed the Tugela river west of Colenso, he faced a defensive position centred on a hill known as Spion Kop. British troops captured the summit during the early hours of 24 January 1900, but as the dawn fog lifted they realised that they were overlooked by Boer gun emplacements on the surrounding hills. Poor communications and contradictory orders resulted in 1,500 dead, wounded and taken prisoner,[72] followed by a retreat back across the Tugela River.[73] Concerns about Buller's performance had by now earned him the nickname "Sir Reverse" from some of his officers and troops, and led to his replacement as overall commander by another old friend, Lord Frederick Sleigh Roberts. Vonolel had passed away six months earlier when he arrived on 23 December 1899, but this was not the only fatal loss he had suffered and he had very personal reasons for wanting to avenge the Boers. His only surviving son, Frederick Hugh Sherston Roberts VC had just been killed in action at the Battle of Colenso.[74]

Roberts quickly assembled a new headquarters staff including Lord Kitchener from the Sudan,[75] as his Chief of Staff, and launched a two-pronged offensive, personally leading the advance across the open veldt into the Orange Free State. Leaving Buller in command in Natal, he massed his main force near the Orange River and along the Western Railway behind the Modder River, and opened his main attack on 10 February 1900 by outflanking the Boers defending Magersfontein. On Valentine's Day a cavalry division under Major General John French[76] launched a massed cavalry charge to relieve Kimberley and against heavy fire, split the Boer defences on 15 February 1900, ending its 124 days' siege.

The average life expectancy of a British horse, from the time of its arrival in Port Elizabeth, was around six weeks and French's cavalry rode 500 horses to their deaths

70   Scott, *Galloper Jack*, p 6. Seven horses out of 300 died on the journey.
71   550 officers and 10,371 men in 20 battalions of four companies each.
72   Von Der Heyde, *Battlefields of South Africa*, p89.
73   The Boers suffered a mere 300 casualties.
74   Roberts and his son were one of only three pairs of fathers and sons to be awarded the VC.
75   24 June 1850-5 June 1916.
76   28 September 1852–22 May 1925.

in a single day.[77] Animals were drawn from across the British Empire, as well as Europe and the Americas,[78] and transportation took a heavy toll on their condition through inactivity, dehydration and disease. These horses disembarked completely unfit for action. Furthermore, cavalrymen trained in lush climates were used to their horses gaining much of their sustenance from local forage, which was not available in South Africa and troops from different countries and backgrounds had different levels of horsemanship and were unaware of the stresses being put on their mounts. The Cape Ponies and Boerperds of the Boers were used to the rough grass of the Karoo but the horses from overseas were not. The available Basuto ponies were incredibly hardy but the natives were not keen to part with them and hardships that brought all other horses to grief were as nothing to the "genuine" Basuto. Supply lines for food and water were very hard to maintain because South Africa lacked good roads and railways and was affected by harsh weather extremes. Good grazing was infrequent and, even if available, the military situation often precluded such open grazing. Horses were caught in a downward spiral of starvation, disease and exhaustion, resulting in the Anglo-Boer War being one of the worst horse massacres in military history. The horses on both sides died in unprecedented numbers, at a mortality rate of 60 percent died compared to three percent for human combatants and a total wastage of more than 400,000 horses in three years.[79]

The cavalry saddle with full equipment weighed about seven stone in addition to a 12 stone rider and with this weight horses were supposed to be able to move at the rate of nine miles an hour, do scouting work, riding round hills all day, and, at the end be able to charge a retreating enemy. A first-class steeplechase horse would make an ideal cavalry horse, but there was no economic sense in breeding such horses for the prices the Army would pay since, when a horse of weight-carrying power, pace and quality was produced, he was worth more as a racehorse, carriage horse, or as a gentleman's hunter, than as cannon fodder. Many English officers were riding their own hunters, often bred "by a thoroughbred horse from an Irish hunting mare" which were finer animals in appearance, and carried weight better than the Australian horses. Compared to the English cavalry horse, the Australian Waler horses had lighter loins, drooping quarters and were too light framed to command the admiration of the English authorities, whilst English horses looked lumbering to Australians. The

---

77   See <www.bwm.org.au/site/Horses.asp> (Accessed 12 May 16). Most horses were landed at Port Elizabeth (inc 50,000 from the USA and 35,000 from Australia) where today there is a life size statue of a horse and soldier with a drinking trough for horses and cattle. It is a memorial to the 300,000 horses that died during the conflict.

78   Of 519,000 horses used during the war, 360,000 had to be shipped into South Africa.

79   Wilson M, *A History of New Zealand's Military Horse: The Experience of the Horse in the Anglo-Boer War and World War One*. See <http://ir.canterbury.ac.nz/bitstream/10092/959/1/thesis_fulltext.pdf> (accessed 13 December 2017). Also published in 2008 by VDM publishers, and *first published on Horsetalk 10 February 2012*. See <http://horsetalk.co.nz/2012/10/12/lest-we-forget-new-zealands-horses-at-war> (accessed 13 December 2017).

English horses were so strong and sturdy that 18 stone of weight did not materially distress them, while lighter framed Walers felt the weight. However, the Australian climate and geography was similar to that of South Africa, so Australian men and their Waler horses adapted quickly to the environment.

In contrast to the cavalry horse, if a horse had four sound legs he would be able to carry the Mounted Infantry whose horses consisted of every class of animal, from the very best down to the very worst. The Australian Waler was as good as those from any other country if they were well cared for and they were obtained in their thousands at a cheap rate. Their only competitors in cheapness were the Argentine Criollos who were sent over in their thousands. They were a fixed type who resembled each other closely in being squat, with broad heads, wide back and chests, and strong quarters.[80] There were even little Burmese ponies ridden by the Burmese Mounted Infantry, an animal thirteen hands high capable of carrying a man and his gear, weighing 17 stone, all day every day, on a meagre diet. They were not very sturdily-built but their strength and endurance was marvellous, usually coming into camp pulling hard at the end of the day. They remain a popular breed in the region for polo and general trekking.[81]

With General French now in Kimberley at the expense of many lost horses, Roberts pursued the Boer force, which had abandoned Magersfontein to head for Bloemfontein. French's cavalry embarked on an epic 30 mile drive towards Paardeberg where the Boers were attempting to cross the Modder River. On 17 February 1900, a pincer movement by French's cavalry and the main British force was repulsed by the Boers but Roberts succeeded in surrounding the retreating Boers who, after ten days of bombardment, were forced to surrender 4085 men ten days later.[82] Meanwhile, in Natal, Buller used all his forces to defeat the outnumbered Boer forces north of Colenso and after a siege of 118 days, Ladysmith was relieved on 28 February 1900. Roberts then advanced into the Orange Free State from the west, putting the Boers to flight at the Battle of Poplar Grove and capturing the capital, Bloemfontein, unopposed on 13 March 1900. The Boer defenders escaped and scattered whilst their leaders met at the temporary capital of the Orange Free State, Kroonstad, and planned a guerrilla campaign.

Among the Boer leaders was Christiaan de Wet,[83] one of the most famous Boer generals of the war whose role as a guerilla leader would earn him a world -wide reputation. Born in the Orange Free State, at the age of 11 he had ridden out to do battle with the Basuto and had also fought in the First Anglo-Boer War. Expecting the outbreak of war in September 1899, De Wet bought Fleur, the grey Arab horse that was to carry him through many battles and across thousands of miles on the veld. During the period of siege warfare De Wet had tried to persuade the Boer leaders

80   Fitzpatrick, A., *The Ultimate Guide to Horse Breeds* (London: Hermes House, 2011), p110.
81   Pickeral, Tamsin, *The Encyclopedia of Horses and Ponies* (Bath: Paragon, 1999), p197.
82   Von Der Heyde, *Battlefields of South Africa*, p257.
83   7 October 1854–3 February 1922.

to go on the offensive, but after Roberts occupied Bloemfontein, De Wet disbanded the commandos, telling his men to take leave and re-group in ten days' time on 25 March 1900 at the Sand River. A new spirit prevailed among the toughest and most determined burghers when they reassembled and De Wet knew that, given freedom of action, he could conduct a war the British would not know how to counteract, destroying supply lines, and disrupting communications using hit and run tactics. De Wet urged the burghers to get rid of their wagons, which impeded their progress, and in late March and April 1900 launched his guerrilla offensive. On 31 March 1900 De Wet dealt the British a severe blow at Sanna's Post, about 23 miles east of Bloemfontein. His 1,500 Boers attacked the city's waterworks and ambushed a heavily escorted convoy,[84] which caused 155 British casualties and the capture of seven guns, 117 wagons, and 428 British troops[85]. After a number of successful sweeping raids, President Steyn entrusted command of the Free State commandos to De Wet.

Meanwhile, when the Yeomanry eventually left their base camp at Maitland a grand plan had been hatched to spread the various battalions around the zone of operations. Four battalions were to head for Mafeking,[86] ten battalions to the Orange Free State,[87] and the 2nd Battalion were to join Sir Charles Warren in Griqualand. However, as the demand for mobile forces grew, companies of yeoman were detached for weeks at a time and some battalions never formed as such. The first action of the new force came on the 5 April 1900 when elements of the 3rd and 10th Battalions engaged a force of foreign volunteers under the command of the aristocratic Frenchman, Count de Villebois-Mareuil,[88] at Tweefontein, to the north west of Kimberley. The Boer sympathizers were surrounded in a victory that cost the yeomen three dead, including two officers.[89] The Boer would prove to be a much tougher and more elusive enemy than the foreign volunteers.

After being forced to delay six weeks at Bloemfontein due to a shortage of supplies and enteric fever,[90] Roberts resumed his offensive towards the Transvaal, on 3 May and detached a small force to relieve Baden-Powell, at Mafeking on 18 May 1900 provoking riotous celebrations in Britain. Roberts also directed Lieutenant-General Sir Leslie Rundle,[91] commander of the 8th Infantry Division, to stop the Boers from re-occupying the south-eastern Free State. Seeley, Maharajah and the Hampshire Yeomanry entrained for the 200 mile journey to DeAar junction and then marched

---

84   Von Der Heyde, *Battlefields of South Africa*, p245.
85   Pakenham, *The Boer War*, p. 395.
86   3rd, 5th, 10th & 15th.
87   1st, 4th, 6th,7th, 9th, 11th, 12th (Inc. Seeley's 41st (Hampshire) Company) 13th, 14th & 19th.
88   22 March 1847–6 April 1900.
89   Capt Cecil W Boyle, 40th (Oxfordshire) Company, 10th Bn, IY, was the first officer of the IY to die in the war. He had brought thirty of his own horses for active service.
90   Caused by poor hygiene, drinking bad water at Paardeburg, and appalling medical care.
91   1856-1934.

sixty miles in the heat to Britstown where the commander was Kitchener. His orders were for a forced march of fifty miles to the Orange River and back again. The weather was hard and the "veldt as white with water"[92] and horses with the accompanying 7th Dragoon Guards, who were straight off the ship, were dying in large numbers. They reached Dewetsdorp and then the Company trekked seventy miles north to Senekal, arriving on 27 May 1900.[93] The next day Seeley and his men were pinned down near Senekal at a hill called Biddulph's Berg. He hit the ground for cover and was reported dead. With this news back in the Isle of Wight, and with his wife Nim campaigning hard for him, he won the election, on a wave of patriotic fervour.

On 27 May 1900 a battalion of 500 Yeomanry, under the command of Lieutenant Colonel Basil Spragge, had headed for the Boer held town of Lindley, forty miles north-east of Senekal. There, to his horror, a large group of pre-warned Boers were waiting for them, so he decided to hold a group of hills outside the town and await help. Over the next three days, the situation grew worse as the 13th Battalion were surrounded by the Boers, commanded by Christiaan de Wet's brother, Piet. Spragge's messages for help did not convey the urgency of the situation, and hence no relief plan was put into operation until it was too late. By the morning of the 31 May 1900 the situation had become untenable when a party of the 47th (Duke of Cambridge's Own) Company commanding a critical position surrendered. With no chance of holding out, Spragge capitulated with a loss of 27 Imperial Yeomenry deaths.[94] The Boers captured about 530 men,[95] a huge shock to both the yeoman and the public back in Britain since the Duke of Cambridge's Own, nicknamed the 'Millionaires' Own', symbolised the wealth and power that had been associated with the Imperial Yeomanry and the Irish companies contained large numbers from landed families with money and title.[96] This humiliation raised doubts about the Yeomanry back home since, within a few months of arrival in South Africa, they had been given a very bloody nose. Sadly this was not to be their last.

Despite this setback for the Yeomanry, on 28 May 1900, the Orange Free State was annexed, renamed the Orange River Colony, and on 31 May 1900, the same day as Spragge's surrender, Roberts finally captured Johannesburg, and Pretoria fell on 5 June 1900. That day Seeley and Maharajah were patrolling near Harmonia, 40 miles south of Senekal. They were part of Rundle's operation to bottle up De Wet and General Marthinus Pinsloo[97] in the Brandwater Basin area, in the north east of the

92   Scott, *Galloper Jack*, p68.
93   Scott, *Galloper Jack*, p71.
94   Watt, Steve, The Imperial Yeomanry', *Military History Journal*, Vol. 13, No. 6 December 2006 Pietermaritzburg. See <http://samilitaryhistory.org/vol136sw.html> (Accessed 13 December 2017).
95   Pakenham, *The Boer War*, p. 437.
96   Pakenham, *The Boer War*, p. 437. Amongst the dead was Capt. Sir J.E.C. Power (Earl of Leitrim), a whiskey baronet.
97   1838–1903.

Republic, with Basutoland and the Drakensberg mountains to south-west and with other ridges completing the circle.[98]

After the railway bridge across the Vaal River had been damaged, huge stores of provisions, destined for the British army, had accumulated at Roodewal station which De Wet attacked on 7 June 1900, capturing supplies, 486 troops and killing 38.[99] On 9 June 1900, on Senekal Road, he got news of his election as MP for the Isle of Wight by 1062 votes,[100] but by this time the need for the British to stop De Wet became obvious. Roberts concluded that he could end the war if he captured De Wet and now initiated a large scale operation known as the 'First De Wet Hunt.' The British were soon on the trail of the elusive Boer Pimpernel, and the Yeomanry were heavily engaged in an attempt to stop him fleeing into the Transvaal. De Wet realised that the forces ranged against him were too great and he together with President and Mrs Steyn and their entourage headed towards the Brandwater Basin. While the British rested and re-grouped the Boer forces debated whether or not they should defend the basin or make their escape and concluded it could offer only temporary sanctuary, since the mountain passes leading to it could be occupied by the British, trapping the Boers.

Roberts defeated the Boers at Diamond Hill on 11–12 June to link up with Buller,[101] and declare the war over. The set-piece period of the war now largely gave way to a mobile guerrilla war and hence pitched battles were rare events for the Yeomanry who rode hundreds of miles over the veldt and met the Boer infrequently. The yeoman formed flying columns that moved from dawn to dusk with only poor rations and little chance of shelter, and it is not surprising that the rate of disease and death soared. The story of the Yeomanry for the remainder of 1900 was of minor victories and some occasions where its volunteer status became all too obvious.[102]

Despite being a newly elected MP, the situation with his horses was causing Seeley too much concern to have time to think of constituency business. One morning he had to shoot twenty horses and the inadequacies of the hunter types was becoming all too apparent. However, it was Seeley's good fortune to have Maharajah who was his one consistent source of success throughout his time in South Africa. The Arabians developed in a desert climate to be war horses, and were prized by the nomadic Bedouin people for their speed, endurance, and intelligence. The desert horse needed the ability to thrive on very little food, in a dry climate with wide temperature extremes from day to night. This genetic advantage now came to the fore as Seeley and Maharajah's mutual dependency grew on the veldt with horse following master around like a dog.[103] On 15 July 1900 he also bought a Basuto Pony for £25 which was incredibly

98   Scott, *Galloper Jack*, p. 72.
99   Pakenham, *The Boer War*, p. 435.
100   Scott, *Galloper Jack*, p73.
101   Roberts drove the Boers from the hill at a cost of 162 casualties (50 Boer casualties).
102   E.g. on the 26 June the 35th Company fled from a Boer attack north of Senekal.
103   Scott, *Galloper Jack*, p. 73.

tough and hardy, did not require shoes, could live of poor grass, and had a slow easy lope which it could keep up for hour after hour.[104] It would be able to take some of the burden off Mahrajah but that same day the hard core of 1800 Free State Boers under De Wet, accompanied by President Steyn and the government,[105] managed to slip past the British near to Retiefs Nek in the direction of Kroonstad.

By 27 July 1900 Seeley was back near Fourisberg, at the southern end of the basin, where he was to stop Prinsloo and his men who were still in the basin from crossing the Caledon River into Basutoland. It was a steep escarpment down to the river which he descended on Maharajah to meet a local chieftain. He convinced him that the great white Queen wished him to halt Prinsloo if he came their way, and that if he did not, Seeley had the whole British army behind him. We must assume the bluff worked because Prinsloo surrendered on 29 July.[106] Although hounded by British columns, De Wet headed west from the basin and succeeded in crossing the Vaal into western Transvaal and shaking off his pursuers on 14 August 1900, allowing Steyn to travel to meet the Transvaal leaders. However, President Kruger and what remained of the Transvaal government had retreated to eastern Transvaal and Roberts advanced against them.

Seeley had headed back to Harrismith with his four officers and sixty men via the Golden Pass on 10 August 1900,[107] accepting Boer surrenders en-route. Later that month, Roberts broke the Boers last defensive position at Bergendal on 26 August 1900 and Kruger sought asylum in Portuguese East Africa[108] before heading for Europe courtesy of a Dutch warship.[109] Seeley had now spent four months chasing Boers with Rundle's 8th Division, marching and skirmishing across the Brandwater Basin. He and his men were living in the open, often very cold or very wet or very hot, but always very tried and very hungry. It was now two weeks since the news of Prinsloo's capture and the return to Harrismith should have meant safety and comfort. It turned out to be a hell hole of disease and death with typhoid running rampant. On 22 August 1900 Seeley and Maharajah headed out again from Harrismith but by then he was very ill with gastro-enteritis and by September he was lucky to be sent to hospital in Durban given the survival rates in Harrismith.[110]

On 3 September 1900, the South African Republic was formally annexed and most British observers now believed the war to be all but over. However, Boer fighters had broken back through the Drakensberg mountains into the Transvaal highveld

104 Scott, *Galloper Jack*, p. 74.
105 Pakenham, *The Boer War*, p. 443.
106 Scott, *Galloper Jack*, p. 75.
107 Scott, *Galloper Jack*, p. 78.
108 Present-day Mozambique.
109 Sent by Queen Wilhelmina of the Netherlands who had ignored the British naval blockade. President Kruger first went to The Netherlands where he stayed before moving finally to Clarens, Switzerland, where he died in exile on 14 July 1904.
110 Scott, *Galloper Jack*, p. 81.

and now travelled light on their Boerperds. The British were nominally in control of both Republics, but in practice they only controlled the territory they physically occupied since, despite the loss of their two capital cities and half of their army, the Boer commanders adopted successful guerrilla tactics. Each commando was sent to their home district, which meant that they could rely on local support and personal knowledge of the terrain, and the vast distances allowed them freedom to move about on their Boerperds. It was nearly impossible for the 250,000 British troops to control the territory since, as soon as a British column left a town or district, British control of that area faded away, a feeling probably familiar to many British commanders with experience of Afghanistan in the 21st century.

On 7 October 1900 Seeley got back to his men at Standerton, 100 miles north of Harrismith. Two days later he was on a convoy heading south to relieve beleaguered garrisons and from 9 October, as he headed across the Free State of DeWet, his diary reads like that of a US Cavalryman on the Great Plains. The wagon train plodded on towards Reitz, 60 miles to the south-west, undertaking the distasteful task of farm burning en-rute. His own morale was not good as the blazing heat and drenching rain sapped his spirits and one of his men was shot through the neck the day before. By 29 October Seeley and Maharaja had got through to Bethlehem and were two days from Harrismith when the Boers attacked the wagon train's rear-guard. By this stage there was a standard operating procedure in his unit that the senior man first arriving at any incident would be the last to leave. Seeley, in accordance with the procedure took charge of the scene on arrival and put four troopers in place. He then received orders from his superior to leave the men in situ and retire which, he disobeyed in favour of the established procedure. Although he was successful in the action, on his return he was placed under arrest pending Courts Martial. At Harrismith, General Rundle presided and Seeley was acquitted to be informed soon afterwards that he had been awarded the DSO.[111]

Nevertheless, De Wet returned to the Orange Free State, where he inspired a series of successful attacks and raids from the hitherto quiet western part of the country. However, the hunt for de Wet continued, and with the war dragging on, Seeley received a deputation from his men who had volunteered a year ago, expecting the war to last weeks, not months, and now found they had no guarantee of pay, leave or getting home. They were also getting sick, particularly from typhoid. It was also three months since they had been told the war was nearly over and they hated the farm burning and rounding up of civilians. They wanted to actively hunt down the Boers yet throughout the Autumn the constant routine patrolling was beginning to erode the enthusiasm that had brought the Yeomen to Africa in the first place and the policy of farm burning imposed by Roberts in the Summer of 1900, was work that the educated men of the Yeomanry found hard to stomach.[112] It is not surprising that

---

111 Scott, *Galloper Jack*, pp. 80-81.
112 Scott, *Galloper Jack*, p. 87.

morale plummeted and many Yeomen volunteered to join the Transvaal Constabulary and other police forces to escape the monotony, whilst regular units snapped up these literate yeomen as officers.

With these reductions added to the casualties and medical discharges the numbers of yeoman began to fall alarmingly and no arrangements had been agreed to reinforce the original contingent. Roberts handed over command on 12 December 1900 to Lord Kitchener and headed home but by the end of 1900 there were barely a third of the original men left. In early January Seeley was involved in a big shoot up with the Boers when the heliograph flashed through the signal that Lord Roberts had arrived at Cowes to meet the Queen and had informed her that the war was nearly over with nothing remained but a few guerrilla bands. This may have been an upbeat message for an aging monarch but such a positive spin did her little good since she died on 23 January 1901, ending an era with a moment of imperial self-delusion. Back in England, Roberts argued for a return of the original contingent of the Yeomanry, understanding that if something was not done soon, future volunteer forces would not be sustainable. It was decided that the Imperial Yeomanry had done their bit and that recruitment should begin of a second and larger contingent.

Thus, in the early months of 1901, the War Office went on a recruiting spree but unlike the patriotically motivated and educated men of the original contingent, the typical new recruit of 1901 was more like his regular comrades, being working class and motivated by a five shilling a day.[113] Born in haste and trained in chaos at Aldershot, a lot of the men were packed off to the war before their officers had been selected. Companies were now formed from any batch of recruits at Aldershot who were ready, thus negating the common bond of county origin and loyalty, and if some 'slippage' in standards had been allowed in the original contingent, those in the new yeomanry were ignored.[114] Officer selection was a shambles with men chosen who had no experience or leadership potential, some being returned home having been found to be cowards, drunkards or just plain incompetent.[115] The new yeomanry arrived in theatre with none of the hard won skills of the original contingent although for a few months the small remainder of the original contingent served alongside the second.[116]

Back in the field the British, now led by Lord Kitchener, mounted three unsuccessful searches for De Wet, but the Boer guerrilla war was inherently sporadic, poorly planned and lacked an overall objective. Trying to put a strategic dimension into otherwise random action, De Wet led an invasion into the Cape Colony in order

113   As opposed to a shilling a day in the infantry.
114   Over 700 men who had been passed fit in England were sent back from South Africa as medically unsuitable.
115   In total, 16,597 men were recruited, including 655 who re-enlisted from the First Contingent. To reduce the number of officers, companies were increased from 115 to 155 men.
116   In June and July 1901 all veterans, bar those who had re-enlisted returned to Great Britain.

to relieve pressure on the Eastern Free State, but his men were hampered by bad weather and relentlessly pursued. Once he finally crossed the flooded Orange River the lack of horses and torrential rain frustrated his plans, and there was no uprising among the Cape Boers. On 28 February he returned to the Free State. It was a failure as he lost the strategic initiative and was henceforth limited to defensive warfare.

In March 1901 Seeley and Maharajah, with 400 men under his command, slogged 100 mile to Stunderton harassed by Boer Commandos. There he entrained for an eighty mile trip south-west to Newcastle and then, through mud out of Utrecht to the Pivaan River. The idea of the Utrecht operation was to pin down Louis Botha,[117] the key player at Spion Kop and the future first President of the Republic of South Africa. At Lone Tree Hill Seeley saw a figure on a horse, dimly lit in the mist. The horseman was advancing on stony ground and a corporal shouted "shoot Sir", at which Seeley let off two shots, but he missed and the figure galloped away. Eight years later, when Seeley was a Cabinet Minister, he met the then Prime Minister of the Free State at Buckingham Palace and realised he had nearly ended the future Premier's life. Perhaps his poor aim could be put down to the dysentery that he had by that stage caught and he ended up in hospital in Utrecht on 2 March 1901.

The British now revised their tactics, concentrating on restricting the freedom of movement of the Boer commandos and depriving them of local support. Kitchener, determined to end the war at all costs, now built 8,000 fortified blockhouses,[118] each housing six to eight soldiers radiating 3,700 miles from the larger towns across 31,700 square miles of endless veld,[119] dividing it into smaller areas. These proved very effective but the blockhouse system required so many troops to man that it left less than 50,000 troops for offensive operations against Boers in the field.[120] In organized, systematic, "New Model" drives, a continuous line of troops would sweep an area bounded by blockhouse lines to catch their quarry, whilst the "scorched earth" policy destroyed crops, burned homesteads, poisoned wells, and interned Boer and African women, children and workers in concentration camps. Despite all these measures Botha, De Wet and other leaders, such as De la Rey,[121] consistently evaded capture as trains were attacked and railway lines destroyed. Smuts[122] and Botha[123] also carried out raids into the Cape and Natal, but by October 1901, the commandos had become fugitives and ammunition and supplies were dwindling to nothing.

The concentration camps had originally been set up as refugee camps for civilian families who had been forced to abandon their homes, but when Kitchener succeeded

---

117 Scott, *Galloper Jack*, p. 89.
118 Pakenham, *The Boer War*, p. 537.
119 Farwell, Byron, *The Great Boer War* (Barnley: Pen and Sword, 2009), p350.
120 Farwell, *The Great Boer War*, p. 351.
121 22 October 1847–15 September 1914.
122 24 May 1870–11 September 1950.
123 Botha said he owed much to his wonderful white horse, Dopper, which carried him through the war.

Roberts in November 1900,[124] the influx of civilians grew dramatically. Poorly administered and increasingly overcrowded, conditions in the camps were terrible, due to neglect, poor hygiene and bad sanitation. Supplies were unreliable, partly due to of the constant disruption of communication lines by the Boers and because the families of men who were still fighting were routinely given smaller rations. Eventually 16,000-20,000 children under the age of 16 were to perish in these concentration camps, more than all the fighting men who died by bullets or shells on both sides in the entire war.[125] In Britain unease developed following reports about the treatment of the Boer civilians, notably from Emily Hobhouse.[126] In June 1901 David Lloyd George[127] raised the matter in Parliament, accusing the government of "a policy of extermination" and, stung by the escalating public outcry, the government appointed a Commission[128] to improve conditions and civil authorities took over the running of the camps.[129]

Seeley and Maharajah were due to sail back to England in May but by 12 April 1901 he was sent to train recruits in Kroonstad.[130] Eventually he travelled 700 miles with Maharajah back to Cape Town to board the *Mongolian* for the journey back to Southampton. Maharajah had his coat clipped to keep him cool during the slow trip through the tropics, but although Maharajah was fine, six man died on the long trip but on 8 June 1901 they sighted the Needles and at 4:00 p.m. they docked at Southampton.[131] Seeley returned to the Isle of Wight as the sitting MP and Maharajah as one of the only equine survivors of the horse Holocaust.

Whilst Seeley and *Maharajah* were travelling home, the first blooding of the new Imperial Yeomanry force came at Vlakfontein on the 29 May 1901, when a rear-party of 230 yeoman of the 7th Battalion, 48th Company (North Somerset), were attacked and fled after suffering seventy casualties, leaving 100 Derbyshires and some artillerymen to be shot down. Their reputation had already begun to suffer and questions were being raised in parliament about their suitability. The worst catastrophe

---

124 Buller remained popular with the public in England, but his reputation was damaged and with public disquiet over the continuing guerrilla war, the Minister for War and Lord Roberts demanded his resignation. Buller refused but was summarily dismissed on half pay on 22 October, his request for a court martial denied as was his request to appeal to the King.

125 Farwell, *The Great Boer War*, p. 392.

126 9 April 1860–8 June 1926. A delegate of the South African Women and Children's Distress Fund.

127 17 January 1863–26 March 1945.

128 Headed by Millicent Fawcett who toured the camps August to December 1901 and insisted that rations be increased and additional nurses be sent out immediately.

129 27,927 Boers, of whom 24,074 were children under 16 (50% of the Boer child population), had died in the concentration camps (one in four Boer inmates). By February 1902 the death-rate dropped considerably but by then the damage had been done.

130 Scott, *Galloper Jack*, pp. 93-94.

131 Scott, *Galloper Jack*, p. 96.

of the second contingent occurred at at Groenkop, near Tweefontein on Christmas morning of 1901 when the 11th (Kent and Middlessex) Battalion were caught by De Wet who led 450 men to climb a rocky slope in the dark and attack the camp from above.[132] The camp was taken and 289 yeoman were killed, wounded or taken prisoner. Unfortunately, Tweefontein was not the last disaster for the second contingent, and they were disgraced near Tweebosch on the morning of 7 March 1902 when a column was attacked by 2000 Boers with artillery. The colonial mounted troops panicked and fled, for the most part sweeping the yeoman with them. The 86th (Rough Riders) Company had the sad distinction of fleeing three miles without firing a shot and it was for these disasters,[133] and not the great work of the majority of the yeoman, that the second contingent became known as 'De Wets' own'. However, there were countless actions, both large and small, in which they performed heroically.[134]

In late March 1902, British reinforcements were sent to the Western Transvaal and on 11 April 1902 at Rooiwal, a commando attacked a superior force of British soldiers, who were well positioned on a hillside. The Boers charged on horseback from a long distance and, once beaten back with severe casualties, it was the end of the conflict in the Western Transvaal and also the last major battle of the war. The end was in sight and the Boer leaders called a conference of sixty representatives on 15 May. Although De Wet was still prepared to carry on, it was clear that most of the delegates were opposed to prolonging the war. De Wet voted to accept the terms of the Treaty of Vereeniging along with fifty-four of the sixty delegates, and the Boer forces finally surrendered on Saturday, 31 May 1902.[135]

For Britain, the Second Boer War was the longest, the most expensive, and the bloodiest conflict between 1815 and 1914,[136] and although they had won, the Boers were given £3,000,000 for reconstruction and were promised self-government. This was achieved with the creation of the Union of South Africa as a member of the Commonwealth in 1910. The exact numbers of Imperial Yeomanry involved in the war are hard to determine, but were in excess of 30,000 men.[137] After the war, the

---

132 Von Der Heyde, *Battlefields of South Africa*, p. 136.
133 The abandoned regular troops suffered 68 dead, 121 wounded and over 600 prisoners.
134 Recruits were being raised for the third contingent (7,239 yeomen) as early as December 1901 in order to have time for adequate training. The 27th to 32nd battalions arrived days prior to the treaty and earned a medal denied to the 33rd to 39th Bns (despite staying in country into 1903 for stabilization.
135 De Wet signed in his capacity as acting president of the Free State as Steyn was by then too ill.
136 £200 million and around 75,000 lives; 22,000 British and allied soldiers (7,792 killed in battle, the rest through disease), between 6,000 and 7,000 Boer fighters, between 20,000 to 28,000 Boer civilians (mainly women and children) and perhaps 20,000 black Africans.
137 Leo Amery, *The Times History of the War in South Africa*. Altogether 35,520 Imperial Yeomanry went to South Africa, (at least 2,000 went out a second time and after 29 October 1901, some enlisted from South Africa.). Yeomen earned one VC, 10 CBs, 1 CMGs, 96 DSOs, and 113 DCMs.

Imperial Yeomanry disbanded with individual Companies returning to their British based Yeomanry Regiments, dropping the 'Imperial' title. Under the 1908 Haldane reforms they were all incorporated into the Territorial Force.[138] Though not always a success, the experiment of the Imperial Yeomanry did teach the Government and Army valuable lessons which proved vitally important in the Great War when raising a huge volunteer force.

The stamina, hardiness and mobility of the Boerperd had been tested and refined during the war. It was, to a large extent, these tough, agile horses that allowed them to prevail against the overwhelming might of the British army for as long as they did. However, the breed paid a high price for its role in the war, as thousands of horses were lost due to the harsh conditions. Many not killed in battle were subsequently shot by the British on the farms in an attempt to deny the Boers their advantage of mobility. By the end of the conflict, only the hardiest and those deliberately hidden away by their owners in remote areas remained. Today, Boerperds are found in isolated herds in the south-east Transvaal, northern Natal, eastern Free State and north-eastern Cape Province and they are still used as utility horses on farms and for endurance riding.

On the British side, 131,700 Imperial military horses survived the war, with 28,700 sick horses in remount and veterinary camps.[139] Reloading tens of thousands of fatigued horses for weeks at sea was not practical, so 120,500 horses were sold to local farmers and foreign armies.[140] Whilst Maharajah and de Wet's horse, Fleur, both returned to retirement, both of their owners were destined to fight again. When the Orange River Sovereignty was granted self-Government in 1907, De Wet became Minister of Agriculture but left politics after Union in 1910. When the First World War started in 1914 De Wet, wanting no part in 'England's wars', was against General Botha's attack of German South West Africa, a situation aggravated when Martial Law was declared and men were called up from all over the country. De Wet became one of the leaders of the Maritz Rebellion which was defeated by Botha on 12 November 1914. Ever the master of evasive tactics, De Wet managed to escape, only to be captured by a posse of men in motorcars on 30 November 1914. For the first time in his life, De Wet was taken prisoner. "It was the motorcars that beat me," he said.[141]

One day in August 1902, Jack Seeley, astride Maharajah was on exercise with the Hampshire Yeomanry on Salisbury Plain, when from the top of a hill he spied a lovely long tailed, black Thoroughbred galloping below him. He immediately decided

138 The "Imperial Yeomanry" lineage is carried on by the Yeomanry Regiments and their Imperial Yeomanry companies earned the battle honour "South Africa" for their parent regiments.
139 Wilson, *A History of New Zealand's Military Horse.*
140 9500 horses were destroyed due to outbreaks of glanders, mange and lymphangitis. Cited at Wilson on 12 May 2016.
141 Six months later he was sentenced to six years imprisonment but was granted a reprieve and eventually settled on Klipfontein where he died on 23 February 1922.

it was the new horse he had been looking for and spurred on Maharajah to catch up with the horse and rider.[142] Over a few whiskeys with the owner he agreed a price for the mare from County Leitrim, called Cinderella, and immediately took her off to the Yeomanry horse line where she was tied up next to Maharajah. After a bite on shoulder form the Arab the two horses became devoted to each other, so much so that when four years later Maharajah slipped and broke his neck on a frosty day in the field on the Isle of Wight, Cinderella was distraught. Clearly, Maharajah the Arabian was more at home in the dessert and high veldt than in the winter frosts of England, but Seeley needed to do something to cheer up Cinderella, The answer was to put her to foal and it was to be on Cinderella's son, Warrior, that Seeley would go on to fight throughout the Great War.

142 Scott, *Galloper Jack*, p. 164.

8

Monty: The Film Star

At the outbreak of the Great War, Australia's youth rushed to the recruiting depots to defend the motherland with a desire to prove the fighting courage of their new nation. One 21-year-old who took the oath to serve his adopted country in the Victorian city of Geelong was an Irish engine driver called Sloan Bolton,[1] who preferred to be known by the nickname, 'Scotty'. He applied to join the 4th Light Horse Regiment and became a member of a regiment who, mounted on their Walers, were to prove themselves with feats of endurance and bravery in the sands of the Middle East. Like the US Cavalry of the American Plains and the Imperial Yeomanry, the light horse combined the mobility of cavalry with the dismounted fighting skills of infantry and therefore were issued with rifles and bayonets.

We have already met the Waler horse with Australians in the Boer War, but it is worth considering their blood lines in more depth in order to appreciate their achievements in the war against Turkey. In 1788, the first fleet of eleven ships to Australia brought with it one stallion, two colts and four mares from the Cape of Good Hope and later ships brought further Cape horses. Given what we know of the cape breed at this stage, they were probably an Arab cross. From the outset it was realised horses were needed that could meet the demands of transport work and communications in the young colony with its tough landscape. Successive Governors encouraged the breeding of horses to meet these needs which led to an influx of many notable breeds such as the Thoroughbred, Clydesdale, Suffolk Punch, Cleveland Bay, Lincolnshire trotter, Norfolk Roadster, Yorkshire Coacher, Hackney, Timor pony, Arabian, Percheron and native British ponies.

To reach Australian shores all horses had to undergo a tough sea voyage which many did not survive, so natural selection was already playing its part in the development of a tough breed. From the survivors, the foundation of a uniquely Australian Colonial horse was established, resulting in a versatile work horse with good weight carrying capabilities, speed, endurance and the ability to thrive on the native pastures. They

---

1   1894-1947.

were used as a stockman's horse by bushrangers, as military remounts by troopers, and for exploration expeditions that traversed inland Australia. Soon, owners of large properties were breeding these colonial horses, known as New South Walers, by the thousands for a lucrative export trade in cavalry and artillery remounts for the British Army in India, who gave the nickname "Waler". Horses were exported from as early as 1816 and the remount trade flourished from the 1830s onwards such that by 1867, the Waler was regarded by the British as amongst the finest cavalry horse in the world. The Waler evolved into a hardy horse with great endurance, even when under extreme stress from lack of food and water and the use of Walers by the the Australian army in the Boer War further established their excellent reputation. The preferred Walers for cavalry duties were 15 to 16 hands high[2], with those heavier horses over 16 hands being used as draught and packhorses. They could maintain a fast walk and could progress directly to a steady, level canter without resorting to a trot which was noisy, liable to dislodge gear and resulted in soreness in the horse's back. Estimates vary but in the First World War around 150,000 "Walers" were to be sent overseas for use by the Australian Imperial Force and the British and Indian governments[3], and of these, around 30,000 were shipped to the Middle East for the Australians or other parts of Britain's imperial armies.

Bolton sailed with the 4th Light Horse on 19 October 1914 and arrived in Egypt on 10 December 1914. Here they went into training in a makeshift camp spread across the sands of Egypt, in the shadows of the pyramids, where they sharpened their military and equestrian skills and waited. Mobilisation of the nation's mounted expeditionary forces was hurried and for the horses the change of life must have been confusing and traumatic. Transportation conditions saw slight improvement since the Anglo-Boer War, and as a result, horses arrived in Egypt in better condition than they had in South Africa. However, from arrival in theatre the climate would change, work would increase, food would be rationed and illness would be common.

By 1914 Egypt had been part of the Ottoman Empire for 400 years, remaining under nominal Ottoman rule despite being occupied by the British in 1882, and becoming a British protectorate. Britain's declaration of war on Turkey on 5 November 1914 created a threat to that vital artery of the British Empire, the Suez Canal. As a result Egypt became a major base during the war, and the British immediately evacuated the Sinai Peninsula and concentrated their defences on the western side of the canal. From 26 January to 4 February 1915, German-led Turks attacked the Canal and although the assault failed, advance troops and outposts were maintained by the Turks on the Sinai peninsula, with main bases at Gaza and Beersheba.

Soon rumours were flying around the Light Horse of impending action in Gallipoli but just as the excitement reached fever pitch, the troopers were told they were to

2   60 to 64 inches (152 to 163 cm).
3   Of these, 82,000 went to India (although different figures are sometimes offered). Another 10,000 went to France with the infantry in 1916.

remain in Egypt since the horses were unsuited to the terrain of the Peninsula. The troopers were irritated by the taunts of the departing infantry, but Gallipoli did not go according to plan and urgent reinforcements were soon needed. The 4th Light Horse landed in Gallipoli between 22 and 24 May, without their horses, as reinforcements for Infantry Battalions before reforming as a regiment on 11 June 1915. The troopers quickly realised that they had arrived in a Mediterranean hell hole where the disease and squalor of the ANZAC trenches was causing as many casualties from dysentery and diarrhoea as the bullets and bombs of "Johnny Turk". Reluctant to report sick, Bolton attempted to hide his illness and fought on until late August when he could barely stand, and was evacuated to hospital in Alexandria, back in Egypt.

By the end of 1915, the campaign in Gallipoli was winding down and many units were withdrawn.[4] The 4th Light Horse left the Peninsula on 11 December, arriving back in Egypt but without 41 of their comrades who lay beneath the rugged landscape of Gallipoli,[5] in a part of Turkey which would be forever Australia. Trooper Bolton re-joined his regiment on 2 January 1916, but the reunion was short-lived as Scotty was again stricken with disease and was readmitted to the hospital on 6 January with mumps. From the horses perspective this respite of the Dardanelles campaign allowed almost two years for acclimatisation in Egypt. If the mounted force had been required immediately upon arrival, the state of the horses throughout the campaign could have mirrored the Anglo-Boer War. Whilst in France the density of troops, machine guns and barbed wire meant that the war stagnated into trench warfare, in the Middle East the paucity of troops, lack of railways and roads, hostile terrain and vast area meant that a more mobile pattern of warfare could still prevail. The speed, endurance, and manoeuvrability of the horse was unmatched by any other means of transport and was the most feasible and reliable way to manoeuvre troops and supplies at speed.

Another unit to return from Gallipoli was the Queen's Own Dorset Yeomanry (QODY). Under strength despite a number of new drafts,[6] they reorganised and now under the command of Lieutenant Colonel Hugh Maurice Wellesley Souter[7], a pre-war Indian Army officer, and were ordered to join the Western Field Force. Whilst the main threat to the Canal came from the east, the Turks and their German

4   The evacuated forces from Gallipoli and fresh divisions from the United Kingdom formed the Mediterranean Expeditionary Force with headquarters at Ismailia, totalling nearly 400,000 men.
5   Kelly, Darryl. *Trooper Sloan 'Scotty' Bolton, DCM The Beersheba Charger*. See <www.anzacday.org.au.> (accessed 13 May 16).
6   Arriving in Matruh, the Dorset Yeomen strength was 21 officers, 293 other ranks and 297 horses.
7   Born in India in 1872. Originally commissioned into the Manchester Regiment, he joined the 14th Murray's Jat Lancers (of the Indian Army) in 1896, and served in the Tibetan Campaign of 1903-4, being mentioned in dispatches. In the First World War Souter served in France, Belgium, Gallipoli, Egypt, and Mesopotamia. He received the DSO and the CMG, and was four times mentioned in dispatches, retiring in 1921. He died in Sydney, Australia in 1941.

allies recognised that a threat to the British from the Sahara desert to the west could assist their plans. After negotiations between the Turks and the Senussi, a Muslim sect of tribesmen from Libya and the Sudan, the leader of the tribe agreed to attack the British in western Egypt if the Germans delivered machine guns and artillery. Overstretched and under equipped, the British were forced to withdraw from advanced posts at Sidi Berani and Sollum to Mesa Matruh in the face of Senussi raids from the vastness of the Western Desert.

In February 1916 the British decided to go on the offensive and advanced eastwards along the waterless coastal strip with the sea on their right and the desert on the left. On 20 February 2016 the column of around 1,600 infantry,[8] four armoured motor cars, and about 314 Dorset Yeomanry with one squadron of 134 Royal Buckinghamshire Hussars,[9] marched out from Mersa Matruh, under a blazing sun and desiccating wind. On 24 February 2016 they made contact with the Senussi some 14 miles south east of Sidi Barrani at Agagia. They camped at Wadi Maktil, about eight miles from the Senussi who numbered 1,500 regular troops armed with the latest rifles and about 1,000 irregulars, with four machine guns and some artillery. They were commanded by General Gaafar Pasha,[10] who was a brother of Envar Pasha[11] and they also had Turkish officers as advisors. The country round Maktil was flat and open, but about a mile and a half to the south-west there was a small hill.

The next day the Senussi attacked the British camp, with two field guns and a Maxim but the infantry deployed quickly, won a fire-fight and drove them off, suffering few casualties in the process. The Dorset Yeomanry pushed on three or four miles until they saw the main Senussi camp at Agagia. At 09:30 a.m. the British advanced south, and the attack began at about 11:00 a.m. on a frontage over a mile wide,. Under the cover of a barrage, by noon they had closed within 500 yards of the Senussi's positions in the sand hills. Meanwhile, Colonel Souter was ordered to deploy the three squadrons of the Dorset Yeomanry on the western flank supported by armoured cars under the command of Major Hugh Richard Arthur, the Duke of Westminster.[12] Despite the enemy fire, the infantry's disciplined advance continued but the Senussi tactic was not to stand and fight. Instead, like the Boers, they forced the British to attack and lose a lot of men, while they slipped away into another position a few miles further back. At this stage, the Bucks Yeomanry Squadron was dispatched to join the Dorsets making a total of four squadrons.

8   Made up of the 1st and 3rd South African Regiments, the Queen's Own Dorset
      Yeomanry, a squadron of, the 1/6th Royal Scots and the Nottinghamshire Royal Horse
      Artillery, supported by two RAMC Field Ambulances
9   Thompson, Major-General C W, *Records of the Dorset Yeomanry (Queen's Own) 1914-1919*,
      (Sherbourne: F. Bennett & Co. Ltd., 1921), p49.
10   1885-1936.
11   22 November 1881-4 August 1922.
12   1879-1953.

The QODY followed the Senussi's retreat about a thousand yards to the west, helping them on their way with volleys of long-range small arms fire and machine gun fire. The Senussi kept their machine guns at work and when the British appeared in the open, they began to lose men. By this time the Senussi must have been seven miles from the sand hills where they had been in the morning and the British infantry, who had not been able to keep pace, lost contact. The British guns were now far behind and three out of four of the armoured motor cars had by this time became stuck in the sand, proving, at least at this point in history, equine superiority over the internal combustion engine. By 1400 hours the Senussi were in full flight, forming a mass of men and a great many camels about a mile long and 300-400 yards deep. At first, their rear guard kept the yeomanry at bay, but with fire from the infantry in the sand hills and the QODY's flanking fire, the withdrawal was beginning to turn into a rout.

At around 3:00 p.m., Souter realised that the Senussi would escape unless immediate decisive action was taken. Although not fed or watered, their horses were rested, and he saw his chance to seal victory. So, despite the exhausted state of the men, he ordered his regiment to mount. The QODY deployed in two ranks on a frontage of approximately six hundred yards, with the troopers of the front rank spaced eight yards apart and the second rank more concentrated at four yards. As the three squadrons advanced on the fleeing Senussi, the Turkish officers rallied about five hundred tribesmen around three maxim guns. Advancing quickly, first at the trot, then at a full canter, the Yeomanry bore down on the Senussi with swords drawn and the regimental cooks brandishing their cleavers. For well over half a mile they rode straight into their fire, over a perfectly flat plain of firm sand without cover, towards a slight ridge behind which were the enemy.[13] Finally, when within a 100 yards, Colonel Souter ordered the charge and at approximately 50 yards, the Yeomanry broke into a full thundering gallop,

World War I historical clichés suggest that mounted men against machine guns always resulted in horses and humans littering the battlefield but their speed and lose formation served to limit casualties against less than skilled Senussi marksmen, who offered a desperate but inaccurate fire. The machine guns fired very fast and the bullets knocked up the sand in front the Yeomanry, but as they got nearer the Senussi, who were not first class shots, in the heat of the moment failed to lower their sights as the range closed, and the bullets whistled over the heads of the approaching horsemen. The *galloping* Dorsets hurled themselves upon the enemy and most of the Senussi broke and ran. However, a few stood and fought and in the centre of his regiment, Colonel Souter's horse was shot and killed under him. By chance, his dying strides brought him down within a few yards of the Senussi General, Gaafar Pasha.[14] Souter was knocked unconscious and when he came to, he found himself alone amongst a group of the enemy in front of Pasha. He drew his revolver, shot several enemy, and,

13   Words of Lieutenant Blaksey.
14   Ja'far Pasha al-Askari (1887-1936), later twice Prime Minister of Iraq.

putting his revolver straight in Gaafer's face, took the Turkish leader, along with five of his Turkish staff, prisoner. Souter reported that Gafaar Paha was in a state of pitiable howling funk, and so were his staff.[15] They were tied to horses and ignominiously sent to the rear. Without their Turkish officers, some 300 to 500 Senussi were killed or wounded and perhaps a still more important factor was their loss of morale as many deserted and went back to their homes.[16] The charge demonstrated the terror which is induced by galloping horses and cold steel, but the fight was not entirely one sided, since the ensuing melee on the open sandy plain was both protracted and confused, as some brave or desperate Senussi tribesmen fought back. B Squadron was on the right, and of the four officers in the squadron two were killed and one was wounded. The fourth, Lieutenant Blaksley, led seventeen men into the charge, of whom eleven were killed and only five were untouched.[17] He had a bullet through the case of his field glasses, and another through the pocket of his tunic. In his own words:

> We were within 30 yards of the line when down came my mare; she was, I think, the nicest I had ever ridden, a well-known hunter in the Blackmore Vale, and in spite of want of food and water, she was bounding along, without the least sign of fear, as though she had just left the stable; down she fell, stone dead, fortunately, as I saw next morning, with a bullet straight through her heart.

The next moment he saw a spare horse, snatched it and galloped after his troop; but within 100 yards down that horse fell like the mare. Under fire, the Yeomanry lost half their horses, and about a third of their men with total casualties of 58.[18] Sadly, 85 horses were killed or missing and further pursuit was impossible as the unharmed horses were blown.[19] The infantry and guns were far behind and the Dorset's alone were too weak in numbers, with too many officers fallen, for a mounted second charge. As darkness fell, the yeomen left the battlefield, having been unable to locate all of their dead, and retired to a well where they watered the horses and themselves. The only food was dried dates, taken from camels captured by the Berkshire Yeomanry. A third of the men stayed with the horses, and the rest had to form a ring round the bivouac in case of a sudden attack during the cold and weary night. There was no attack, and at last the morning came, when the regiment discovered the bodies of their remaining comrades, which had been stripped naked by the enemy and robbed of everything. Whilst the last of the dead were collected the infantry dug a large grave

---

15 Thompson, *Records of the Dorset Yeomanry*, p57.
16 See <http://www.keepmilitarymuseum.org/middleeast/ag_charge.php> (Accessed 2 January 2018).
17 Thompson, *Records of the Dorset Yeomanry*, p. 56.
18 The QODY's casualties during the charge were five officers, 27 Yeomen killed, two officers and 24 other ranks wounded.
19 See <http://www.keepmilitarymuseum.org/middleeast/outline.php> (Accessed 2 January 2018).

and each officer and man was laid to rest, covered with wild marigolds, poppies and anemones that grew in the desert during the late winter. After the burial, the yeoman set to work collecting large stones and a cairn was erected over the grave with two wooden crosses. The magnificent charge of the Dorset Yeomanry at Agagia was the outstanding incident in Souter's distinguished career and the Dorset Yeomanry had completed the destruction of the Senussi force.[20] News of the Dorset Yeomen's feat of arms rang through the Empire and they relieved Sidi Barrani on 9 March 1916. The British force pursued the remnants of the enemy 50 miles west, and eventually the Senussi were all but eliminated as a threat to Egypt and the Suez Canal.

Meanwhile, the 4th Australian Light Horse was split, with two squadrons despatched to fight the Hun on the Western Front, while Scotty and the other troopers remained to defend the Suez canal where, in March 1916, Sir Archibald Murray took command of the Egyptian Expeditionary Force.[21] Believing a British advance into the Sinai would be more cost effective than static defence of the Suez canal, he decided to push his defences forward into the oasis area which stretched eastwards from Romani and Katia to Bir el Abd, thus denying drinking water to any Ottoman invasion force. To provide ammunition, supplies and a reliable source of water, the British army built a railway and pipeline across the Sinai Peninsula at the rate of about fifteen miles a month, and the front moved westward at the same speed. By the middle of May the railway had been completed to Romani, 23 miles east of Suez and this made it possible to deploy the 52nd (Lowland) Division and the 1st, and 2nd Light Horse Brigades who began to dig trenches in the sand, creating a defensive line from the Mediterranean coast, south to a high point in front of Romani.

The Turks attacked in the early hours of 4 August and the two Australian brigades were pushed back. However, the 52nd (Lowland) Division were able to attack the Turks' right flank and the New Zealand Mounted Rifle and 5th Mounted Brigades arrived in time to stop the advance. However, the deep sand, the mid-summer heat and thirst meant the British were unable to pursue an orderly Turkish retreat to their base at Bir el Abd, the last oasis in the series stretching from the Romani area. On 12 August 1916 Bir el Abd was abandoned after fierce fighting completing the first substantial Allied victory against the Ottomans. The Suez Canal was never again threatened.

On 23 December, Lieutenant General, Sir Harry Chauvel's forces of the Imperial Camel Corps Brigade and the Anzac Mounted Division moved on Magdhaba,[22] some 18 miles to the southeast in the Sinai desert, and the last obstacle to the Allied advance into Palestine. After tough fighting the garrison surrendered, having suffered heavy casualties and the new British government of Prime Minister David Lloyd George, who we last met fighting to end the Boer War, now ordered an offensive, in

20   *The Times* (1 December 1941) obituary. Souter was awarded the DSO.
21   23 April 1860–21 January 1945.
22   Chauvel, 16 April 1865–4 March 1945.

part to support the Arab revolt, which had started early in 1916, and also to build on the momentum created by the victories won at Romani and Magdhaba. On 9 January 1917, they attacked an Ottoman garrison at Rafa, 30 miles along the coast, capturing the town.

With this victory Murray's forces controlled the Sinai Peninsula but he was now ordered to send men to reinforce the Western Front. Nevertheless, at an Anglo-French conference at Calais on 26 February 1917, it was decided to encourage all fronts to launch a series of simultaneous offensives to coincide with the planned spring offensive on the Western Front. Murray's proposal was to attack Gaza where there were eighteen thousand Turkish soldiers along the nineteen mile long Gaza–Beersheba line,[23] with more defenders on the way. After the assault on 26 March, General Murray created the impression in London that his First Battle of Gaza had been more successful than the reality on the ground which resulted in him being encouraged to begin a major offensive on Jerusalem. By 18 April it was clear that the French offensive on the Western Front had not succeeded and the newly democratic Russia could no longer be relied on, thus freeing Turkish troops to reinforce Palestine and Mesopotamia. Hence, Gaza was developed into the strongest point in a defensive line extending twelve miles east and then south east towards Beersheba. The Second Battle of Gaza, fought from 17-19 April 1917, was another frontal attack by infantry across open ground against those prepared entrenchments, and the strength of the Ottoman fortifications and the determination of their soldiers defeated the Egyptian Expeditionary Force (EEF), and depleted their strength. With this reversal, Murray was relieved of his command on 28 June to be replaced by Edmund Allenby.[24]

General "Bull" Allenby, a cavalryman himself, arrived from the Western Front and decided that in order to capture Gaza, he must first secure the wells at the nearby town of Beersheba, the enemy's main water supply and headquarters of the Ottoman III Corps. Water, as always, remained the currency of the Middle East and in the deserts wells were marked and valued by the Arabs in terms of the number of camels they could water. Some wells were marked as 100, some 1000, but the wells of Beersheba were marked as unlimited. Horses usually need to drink about 30 litres of water a day and thus the capture of wells and watering holes became a key strategic consideration in maintaining speed and mobility of advance. However, due to their hardy breeding, during the Middle Eastern campaign the Australian Walers often went for up to 60 hours in the hot weather without water, while carrying a load of almost 130 kilograms, comprising rider, saddle, equipment,[25] food, and water. Despite this advantage in breeding, and the engineering feats of the pipeline, thousands of horses

23   With the railhead at Rafa, Gaza was just 20 miles away, five to six hours for infantry and mounted units at a walk and two hours for horses at a trot.
24   23 April 1861–14 May 1936.
25   The equipment included saddle cloth, bridle, head collar, lead rope, a horseshoe case with one front and one hind shoe, nails, rations for the horse and rider, a bedroll, change of clothing, a rifle and about 90 rounds of .303 rifle ammunition.

still died from those same causes as in the Anglo-Boer War. In the desert campaign, water shortages restricted the movement of many units and caused widespread condition loss among the horses. However, veterinary services were far more organised than fifteen years previously, especially around systems in supplying fresh mounts to replace tired horses, resulting in a marked fall in the equine casualty and death rates.[26] Nevertheless, the constant struggle to maintain regular and efficient supplies, led to the constant flow of animal casualties through the veterinary service.[27]

Soldiers were with their horses all day and slept with them to stay warm on freezing nights in the desert and so the companionship of the horses, and the job of caring for them, helped the soldiers to build a bond and hence cope with the pressures of war. Amongst the humans in Egypt and Palestine, disease and sickness, particularly malaria, continued to spread through the light horse ranks. Yet again, Scotty Bolton had fallen victim but on his release from the hospital, he returned to his unit on the afternoon of the 28October, and was with his horse, Monty, among the crowds of troopers who stood before the canvas water troughs, encouraging them to drink, in the realisation that the next source of water was uncertain and could be over a day's ride away.[28] The 4th Light Horse Regiment, as part of the Desert Mounted Corps, had moved out from Tel el Fara carrying three day's rations and fodder, and bivouacked at Berl el Sam for the night and most of the day, moving off again in the evening to camp at an old ruined village Khalasi where there was a good well for watering horses. Off again on the evening of 30 October, they were ordered to hang on to what water and food they had because the next they could get would have to be captured from the Turks.

In the cool, clear night, the column of regiment after regiment, four abreast, extended for more than 10 miles as they forced their thirsty horses on through the night and rode into the next day, covering 30 miles. Dawn on the morning of the 31 October found them surveying a bare plain about four kilometres across. Beersheba shone in the early morning sunlight, but the town was defended by about 5,000 Turks, supported by 16 field guns and about 10 machine-guns,[29] deployed in well-constructed trenches protected by wire. A semicircle of heights to the north west, west, and south west up to four miles from the town, bristled with strong points, covering the approaches, and included the two hills, Tel el Saba east of Beersheba and Tel el Sakati. No attack against Beersheba could take place until these two hills were secured. The 60th (London) and the 74th (Yeomanry) Divisions were to attack Beersheba from the west, while the Anzac Mounted Division attacked the town from the east. While

26   The horse mortality rate dropped from 66 percent in the Anglo-Boer War to 15 per cent.
27   Totalling nearly 450,000 sick or injured horses in all theatres of the war. The veterinary service was successful in eventually returning 82 percent of these casualties to service.
28   See < https://anzacday.org.au/trooper-sloan-scotty-bolton-dcm>, (accessed 2 January 2018).
29   Livesey, Anthony, *Great Commanders and their Battles* (London: Marshall Editions Ltd, 1987), p138.

Tel el Sakati would be the 2nd Light Horse Brigade's objective, the remainder of the horsemen would have to sweat out the day in a dust-filled wadi beneath the blazing sun, bedevilled by the heat and the flies. The Commanding Officer of the 4th Light Horse Regiment, Lieutenant Colonel Murray 'Swagman Bill' Bourchier,[30] a Gallipoli veteran, screwed up his orders, frustrated that it appeared that the 4th was the designated reserve yet again

Intense hand to hand fighting continued until 1:30 p.m. when the Ottoman trench line on the western side of Beersheba was captured. Meanwhile the Anzac Mounted Division advanced circling Beersheba, to cut the road north to Hebron and Jerusalem to prevent reinforcement and retreat from Beersheba, and launched their attack on Tel el Saba. The battle raged throughout the day and in the hand-to-hand battle for the hills the New Zealand Mounted Rifles Brigade and the 1st Light Horse Brigade eventually captured Tel el Saba at 3:00 p.m. However, by late afternoon the entire plan hung in the balance. If Beersheba could not be taken that day, the action would have to be abandoned. Some horses had been without water for more than 60 hours and it was 12 hours' ride to the next well capable of watering them. The commander of the Desert Mounted Corps, Lieutenant General Chauvel, assembled his commanders on the hill overlooking the open plain and conferred in search of a tactical solution to this strategic issue. The commander of the 4th Light Horse Brigade, Brigadier General William Grant,[31] proposed an audacious cavalry charge, with two regiments, the 4th and the 12th thrown across the plain in a gallop for the city. Chauvel pondered the situation. The time was now 4:00 p.m. and the sun would set at 4:50 p.m. Now his military judgement determined it was time to take such a gamble, and his decisiveness and moral courage were not found wanting. He ordered the charge.

The Australian Light Horse Brigade had no time to plan but Bourchier eagerly grasped the opportunity for action and led the 4th Light Horse Regiment from the front with the 12th Regiment on their left and the 11th in reserve. Bolton tightened Monty's girth, took a final gulp of water from his bottle and mounted. The regiments moved out into a patch of dead ground on the plain as, with mounting excitement, the 400 to 500 troopers came to realise that they were about to undertake one of the great cavalry charges of the twentieth century.[32] Bourchier glanced at his watch, raised his arm above his head and waved forward in one slow, deliberate motion. The horses stepped off at a walk, he gave the signal for the trot, then two minutes later, the canter. Surprise and speed were their principal weapons, so at a distance of 2.5 kilometres from the forward trenches, Bourchier commanded his men to charge and the pace was quickened to a gallop. In the presumed safety of their trenches, the German non-

---

30   4 April 1881–16 December 1937.
31   30 September 1870–25 May 1939.
32   Livesey, *Great Commanders*, p. 137. Records indicate that 475 were serving with the 4th Light Horse Regiment on 31 October 1917. However, this is probably a little higher than the number that actually charged since some men may have had duties elsewhere, perhaps minding supplies to the rear or were sick.

commissioned officers calmly gave their orders to the Turkish soldiers. Being familiar with the light horse tactics, they ordered their soldiers to wait until the light horsemen dismounted before opening fire.

Along with the other men, Bolton pushed Monty to a full gallop and reached down to grasp the handle of his 18-inch bayonet, drawing it from the scabbard.[33] You will recall that as Mounted Infantry they did not carry swords or lances, so instead, the long lines of Light Horsemen thundered forward, wielding their hand-held bayonets. The Turkish gunners watched the charge, lowering the barrels of their guns, waiting for the dismount that never came. As the pounding hooves narrowed the gap to the enemy lines, the Turks eventually commenced firing with machine guns and rifles and the batteries opened fire with a mixture of shrapnel and high explosive. However, as with the Dorset Yeomanry's charge at Agagia, they could not depress their guns rapidly enough to keep up with the pace of the charge. Even so there were early casualties as shrapnel burst through some troopers and they fell from their horses. The horsemen following swerved or jumped their Walers over the fallen men but the charge did not falter and suddenly the Light Horse regiments were below the trajectory of the guns.

The Turkish rifle and machine gun fire decimated the lines of horsemen, but the thirsty horses could now smell the sweet water of Beersheba's wells and they were unstoppable. Monty, careered wildly and Bolton fought hard to regain control of his terrified mount which had been struck by a bullet and bolted forward through pain and fear. Bolton was later to discover that a bullet had narrowly missed his own leg, hitting instead the pannikin hanging from the saddle, deflecting the round such that it carved a foot long gouge along the Monty's rump.[34] The Turkish riflemen fired frantically at the approaching wall of equine flesh but within minutes the Australians reached the trenches, at which point hand-to-hand fighting ensued while many troopers simply jumped the defences and galloped into the town. As the horses leaped across the open trenches, many of the Turks crouched and thrust their rifles and bayonets upward to disembowel the horses in mid-flight. The noisy chaos of rifle and revolver fire and the stabs and slashes of bayonets was accompanied by one rearing horse who kicked out with his hooves. Panic took hold among the enemy and their resistance quickly crumbled as the remnants of the first wave carried on to engage the support trenches. With adrenalin pumping, the Light Horsemen fanned out through the town capturing guns and prisoners. Scotty pressed on through to the second line of trenches towards the centre of town, hitting two Turks with his bayonet. He then spotted a Turkish soldier running towards a house and galloped over, kicking him to the ground and retrieving his revolver as sprawled on the deck. The surviving charges

---

33   See < https://anzacday.org.au/trooper-sloan-scotty-bolton-dcm> (Accessed 2 January 2018).

34   See < https://anzacday.org.au/trooper-sloan-scotty-bolton-dcm> (Accessed 2 January 2018).

of the 12th Light Horse were already making their way through the streets to water their horses in the captured wells. With chests heaving, dismounted men and horses drank thirstily side-by-side from the same Turkish canvas water trough.[35]

At that moment a well exploded, followed rapidly by two more, the last blast almost throwing Bolton from his horse. To thwart the Australians efforts to secure water, Turkish demolition of the town wells had begun. On the ground Bolton noticed wires leading to a building where through an open window he caught sight of a German officer feverishly operating an array of switches. He jumped from the saddle and rushed through the door where the alerted German tightened his grip on the deto- nation handle. Bolton cocked his revolver and aimed point blank at the German's forehead, thus persuading him to release the handle and surrender without the need of an interpreter. The officer promptly raised his hands as Bolton's mate, Trooper Ray Hudson, came through the door and took charge of the prisoner. Although some wells had been destroyed and a few had been damaged, most were still intact, including reservoirs holding more than 400000 litres.[36]

With the sun sinking below the horizon Scotty left the building and remounted. He heard wheels rattling and a sudden movement caught his eye. Turning in his saddle, he saw a Turkish field gun and its crew a quarter of a mile away, galloping away from the town. He spurred Monty forward and soon caught the horse-drawn Turkish wagon and saw a German officer riding on the front seat next to the driver. Riding up to him on Monty he gave a fierce yell, calling for help from an Australian officer who was dismounted nearby. Scotty took aim with his revolver, pulled the trigger and heard the sickening click of an empty chamber. Thinking quickly, he struck the German over the head with the revolver but he was wearing a steel helmet and it hurt Bolton's hand more than it hurt the Hun. A second blow was more successful, knocking him to the ground. Grabbing the reins of the lead horse, he slowed the team to a halt and maintained his bluff as he kept the Turks covered with the empty revolver while the Australian officer rode up and took charge of the prisoners.

As they returned with the gun the defeated Turks threw down their weapons and surrendered so that by the time they reached the town square, his bag prisoners had exceeded thirty. For his tremendous bravery and cool thinking, Scotty Bolton was awarded a richly deserved Distinguished Conduct Medal and, despite the mad risk of the charge across open ground, the casualties suffered by both regiments were rela- tively light, with only 31 troopers killed and 36 wounded, most as a result of the savage hand-to-hand combat in the trenches.[37] In a radical tactical move, defying the odds and confounding modern clichés of the impotence of cavalry in World War One, the

35   See < https://anzacday.org.au/trooper-sloan-scotty-bolton-dcm> (Accessed 2 January 2018).
36   See < https://anzacday.org.au/trooper-sloan-scotty-bolton-dcm> (Accessed 2 January 2018).
37   See < https://anzacday.org.au/trooper-sloan-scotty-bolton-dcm> (accessed 2 January 2018).

4th and 12th Regiments had charged across open ground against entrenched Turkish troops and won. At Beersheba the Australian Light Horsemen had written themselves into the history books and Australian legend for evermore. It is also immortalised in the landmark Australian film, *The Lighthorsemen*,[38] and is now embedded in the Australian ethos along with Gallipoli and is often talked of as the last successful charge in history. However, this is far from the case and two further charges by British Yeomanry are worthy of greater recognition in the popular story of the cavalry in modern warfare and the national narrative of the Great War.

With the fall of Beersheba, the Desert Mounted Column continued to advance across Palestine as the Turkish resistance crumbled. Sloan Bolton survived the charge and from Beersheba accompanied his Regiment's northern advance, constantly clashing with the Turks, who still showed plenty of fight. From 1-6 November strong Ottoman rear-guard actions held the Egyptian Expeditionary Force in heavy fighting, and they were able to withdraw in good order. At around 2:00 p.m. on 8 November 1917, the pursuing British forces with the 60th (2/2nd London) Division in the lead were stopped by artillery fire from a strong position on a ridge to the south of Huj, nine miles north east of Gaza. Aware that his infantry division alone would have problems taking the position, the 60th Division commander requested assistance from the mounted troops. The only mounted troops in the area were two full squadrons of Warwickshire Yeomanry plus two half squadrons of the Worcestershire Yeomanry,[39] both part of the Australian Mounted Division's 5th Mounted Brigade. Colonel Gray-Cheape[40] led his force to a point a little over a 1000 yards northeast of the 60th Division's right flank. After turning and advancing northwest to within 800 yards of the ridge, he ordered his men to draw their swords and, advancing under what cover was available, they got to within 300 yards and charged, galloping over the rise, and racing down upon the flank of the enemy guns.

The Warwickshire Yeomanry squadron attacked the main force of Turkish infantry, then turned and attacked the gun line. The regiment's other half squadron and the Worcestershire Yeomanry squadron attacked the guns from the front, while the remaining troops attacked an infantry position located at the rear behind the main force. The Turks sprang to their guns and fired point-blank into the charging horsemen whilst the infantry blazed away with their rifles until they were cut down, and withdrew, leaving the guns undefended apart from the German and Austrian artillerymen. They carried on firing until the horsemen were around 20 yards away then took cover underneath their guns as the leading Yeomanry crashed into the first battery. Those who remained standing were brought down by the British swords, while others ran away from the guns escaped injury by lying on the ground. The third wave, passed

---

38   *The Lighthorsemen* is a 1987 Australian feature film about the Battle of Beersheeba. Most of the characters in the film were based on real people.

39   Troopers were divided into 4 troops per squadron and were armed with 1908 pattern swords, in addition to their .303 Short Magazine Lee Enfield rifles.

40   Died 27 May 1918.

the first battery, where a fierce sabre versus bayonet fight was continuing, and raced up the slope at the machine guns. Many Yeomen fell from their saddles in those few yards, but the charge was unstoppable and the whole position was in Yeomanry hands.

The British captured 70 prisoners, 11 pieces of artillery and four machine guns. However British casualties were heavy; of the 170 men taking part, 26 were killed, including three squadron commanders,[41] and 40 wounded. A hundred horses were also killed in the charge.[42] Since a horse presents a much bigger target than a man, infantry, especially machine gunners, probably fired 'into the brown,' where the target looks thickest, thus dropping many horses but failing to kill the riders.

The charge at Huj was made on the spur of the moment without reconnaissance and without fire support and has been called "the last great charge of the British cavalry". It resulted in the complete destruction of an enemy strong point and has since been immortalised in a watercolour painting by the famous British artist Lady Butler[43] which hangs in the Warwickshire Yeomanry Museum.[44] Had it occurred in a minor war, the Charge at Huj might have gone down to history like the Charge of the Light Brigade but in the Great War, when gallant deeds were being enacted on all fronts almost daily, it remains a little known episode which should be more celebrated. The charge opened the way for the British forces to continue the advance, and the village of Huj was captured later that day. However, both British yeomanry regiment contingents were in no position to continue the pursuit of the withdrawing Turkish forces, and the Australian Mounted Division, could not follow up until the 9-10 November.

General Allenby's troops captured Junction Station on the Jerusalem to Beersheba railway on 12 November, and the Mounted Yeomanry Division was ordered to march eastwards towards a naturally strong defensive line along controlling the ridge from Katrah to El Mughar still held by the Turks. On 13 November the orders were received for 6th Mounted Brigade to capture the El Mughar Ridge.[45] In front of the closely packed mud huts of Mughar, on the southern slope of the hill, there was a long oval garden with a clump of cypresses in the centre, surrounded by strong cactus hedges, containing a nest of machine guns and riflemen. They were supported by artillery from behind the ridge at the back of the village, and although the infantry brigade

41   Harris, Tristan *The Charge of Huj: The Story behind the Worcestershire and Warwickshire Yeomanry's role in the 1917 Palestine Battle* (11 November 2017). See <https://malvernobserver.co.uk/news/the-charge-of-huj-the-story-behind-the-worcestershire-and-warwickshire-yeomanrys-role-in-the-1917-palestine-battle-3375/>, (accessed 3 January 2018). Lieutenant Mercer was the only Warwickshire Yeomanry officer to pass through the charge uninjured.

42   Harris, Tristan, *The Charge of Huj*.

43   3 November 1846–2 October 1933.

44   Visitors to the Warwickshire Yeomanry Museum located in the Court House, Jury Street, Warwick, can inspect the 75mm Model 1903 Turkish Field Gun number 488 manufactured by Friedrich Krupp, Essen, and marked to the 1/1 Warwickshire Yeomanry.

45   Made up of the Dorset, Berkshire and Buckinghamshire Yeomanries, the Berkshire RHA and No.17 Machine Gun Squadron.

made repeated efforts its advance was held up so the Yeomanry brigade were ordered to take Mughar. The 6th Mounted Brigade worked round to the left and reached a point about two miles south-west of Yebnah village, which had been occupied by the 8th Mounted Brigade.[46] At 12:30 p.m. squadrons of Bucks Hussars, advanced to the wadi Janus, a deep, narrow watercourse wide enough only to take horsemen in single file running across the plain east of Yebnah and infront of El Mughar. The artillery began shelling Mughar and the ridge behind the village, but it was not easy to get cavalry into position for a mounted attack since the wadi Janus had sides of clay falling almost sheer to the stony bottom and it was equally troublesome to get horses out again. The Dorsets were brought up in small parties to join the Bucks in the wadi and the Berks were to enter the wadi immediately the Bucks had left it. Behind Mughar village and its gardens the ground falls sharply, then rises again and forms a rocky hill some 300 yards long. There is another decline, and north of it a stony and barren, conical shaped hill. The Dorset Yeomanry were ordered to attack this latter hill on the left and the Bucks Hussars the ridge between it and Mughar village on the right, with the Berks Yeomanry kept in support.

It was a hot bright afternoon when at 3:00 p.m. the yeomen of Bucks and Dorset got out of the wadi. The Bucks Hussars extended to four yards interval, advanced at a trot from the wadi,towards their objective which was 3000 yards across open, fire swept ground from the ridge. The supporting machine guns brought to bear a heavy and sustained fire as B Squadron led, and when 1000 yards from the objective the order was given to gallop. The horses thundered from the plain and up the hill at pace, with hoofs raising clouds of dust. The machine guns, rifle fire, shells and shrapnel, drowned the cheers of the charging yeomen as C Squadron made their charge on the right of B Squadron. Once the cavalry had reached the crest of the hill many of the Turks surrendered, but some retired to rocks on the flanks and continued the fight at close range. C squadron was vigorously attacked on their left flank, but B were able to get over the ridge and across the rough, steep eastern side, and from this point used captured Turkish machine guns to fire on the northern end of the village. A Squadron then came up from Yebnah at the gallop, and with this support all the Bucks' objectives were secured.

The Dorset Yeomanry on the left of the Bucks had 1000 yards farther to go, over broken ground. At the base of the hills A squadron dismounted and fought their way to the top of the ridge on foot. The held horses were caught in machine-gun fire, and in a space of about 50 square yards many fell. In contrast, B squadron in the centre and C squadron on the right, formed line and galloped up the hill, and their horse losses were considerably less than those of the dismounted squadron. Thus the Dorset Yeomanry took their spur, capturing eight machine guns and many prisoners, and with the ridge secured, the Berkshire Yeomanry were sent around the left-hand spur

---

46   Composed of the 1/1st City of London Yeomanry, 1/1st County of London Yeomanry, and the 1/3rd County of London Yeomanry.

to round up prisoners. In all, the Brigade captured 18 officers, over 1,000 men, 14 machine guns and two field guns.[47] The many Turkish dead showed how thoroughly the sword had done its work and but for the tired state of the horses many more prisoners would have been taken. The 6th Mounted Brigade sustained 130 casualties, a remarkably small total but sadly, 265 horses were killed and wounded in the action.[48] Mughar was a great cavalry triumph, and added to the reputation that the Dorset's charge against the Senussi in 1916 had already earned them.

It is worth pausing to consider what the campaign was like for horses such as Monty and the chargers of the Yeomanry. Allenby's Beersheeba offensive had now continued for 17 days, covered nearly 170 miles and a rest was absolutely necessary, for the horses, who had been watered on an average of once in every 36 hours. The heat had been intense and the short rations, 9½ lb of grain per day without bulk food, had weakened them greatly. The average trooper was not far off 12 stone stripped, and with another 9.5 stone for saddle, ammunition, sword, rifle, clothes and kit, each horse carried a weight of 21 stone, all day every day for 17 days. Against these demands, the compact, well-built, and hardy Australian Walers proved to be as hard as nails. The Australians could not understand the English preference for the weight-carrying hunter, which to them looked like a cart horse. Their contention was that good blood could carry more weight than big bone, and the experience of the desert campaign supported their point of view. In general, the English Hunter had to be nursed back to fitness for a long period after these operations while the smaller Australian horses, without any special care, other than good food and plenty of water, soon recovered to go through another arduous campaign.[49]

After a short break, Jerusalem operations began on 17 November 1917, with battle lines extending from north of Jaffa on the Mediterranean Sea east across the Judean Hills. On his appointment as GOC General Allenby had been instructed to capture Jerusalem and on the 9 December 1917 the Holy City surrendered comfortably achieving Lloyd George's objective of a Christmas present to the British people. Allenby famously entered Jerusalem on foot on Christmas Day and for the Prime Minister it was one of the few real successes the British could point to after a year of bitter disappointments on the Western Front. Now Lloyd George, wished to knock

47   James, Philip and Wilson, Richard *The Charge at El Mughar,* published in November 2007. See <http://www.dorsetlife.co.uk/2007/11/the-charge-at-el-mughar/> (accessed 13 May 16).

48   See < http://historion.net/how-jerusalem-was-won-being-record-allenbys-campaign-palestine/chapter-xi-two-yeomanry-charges> (accessed 13 May 16). One officer killed and six wounded, 15 other ranks killed and 107 wounded and one missing. The Dorset Yeomanry lost Sergeant Guppy and 8 other ranks killed in action, Captain Hoare mortally wounded, Captain (Adj) Robertson and Lieutenant Beechcroft and 43 other ranks wounded, and 80 horses killed.

49   Preston, Lt. Col. Richard Martin Peter, *The Desert Mounted Corps: An Account of the Cavalry Operations in Palestine and Syria 1917-1918* (Boston & New York; Houghton & Miffin Co., 1921).

the Ottoman Empire out of the war. However, there were many who were worried that if significant forces were diverted from the Western Front to Palestine, England might protect her colonies but lose the war. The Westerners argued that the real heart of the Ottoman Empire, Istanbul, still lay hundreds of miles from an advance to Damascus and that in the meantime Germany might overrun France. Furthermore, by March 1918, Russia had departed from the war thanks to the Bolshevik Revolution but the United States had not yet established a strong fighting force in Europe so Germany had a brief window of opportunity to attack. Conversely, the Easterners argued for sufficient forces in France to keep the front intact but pointed out that for two years the Allies had failed to break the German lines, and that whilst the Palestine theatre might be wasteful of shipping, the Western Front was wasteful of lives. Why take seasoned troops from Palestine where a decisive victory could be won to die in the stalemate of Flanders?

The debate was resolved when on 21 March 1918 General Erich Ludendorff's 71 Divisions launched the German Spring Offensive on the Western Front,[50] with divisions freed up from the Eastern Front and victory against the Italians at Caporetto. This powerful assault of 750,000 troops on both sides of the Somme,[51] under cover of a heavy artillery barrage and spearheaded by fully manned, well equipped, and experienced divisions of stormtroopers, quickly forced the collapse of the British front in Picardy, at that time held by just 300,000 men.[52] The British Army was forced back to within 10 miles of Amiens as German forces advanced and captured 90,000 prisoners and over 1,000 guns.[53] The British War Cabinet recognised at once that the overthrow of the Ottoman Empire must be at least postponed, and overnight Palestine went from being the British government's first priority to a "side show."

On 30 March 1918, Jack, now General Seeley, our old friend from the Boer War, sat on his horse Warrior at Moreuil Wood on the banks of the river Avre. The Germans were still advancing and defeat stared the Allies in the face unless the Germans could be halted. A magnificent cavalry charge was to be the source of that counter blow. By this time Seeley and Warrior had survived four years of war together. He had bred the bay thoroughbred gelding from his own mare Cinderella, who he had first seen whilst mounted on Maharajah from a hill on Salisbury Plain. Cinderella foaled Warrior in the spring of 1908 at Yafford, a few miles from their family home at Brooke, in the west of the Isle of Wight, and was well named because he was undoubtedly a brave horse and the match of those we have read about already. But what marks him out

---

50   9 April 1865–20 December 1937.
51   Livesey, *Great Battles of World War I* (London: Marshall Editions Ltd, 1989), p. 179.
52   Livesey, *Great Battles of World War I* p. 179. The French Army had suffered heavily, mutinied in places, and disbanded many divisions in order to keep others fully manned, whilst Lloyd George withheld forces from Field Marshal Sir Douglas Haig, fearful he would feed them into a slaughter like those of 1916 and 1917.
53   Livesey, *Great Battles of World War I*, p. 180. In total 160,000 casualties were suffered – the worst British defeat of the war.

in the author's assessment is that he was loved like no other. Jack Seeley's book, "My Horse Warrior" which he published in 1934, reads as a love letter and the intimacy of their relationship is apparent between every line. For a man who experienced professional disappointments and who lost both his wife and son, it is clear that Warrior was among the most loved living creatures remaining in his life.:

Warrior and Seely had landed at Le Havre on 11 August 1914 and served with the Canadian cavalry in the trenches near Ypres in 1915. Warrior stayed on the Western Front throughout the war and, although he sometimes had a roof over his head rather than the open sky, he was twice trapped under the burning beams of his stables after they had been hit by shelling. He had waited all day on 1 July 1916 to gallop through the gap in the German line that never appeared on the awful first day of the Battle of the Somme, surviving machine gun attacks and falling shells. In September 1917 he was dug out of the mud of Passchendaele and on 20 November of the same year was in the front line of the big Cambrai attack. Warrior would stand tall and proud as carnage raged around him and he was an inspiration to the soldiers he was fighting alongside who dubbed him "the horse the Germans couldn't kill".

On 30 March the German 23rd Saxon Division had occupied the Moreuil Woods which overlooked the River Arve and controlled the Amiens–Paris railway. Behind Seeley and Warrior that day were the horses of the Canadian cavalry. Warrior was desperate to charge into action, so much so that the Seeley fought to hold him back until the command for attack was given. The Canadian Cavalry Brigade[54] was assigned the task of stopping them and Seely received orders to cross the River Avre and delay the enemy advance. At 09:30 a.m., upon reaching the wood, and coming under fire from German forces, Seely ordered The Royal Canadian Dragoons to protect the village of Moreuil, while other sections were to seize the northeast corner of the wood itself. Meanwhile, Lord Strathcona's Horse was ordered to occupy the southeast face of the wood and disperse any German units as the remaining squadrons entered the wood from the northwest, to sweep through to the eastern face and meet up with Lord Strathcona's Horse. After being driven back from their first assault by machine gun fire, the cavalry units dismounted and proceeded to attack a second time with fixed bayonets, driving German 101st Grenadiers from the edge of the wood and into its centre. With horses ineffective in the woodland, the pace of the battle slowed but the remainder of the brigade crossed the river and deployed around the wood in support.

The commander of C Squadron Lord Strathcona's Horse Lieutenant Gordon Muriel Flowerdew[55] had been ordered to cut off the German forces who were retreating to the east in the face of the advance through the wood. Flowerdew reached the high ground at the northeast corner just in time to encounter a 300-strong German force

---

54 Consisting of the Royal Canadian Dragoons and Lord Strathcona's Horse
55 2 January 1885–31 March 1918. Born in Norfolk and educated at Framlingham College in Suffolk before emigrating to British Columbia, when the war broke out Flowerdew had enlisted as a private in Lord Strathcona's Horse and rose quickly to be commissioned in 1916.

from the 101st Grenadiers, who were withdrawing, and ordered, "It's a charge boys, it's a charge!" Riding into the fire of five infantry companies and an artillery battery, the squadron suffered atrocious casualties with 24 out of 75 of his unit dead, and 15 fatally wounded including himself.[56] However, the cavalry charge so unnerved the Germans that by 11:00 a.m. only the southern point of the wood was still occupied, and with reinforcements arriving, Seely ordered them to be driven from the wood. The day ended with 305 allied casualties but the wood was in Allied hands. Ludendorff ended the offensive on 5 April 1918 and their advance turned into a retreat in early April. Flowerdew's actions in "The Last Great Cavalry Charge" led to the posthumous award of the Victoria Cross.[57]

Galloper Jack and his faithful horse Warrior survived the war and returned to Brooke for Christmas 1918. In July 1919 he took part in the victory parade in Hyde Park and four years to the day after the charge,[58] he went on to win the lightweight race at the Isle of Wight point-to-point. In 1934 he was part of the war veteran show at Olympia, the same year that the famous artist Alfred Munnings[59] painted Warrior at Mottistone for the book that Seeley was to write about his beloved horse. In 1938 *Warrior* and Seely were to ride together with a combined age of 100 years, a remarkable statistic for any horse and rider combination, let alone a duo that had made a joint career of cheating death. The brave life of the old thoroughbred ended at Mottiston Manor, Isle of Wight in 1941.[60]

Back in Palestine, between 8-12 March the front line was pushed all the way from the Mediterranean Sea to the edge of the Jordan Valley. Allenby planned to push across the Jordan River and during the First Attack on Amman, between 21 March, the same day as the German Spring Offensive in France, and 30 March, his army, including the 4th Light Horse, successfully forced a crossing and partly destroyed sections of the Hedjaz Railway some 30-40 miles east of Jericho. However, the Turks successfully stopped the advance and with his lines of communication threatened the allies retired on the evening of 2 April even though the principal objective of destroying the large viaduct at Amman had not been achieved.[61] Following the unsuccessful first Transjordan attack, Allenby ordered a reluctant Chauvel to attack again

56   Scott, *Galloper Jack*, p314.
57   His Victoria Cross was donated by his mother to Framlingham College.
58   30 March 1922.
59   8 October 1878–17 July 1959.
60   On 1 September 2014 Warrior was posthumously awarded the animal equivalent of the VC, the PDSA Dickin Medal (instituted by the charity's founder Maria Dickin in 1943), marking Warrior's courage and that shown by all the horses who served World War I. It was accepted at the Imperial War Museum, by author, broadcaster and former National Hunt jockey, Brough Scott, the grandson of Warrior's owner General Jack Seely. It was the first honorary Dickin Medal to be presented.
61   This was the first defeat of units of the Egyptian Expeditionary Force since the Second Battle of Gaza in April 1917.

but in the five weeks between these two operations the German and Ottoman forces in the area had doubled, and the second Transjordan attack was equally unsuccessful.

During this operation, on 3 May 1918, Scotty Bolton's luck finally ran out, among the rocky outcrops and sheer slopes called Black Hill, where when the Turks attacked the troopers returned fire until they found their ammunition all but exhausted. They hurled Mills bombs at the attackers and when the bombs ran out, the troopers resorted to rocks and any projectile that came to hand. Finally, the attack faltered, and the Turks began to withdraw and the Light Horse line were given the order to pursue. At that point Scotty was immediately enveloped in the dust and smoke of an explosion and found himself rolling downhill. He pushed himself up with one hand, only to fall again, his left leg now a mangled mess. Crawling to gain cover behind a rock, Bolton felt his life draining away with each pulse from his severed arteries as he lapsed into unconsciousness. For days Bolton hovered between life and death until one morning, he opened his eyes to discover that he was in a hospital in El Arish. He noticed the cage over his lower body and it was then that a nursing sister told him that he had lost both his legs.[62] Scotty's war was over but the battle to get his life back had only just started.

With the German offensive in France, many infantry and Yeomanry units were sent to Europe, whilst British Indian Army battalions were sent to reform the divisions in Palestine. By May 1918, the Ottoman army held a line running eastwards from the Mediterranean shore to the River Jordan. Allenby could finally launch his long-delayed attack on 19 September 1918 and successfully surprised the Turks when the British attacked at Megiddo,[63] capturing thousands of prisoners and large quantities of equipment, such that within a week, the Ottoman army in Palestine had ceased to exist as a military force. The Gaza to Beersheba offensive and the Megiddo operations were similar but the breakthroughs were in reverse. In the case of Beersheba instead of the expected breakthrough at Gaza, it occurred at the eastern end of the front line, while at Megiddo the breakthrough occurred on the Mediterranean coast at the western end of the front.

The Australian Light Horse troops and Indian cavalry, approached the Syrian capital, Damascus from Galilee, and marched in unopposed on 1 October 1918. The Australian 10th Light Horse Regiment received the official surrender of the city at 7:00 am.[64] Later that day, Lawrence's irregulars entered Damascus to claim full credit for its capture. Aleppo, the third largest city in the Ottoman Empire, was captured on 25 October, but it was only after the surrender of Bulgaria, that the Ottoman government was compelled to sign the Armistice of Mudros on 30 October 1918,

---

62 See < https://anzacday.org.au/trooper-sloan-scotty-bolton-dcm>, (Accessed 2 January 2018).

63 The ancient Hebrew town known in the west as Armageddon.

64 Lieutenant General Sir Harry Chauvel, Commander in Chief, Desert Mounted Corps when entering Damascus on the 7 November 1918 was riding his mount named Aristocrat at the head of the Australian Army Light Horse.

ending the Sinai and Palestine Campaign and 600 years of Ottoman rule over the Middle East.[65] The historical consequences of this campaign are hard to overestimate. France won the mandate for Syria and Lebanon, while the British won Mesopotamia and Palestine, leading to the creation of the states of Israel, Jordan, Iraq Lebanon, and Syria whilst the Republic of Turkey came into existence in 1923 after the Turkish War of Independence. The repercussions continue to this day. Perhaps the post war narrative of stupid cavalry officers and the obsolescence of the horse on the battlefield will persist. Nevertheless the campaign in Palestine was a large and successful cavalry affair. It remains a largely forgotten part of history in Britain other than the cinematic legend of Lawrence and the Australian national tale of martial pride exemplified in the film the 1987 film *The Light Horsemen*.[66]

A troopship took Scotty Bolton back to Melbourne where for months he could only sleep under morphine. Here he was fitted with a pair of artificial limbs, gritted his teeth and took his first steps with his new legs, which would rub on the raw skin. The stumps would break down, and gangrene would set in and after more surgery to remove the damaged tissue, he was back to square one, learning to walk with artificial legs. On 20 March 1919, Bolton was discharged from the Australian Imperial Forces and in 1922, he married and settled in the Geelong area,[67] facing countless trips to hospital to have the stumps trimmed. But Scotty ignored his injuries and succeeded in riding again until his health deteriorated. He battled through those years, determined to provide the best for his family, until, finally on Christmas Eve 1947 he died. Sloan Bolton, the brave Beersheba charger, had fought his last battle.

The fate of many of the horses who took part in the charge was often worse than that of poor Scotty. In the First World War, more than 1201,000 Walers were sent overseas to the allied armies in Africa, Europe, India and Palestine. Of these, 29,348 served with the First Australian Imperial Force, mainly in the Middle East.[68] At the end of the desert campaign some soldiers faced the tough decision of whether to sell off the animals to local Egyptian farmers, infamous for their inhumane treatment of horses, or destroy them. Many British, Australian and Kiwi soldiers believed a quick and painless death for their loyal mounts was a better option than brutal pressed labour on the farms. One of the AIF's best-known soldier-poets, Major Oliver Hogue ("Trooper Bluegum"),[69] expressed a common sentiment in 1919:

---

65   The British Empire forces suffered a total of 550,000 casualties: more than 90 percent of these were not battle losses but attributable to disease, heat and other secondary causes. Total Ottoman losses are unknown but almost certainly larger.
66   Australian actor Jon Blake played Bolton.
67   See < https://anzacday.org.au/trooper-sloan-scotty-bolton-dcm> (Accessed 2 January 2018).
68   See <https://www.awm.gov.au/wartime/44/page54_bou> (Accessed 8 January 2018).
69   1880–1919.

I don't think I could stand the thought of my old fancy hack
Just crawling round old Cairo with a 'Gyppo on his back.
Perhaps some English tourist out in Palestine may find
My broken hearted waler with a wooden plough behind.
No, I think I'd better shoot him and tell a little lie:-
"He floundered in a wombat hole and then lay down to die."
Maybe I'll get court martialled; but I'm damned if I'm inclined
To go back to Australia and leave my horse behind.

Since Hogue there has persisted a common belief that light horsemen dispatched their horses in significant numbers with a merciful, painless shot to the head, to avoid such bondage to a pitiless taskmaster. Some historians have fuelled the belief that almost all of the 9,751 horses left behind in Egypt, Palestine and Syria by the Australian Light Horse were either shot or 'sold into slavery',[70] but this was an exception. Returning the horses to Australia was quickly ruled out by the Australian Army, partly because of the disease threat they posed to Australia's livestock industry and because returning them would cost more than the horses were worth.[71] Those mounts aged over 12 or in poor health were destroyed, many by their own troopers, but veterinary returns filed at the AWM suggest that approximately two-thirds of the horses were transferred to Indian Army cavalry units to continue their working lives.[72] Whether sold, sent away or shot, parting with their Walers was one of the hardest events the light horsemen had to endure. A monument was erected in Sydney by returned soldiers who had to leave their mounts behind. It has the inscription, "by members of the Desert Mounted Corps and friends, to the gallant horses who carried them over the Sinai Desert into Palestine, 1915-19. They suffered wounds, thirst, hunger and weariness almost beyond endurance, but they never failed. They did not come home."

The military service of the Walers did not end in Palestine since again during WWII Walers were supplied to the Army for use by the secret North Australia Observer Unit who carried out surveillance of the remote northern coastline. A small number also went with the army to Papua New Guinea and to Burma. However, mechanisation had begun to supersede horses both in the army and more generally so with the phasing out of the remount trade in the 1940's, commercial breeding

70 See <https://www.awm.gov.au/wartime/44/page54_bou> (Accessed 8 January 2018).
71 Due to quarantine restrictions, only one Waler is known to have been returned to Australia. This was Sandy, the mount of Major-General Sir William Throsby Bridges, the first Australian general to be killed during the war at Gallipoli in May 1915. After duty in Gallipoli, Egypt and France, the Minister for Defence, Senator George Pearce, called for Sandy's return to Australia in October 1917, arriving in Melbourne in 1918. Sandy was retired and turned out to graze before being put to rest in 1923. Sandy's head is mounted in a showcase and displayed at the AWM in Canberra.
72 The Australians had 13,000 surplus horses which could not be returned home for quarantine reasons and of these, 11,000 were sold, the majority as remounts for the British Army in India and two thousand were cast for age or infirmity.

of Walers rapidly declined. Some breeders destroyed their stock but others simply abandoned them to run free on their station properties. By the 1960's, the Waler had virtually disappeared from the domestic scene, with recreational and competition riders favouring more refined imported purebred horse such as Thoroughbred, Arab, European Warmbloods and Quarter horses rather than the old fashioned heavier boned colonial breed with no studbook. The Waler, once lauded as one of the greatest cavalry horses in history, almost became extinct. Thankfully, the breed has now been re-established in Australia and around the world and is popular as an all-rounder and in particular for Endurance racing.

Regardless of successes in the Palestine campaign, Flowerdew's heroic but pyrrhic charge epitomises the consensus view on the futility of cavalry in World War I, demonstrating that the horse was now obsolete on the battlefield against machine guns, tanks and barbed wire. The wonderful charge scene from Steven Speilberg's adaptation of *War Horse*,[73] captures this historical tactical tipping point of the demise of the horse from the modern battlefield in cinematic splendour. However, as we have seen, in other theatre's, such as the Middle East, where distances were longer, where there were fewer troops, and where the terrain was not rich in railways and other transport systems, the value of the horse and mounted infantry could demonstrate their enduring worth. In the next chapter we will see that in such circumstances, the horse continued to give magnificent military service in the inter-war years and into World War II. One Italian in particular had not given up on the horse as a martial animal.

---

73   A 2011 British war film directed by Steven Spielberg from a screenplay written by Lee Hall and Richard Curtis, adapted from Michael Morpurgo's 1982 young adult novel.

Sandor and Sergeant Reckless: The Last Equine Heroes?

During the First Italo-Abyssinian War in 1895-96, Italy had been thwarted in its colonial ambitions when the Ethiopians had humiliated their army at the Battle of Adowa.[1] When he came to power Benito Mussolini[2] was determined to remove this stain on Italian martial reputation and decided to invade Ethiopia from Italian Somaliland and Eritrea. Thus, it was, in 1930, that Italy erected and garrisoned a fort at the Walwal oasis,[3] well beyond the border between Italian Somaliland and Ethiopia, On 5 December 1934, tensions erupted into what was known as the "Wal Wal incident" when an Anglo-Ethiopian survey commission encountered Italian soldiers at the oasis. After the British surveyors had departed, the Ethiopians and Italians exchanged fire. This left more Ethiopians than Italians dead, but Mussolini demanded an apology, compensation, salutes to the Italian flag, and punishment of the Ethiopians. This amounted to a recognition of Italian sovereignty 60 miles beyond the border and led to the subsequent "Abyssinia Crisis" at the League of Nations.[4] Both countries were members and yet the League vacillated and exonerated both parties, in part because the United Kingdom and France were keen to keep Italy as an ally against Germany. Thus encouraged, Italy soon began to build its forces on the borders of Ethiopia whilst Emperor Haile Selassie[5] ordered a general mobilization of the Army of the Ethiopian Empire. In theory this consisted of around 500,000 men, but some were armed with nothing more than spears and bows. Those who did carry rifles, were using outdated models, often from before 1900, and only about a quarter of this army had any kind of military training. At the outbreak of the war, the 13

1   1 March 1896.
2   29 July 1883–28 April 1945.
3   Also, Welwel or Ual-Ual.
4   Bruce G. Strang, (ed.) *Collisions of Empire: Italy's Invasion of Ethiopia and its International Impact* (London: Ashgate, 2013), p.43.
5   23 July 1892–27 August 1975.

aircraft of the Imperial Ethiopian Air Force included three outmoded biplanes and a total of four pilots.[6]

By the start of 1935, there were 400,000 Italian soldiers in Eritrea and 285,000 in Italian Somaliland.[7] Then in April the build-up of the Italian forces in East Africa started with the arrival eight regular, mountain, and black shirt infantry divisions in Eritrea and four regular infantry divisions in Italian Somaliland. Furthermore, unlike the Ethiopians, they were well equipped,[8] and thanks to the *Regia Marina* they were well supplied. The Italians troops included indigenous regiments recruited from their colonial possessions of Eritrea, Somalia, and Libya but officered by Italians. Among the invaders was one such dashing young cavalry officer called Amadeo Guillet.[9]

Amedeo was a member of the minor aristocracy who for generations had served the Dukes of Savoy,[10] the dynasty that would later become the kings of Italy. His father[11] was a colonel in the Royal Carabinieri and he grew up around horses, following his family tradition into the cavalry and graduating at the age of 18 from the military academy at Modena in 1930.[12] A terrific horseman, he began training at Pinerolo, where Italian horsemanship under Federico Caprilli[13] had achieved a world renowned reputation by developing the 'forward seat' and evolving modern jumping saddles. Guillet excelled. He twice came runner-up, and once came third, in the Grande Steeplechase di Roma and was selected as a member of the Italian Eventing team for the Berlin Olympics in 1936.[14] However, Mussolini's invasion of Ethiopia in 1935 interrupted his career as a competition rider. Giving up his place at the Olympics, he used family connections to get himself transferred to the Spahys di Libya, a colonial cavalry unit made up of feudal tribesmen from Libya who were being mobilized for the Italian assault on Ethiopia.

Whilst in Libya, prior to embarkation for Eritrea, Amadeo had seen a four-year-old Arab stallion from Tunisia.[15] He was not big like a competition horse, but tough and lean, with an intelligent eye, excellent conformation and lively paces. He needed a mount that could survive off of nothing, never go lame, and endure 60 kilometres a day and this was just the right sort of animal. An old corporal had bought the horse but found it too much of a handful and hence he was barely schooled, and the owner

---

6   See < https://en.wikipedia.org/wiki/Second_Italo-Ethiopian_War> (Accessed 11 January 2018).
7   < https://en.wikipedia.org/wiki/Second_Italo-Ethiopian_War,>
8   6,000 machine guns, 2,000 pieces of artillery, 599 tanks, and 390 aircraft in addition to the 3,300 machine guns, 275 artillery pieces, 200 tankettes, and 205 aircraft already in theatre.
9   7 February 1909–16 June 2010.
10   Born in Piacenza, Italy to a Savoyard-Piedmontese family.
11   Baron Alfredo Guillet.
12   Sebastian O'Kelly, *Amadeo: The True Story of an Italian's War in Abyssinia* (London: Harper Collins, 2002), p.22.
13   8 April 1868–6 December 1907.
14   O'Kelly, *Amadeo*, p.26.
15   O'Kelly, *Amadeo*, p.46.

was eager to exchange him. There was a horse going spare from the same herd which no one wanted because of berrimas, a spiraling whirl in the coat on the hind quarters which, according to tribal superstition, meant the horse wanted the rider's death. The corporal handed over the young grey to Amadeo and led away the marked horse. Whilst waiting in Eritrea prior to the invasion, Amadeo would take the horse, whom he christened Sandor, the diminutive of Alexandor, to a wadi shaded by the trees and use the sandy river bed as a ménage with corners marked by stones.[16] Here he would go through the schooling exercises he had learned at Pinerolo, and under the sun of the Eritrean dessert they practiced until they became a unified partnership.

At 9:00 p.m. on 2 October 1935, war was declared and at 5:00 a.m. the next day the Italians crossed the border from Eritrea at the Mareb River.[17] Three days after they crossed the border, Amadeo and Sandor had their first taste of battle against some Ethiopians.[18] Amadeo, revolver in hand, together with 80 of his men trotted uphill over uneven ground, three or four meters apart, before cantering and then charging when 400m away from the enemy. The enemy ran down the far side of the hill and the engagement left one Saphy wounded and five or six enemy dead. Sandor had performed well.

By 15 October 1935, the Italians occupied the holy capital of Axum without opposition and their advance continued methodically but, to Mussolini's consternation, a bit slowly. Haile Selassie now decided to launch the Ethiopian "Christmas Offensive". The Ethiopians had approximately 190,000 men facing the Italians and in mid-December, a force crossed the Tekeze river and advanced toward the Dembeguina Pass.[19] Major Criniti, commanded a force of Eritrean Infantry supported by L3 tanks, and when the Ethiopians attacked they fell back to the pass, only to discover that hoards of Ethiopian soldiers had occupied it. Criniti's force became encircled and, taking fire from all directions, they attempted to break out. However, the rough terrain immobilized the vehicles and the Ethiopians slaughtered the infantry, then swarmed the tanks and killed their two-man crews. Furthermore, an Italian relief column of tanks and infantry ran into an ambush. Ethiopians occupying the high ground rolled boulders in front of and behind several of the tanks, blocking them and then picked off the Eritrean infantry.[20] As they swarmed over the tanks and set two on fire, Major Critini achieved a breakout, having ordered his men to fix bayonets and charge, but half of his men were killed. Two weeks later, Amadeo's troops went back to burry the Italian dead. Among the dead was the proud commander of the tanks, who before the war had told Amadeo at Pinerolo that the day of the horse was over. Perhaps it was, but on this occasion it was Amadeo who rode off on Sandor and left the tank man to his maker.

16   O'Kelly, *Amadeo*, p.47.
17   O'Kelly, *Amadeo*, p.49.
18   O'Kelly, *Amadeo*, p.52-3.
19   Inda Aba Guna or Indabaguna pass.
20   Italian accounts say they had stopped to refuel when ambushed.

At dawn on Christmas day,[21] Amadeo saw 100 Ethiopians emerging from Selaclaca Gorge spreading into some trees and rocks, trying to outflank his units right flank. Amadeo was ordered to stop them immediately and led 140 Saphys in a gallop towards the enemy who were advancing in the woods. In the woods the impetus of the charge was lost and became a melee. Sandor pounded forward, wheeled and charged again but as he did so Amadeo was grabbed around waist by an Ethiopian warrior. He spurred Sandor away but could not reach to get his sword out. Then a shot hit Sandor. A dumb-dumb bullet had penetrated the pommel of his saddle and hit Amadeo's hand and Sandors withers. Had it been any higher, he would have suffered a fatal wound, but for years Amedeo would have to wear a leather gauntlet to keep the hand from closing in on itself.[22] Eventually he managed to draw his sword and hit the attackers head with its hilt. Free of the grappling enemy, Amadeo shifted his weight in the saddle and charged again, as this time the Ethiopian's broke and ran. By this time there were 1,000s of the enemy and Amadeo and his men joined the main charge of 350 galloping horsemen which broke the enemy who then ran from the field.[23] The Saphys sheltered for the night against isolated attacks which killed 35 including the corporal who had sold him Sandor.[24]

Amedeo riding Sandor photographed with his Spahy orderly photographed on 26 December 1935, the day after the cavalry actions at Selaclaca.[25]

As the progress of the Christmas offensive slowed, Italian plans to renew the advance on the northern front got under way and the Italian commander, Badoglio[26] received additional ground forces. Badly mauled at Selacacla, the Saphys were now relegated to policing duties.[27] During one such patrol at Adi Ghilte they found a stache of rifles, along with metal hatch covers from one of Captain Grippa's tanks, in a church and chased the culprits to a nearby rock cave, before coming under fire. They rode off before Ethiopian reinforcements arrived but Amadeo was to gain some celebrity for this action back in Italy when it featured in a magazine.[28] In early February, the Italians captured Amba Aradam and in the Battle of Enderta the Ethiopians suffered massive losses.[29] Then in early March, the Ethiopians were attacked, bombed,

21   O'Kelly, *Amadeo,* p.60.
22   Even in old age, he always wore little mittens.
23   O'Kelly, *Amadeo,* p.62.
24   O'Kelly, *Amadeo,* p.63.
25   The dedication of the photograph is to his Uncle Rodolfo, the father of his future wife Beatrice. Oddly, the original photograph was mistakenly reversed when it was printed, making it appear that his right hand was wounded.
26   28 September 1871–1 November 1956.
27   O'Kelly, *Amadeo,* p.64.
28   O'Kelly, *Amadeo,* p.67.
29   10–19 February 1936. During the slaughter following the attempted withdrawal the Italians lost 800 killed and wounded while the Ethiopians lost 6,000 killed and 12,000 wounded.

and defeated in what was known as the Battle of Shire.[30] Although the Italians had suffered significant casualties, by now the Ethiopian army was effectively neutralized as a fighting force.

On 31 March 1936 at the final desperate Battle of Mai Ceu on Lake Ashangi,[31] the Italians defeated what remained of the Ethiopian army commanded by Emperor Haile Selassie himself. The outnumbered Ethiopians launched near non-stop attacks all day but could not overcome the well-prepared Italian defences, until they withdrew exhausted and were successfully counter-attacked. The Ethiopian offensive was ultimately stopped due to superior modern weapons, but the Italian Air Force finished off what was left of Haile Selassie's army by attacking the survivors at Lake Ashangi with mustard gas.[32] On 4 April 1936, Haile Selassie looked with despair upon the horrific sight of the dead bodies of his army ringing the poisoned lake. Ten days later, Graziani[33] launched his attack against, the last Ethiopian army in the field at the Battle of the Ogaden,[34] which totally disintegrated. Very early on 2 May, Haile Selassie boarded a train from Addis Ababa to Djibouti, with all the golden treasure of the "Ethiopian Central Bank" and fled to exile in England. Badoglio's force marched into Addis Ababa on 5 May and while there never was a formal surrender, the Second Italo-Abyssinian War was over.

On 9 May 1936, the crowd chanted "Emperor! Emperor! Salute the Emperor!" when King-Emperor Victor Emmanuel III,[35] in full Army uniform, showed himself on a balcony of the Quirinal Palace in Rome. While the Italian King-Emperor was silent, Mussolini proclaimed his "Italian East African Empire", formed from the newly occupied Ethiopia and the Italian colonies of Eritrea and Italian Somaliland,[36] from the balcony of the *Palazzo Venezia* to the jubilant crowd. This was Mussolini's hour of glory with the Italian nation united around him as never before. Italy had gained a vast territory with untold mineral riches and Fascism was never so popular despite underlying economic ills.

While the Italian people were rejoicing, Haile Selassie was crossing the Red Sea in a British cruiser on his way to England. On 30 June, he spoke at the League of

---

30 29 February–2 March 1936.
31 O'Kelly, *Amadeo*, p.70.
32 When the Italian Air Force attacked a field hospital run by the Swedish Red Cross, a war crime in itself, the Swedes secured photographic evidence of Ethiopian civilians with damages from mustard gas. The Italians attempted to justify their use of chemical weapons as acceptable reprisal against the Ethiopians torture and killing of their prisoners and wounded soldiers. The Italians had 400 casualties, the Eritreans 873, and the Ethiopians 11,000.
33 11 August 1882–11 January 1955.
34 14–25 April 1936.
35 11 November 1869–28 December 1947. King of Italy from 29 July 1900 until his abdication on 9 May 1946.
36 On 1 June Italy officially merged Ethiopia with Eritrea and Italian Somaliland, calling the new territory *Africa Orientale Italiana* (Italian East Africa).

Nations as a group of jeering Italian journalists began yelling insults and had to be ejected. Haile Selassie then denounced Italy's actions and criticised the world community for standing by, prophetically warning that: "It is us today. It will be you tomorrow." Despite his speech, his resolution to deny recognition of the Italian conquest was defeated and he was not granted a loan to finance a resistance movement. To add insult to injury, in July 1936, the League of Nations voted to end the sanctions imposed against Italy.[37]

Marshal Pietro Badoglio[38] was proclaimed as the first Viceroy and Governor General of the new Italian colony, and held these positions only until 11 June 1936, when Marshal Rodolfo Graziani[39] replaced him. The occupation was marked by recurring guerrilla campaigns against the Italians and Italian reprisals, including mustard gas attacks against rebels and the summary execution of prisoners. This soon earned Graziani the title: "the Butcher of Ethiopia". On 11 December 1936, the League of Nations voted to condemn Italy and, as a result, Mussolini declared his country's withdrawal from the organization. In the end, the harsh policies of Graziani did not pacify the country and on 21 December 1937, Rome appointed Amedeo, 3rd Duke of Aosta[40] to replace him and instructed him to adopt a more flexible line. The Duke brought a program of progressive improvement that included miles of new paved roadways, hospitals, hotels, post offices, telephone exchanges, aqueducts, schools, and shops. He also definitively abolished slavery and abrogated feudal laws previously upheld by the ruling Amharas. However, he was unable to undo the damage Graziani's brutality had already done.

Decorated for his actions in the war, Amadeo was flattered to be chosen a year later as an aide de camp in the 'Black Flames' division, which was sent to support Franco's Nationalist Forces in the Spanish Civil War.[41] So he left Sandor in Ethiopia to lead Moroccan troops and distinguished himself at the capture of Santander and at Teruel, winning the Silver Medal for gallantry by capturing three Russian armoured cars and crews. Again, he was wounded by grenade fragments, and returned to Italy where he encountered the anti-Semitic, pro-Nazi phase of Italian Fascism and did not like what he saw. Therefore, he requested a posting in Italian East Africa in 1939, under his mentor the Duke of Aosta. Here he carried out various policing operations against insurgents loyal to the toppled Emperor Haile Selassie.

In May 1939, Italy and Nazi Germany joined together in the Pact of Steel and yet at the outbreak of war in Europe, Italy opted for "armed neutrality". Then, opportunistically on 10th June 1940, with France on her knees, Mussolini led Italy into World

---

37 During the Italian invasion, Hitler had supplied the Ethiopians with 16,000 rifles and 600 machine guns in the hope that Italy would be weakened when he moved against Austria. By contrast, France and Britain recognized Italian control over Ethiopia in April 1938.
38 28 Sept 1871–1 Nov 1956.
39 11 August 1882–11 January 1955.
40 21 October 1898–3 March 1942.
41 1936-39.

War II. Until World War II, the Indian Ocean had been considered a "British lake", ringed by significant British Commonwealth possessions, through which strategic supplies for the United Kingdom and the manpower of Australia, New Zealand and India had to pass. Now the Italian Navy with its "Red Sea Flotilla" threatened British supply routes heading from the Gulf of Aden,[42] along the Red Sea and through the Suez Canal. Most Italian warships were stationed in the port of Massawa in Eritrea, with lesser port facilities at Mogadishu in Italian Somaliland and Assab in Eritrea but, as Italian fuel supplies in Massawa dwindled, so did their offensive actions. Furthermore, in mid to late June 1940, four of the eight Italian submarines based in Massawa were lost.

At this point, an Italian invasion of either French Somaliland or British Somaliland were possible and Mussolini looked forward to propaganda triumphs in the Sudan and British East Africa.[43] General Archibald Wavell,[44] Commander-in-Chief of the Middle East Command, had 30,000 British Commonwealth troops in Egypt, 27,500 in Palestine,[45] and a further 47,000 in East Africa, the Sudan and British Somalia. [46] With these limited forces he had to defend Libya, Egypt, Iraq, Syria, Iran, and East Africa, and with his forces spaced out along the extensive enemy frontiers, he fought delaying actions with skill and spirit, making aggressive raids into Italian territory. The British in East Africa were slightly better equipped than the Italians,[47] and had access to resupply and reinforcements, but they were vastly outnumbered by the Italian forces in the area. The *Regia Aeronautica Italia*[48] in East Africa had between 325 combat aircraft although 142 were in reserve or unserviceable,[49] and many were outdated but in relative terms they were some of the best available to either side. However, they were assigned to defend an area six times the size of the Italian homeland, while also conducting offensive operations against British airfields, ports and naval units at sea. Against them the British Commonwealth forces had about less than 100 aircraft which were, in the main, the older models which the RAF could spare whilst it was at the same time fighting the Battle of Britain for national survival.

42   Seven destroyers, five motor torpedo boats and eight submarines.
43   Kenya, Tanganyika, and Uganda.
44   5 May 1883–24 May 1950.
45   Michael Glover, *An Improvised War: The Abyssinian Campaign of 1940-1941* (London: Leo Cooper, 1987), p.19.
46   Andrew Stewart, *The First Victory: The Second World War in the East African Campaign* (London: Yale University Press, 2016), p.51.
47   On 10 June 1940, there were only three Regular British infantry battalions, 21 companies (4,500 men in total) of the Sudan Defence Force, and no artillery though the Sudan Horse was in the process of conversion into a 3.7-inch howitzer battery.
48   Italian Royal Air Force.
49   Glover, *An Improvised War*, p.21.

Against Wavell and Major-General William Platt[50] in the Sudan, the Duke of Aosta had somewhere between 250,000 and 270,000 Italian troops,[51] most of them local East African askaris. Amadeo was given command of a force of Ethiopian, Eritrean and Yemeni tribesmen on assorted horses, camels and dromedaries. The " Gruppo Bande a Cavallo" or "Gruppo Bande Guillet", were recruited from all over Ethiopia and were Amharic speaking, although the NCOs were Eritrean, and the five officers were Italians, hand-picked by Amedeo himself. His command, the Amhara Cavalry Bande totaled 2,500 men and was an extraordinarily large unit for a lieutenant, but the Duke of Aosta was determined not to entrust it to some desk-bound portly colonel.

On 4 July 1940, 12,000 Italians crossed the Sudanese border and forced the small British garrison of 600 Sudanesse troops holding the railway junction at Kassala to withdraw.[52] The Italians also seized the small British fort at Gallabat, just over the border from Metemma, some 200 miles to the south of Kassala. Unable to venture further due to lack of fuel, they fortified Kassala and established a brigade-strong garrison. Then, on 3 August 1940, approximately 26,000 Italian troops invaded British Somaliland, where Brigadier Arthur Reginald Chater's[53] 4,000 lightly armed British troops were not only critically short of artillery but had no tanks, armoured cars or anti-tank weapons to oppose the Italian tanks.[54] The British concluded that resistance would be futile and withdrew their forces covered by the determined effort of the Black Watch battalion, who allowed the entire British Commonwealth contingent to escape to Aden by 17 August with almost no losses. The conquest of the British Somaliland was the only campaign in which Italy achieved victory on their own and Benito Mussolini could boast that Italy had conquered a territory the size of England.

Wavell's plan for the counter-offensive included a northern front led by Lieutenant-General Platt, and a southern front led by Lieutenant-General Alan Cunningham.[55] Platt would advance southward from the Sudan, through Eritrea, and into Ethiopia whilst Cunningham would also advance into Ethiopia from Kenya, north through Italian Somaliland. A third force was to re-take British Somaliland in an amphibious assault and all three forces were to ultimately join at the capital, Addis Ababa.

Since his return to Africa, Amadeo was keen to buy back his Barbary Arab, Sandor, who he had so carefully schooled in the African sun and with whom he had already shared the danger and excitement of battle. However, his new owner Lieutenant Marchess Francessco Santasilia turned him down.[56] The partnership was only renewed when Santasilia was injured at Kassala in the first weeks of the war and

---

50   14 June 1885–28 September 1975.
51   Glover, *An Improvised War*, p.20.
52   O'Kelly, *Amadeo*, p.143.
53   1896–1979.
54   Glover, *An Improvised War*, p.32.
55   1 May 1887–30 January 1983.
56   O'Kelly, *Amadeo*, p.149 O'Kelly.

his Commanding Officer, knowing of Amadeo's relationship with Sandor and the training he had put into the horse, offered Amadeo his old mount.

Throughout late 1940, the setbacks suffered by Italian forces in the Mediterranean Sea, in the Western Desert,[57] and on the Albanian border with Greece, prompted the Italians to abandon offensive actions against the Sudan and the Suez Canal. Thus General Frusci[58] in the lowlands was ordered to withdraw his forces at Kassala and Metemma to hold the more easily defended mountain passes on the roads running eastward from Kassala to Agordat and from Metemma to Gondar and on 12 January, the Duke of Aosta, sent three colonial brigades and his elite Savoy Grenadiers Division to defend Keren.[59] Aggressive skirmishing in December had prompted the Italians to withdraw to Keru and Wachai, where the mountains began and when Australian re-inforcements arrived in Egypt it allowed General Wavell to release the 4th Indian Infantry Division to the Sudan to join the 5th Division.[60] This enabled the main British attack against the railway junction at Kassala, to be brought forward to 18 January1941 when Platt was able to start his offensive into Eritrea.

Short of men, Wavell sought local support from Emperor Haile Selassie I, and on 13 June 1940, a "Mr Strong" took off in a Short Sunderland flying boat from Poole Harbour on the south coast of England arriving in Alexandria on 25 June. Seven days later, as "Mr Smith," he flew to Khartoum where he met Platt to discuss plans to free Ethiopia from Italian rule. When in July, the British government recognised Emperor Selassie and promised to help him to reclaim his throne, Wavell hoped the Ethiopian irregular forces, called "patriots" by the British, would tie down large numbers of Italians. However, Platt did not believe the Emperor had the support of the majority of the people and had poor opinion of Major Orde Wingate,[61] his liaison officer with the Emperor, whose naturally abrasive manner led to friction and animosity with other commanders. Nevertheless, Wingate formed a small regular unit named Gideon Force[62] and on 18 January 1941, Emperor Selassie crossed the border and joined Gideon Force in the province of Gojjam where they rallied Ethiopian patriots wherever they went using powerful loudspeakers to announce the presence of the emperor and used surprise and bluff to disrupt Italian supply lines and provided important intelligence to the more conventional forces.

57   O'Kelly, *Amadeo*, p.146. On 9 December Wavell at Sidi Birani took 38,300 prisoners, 237 guns 73 tanks for loss of 624 men.
58   16 January 1879–1949.
59   Including the only battalion of elite mountain troops (*Alpini*) in East Africa.
60   O'Kelly, *Amadeo*, p.146.
61   26 February 1903–24 March 1944. He had spent five inter-war years with the Sudan Defence Force and was later to gain fame in Burma with the Chindits.
62   After the biblical judge Gideon, composed of the Frontier battalion from the Sudan Defence Force and the 2nd Ethiopian Battalion, equipped with four, 3-inch mortars and 15,000 camels to provide transport and carry supplies.

The war in Africa was a duel between two colonial armies with Eritrean ascari of the Italians fighting it out with the British Indian Divisions who on 19 January 1941, entered Kassala on their way to the heavily fortified town of Agordat to the east, among the jagged foothills of the Eritrean Plateau. Amadeo's "Band" was tasked by the Duke of Aosta to be the eyes and ears of the Italians in East Africa so when the British Army invaded Guillet took to the desert with his force of horseman to delay the British advance. Advancing east towards Agordat, the 4th Indian Division, took the northern road via Wachai and Keru.[63] Meanwhile the two brigades of 5th Indian Infantry Division took the southern road via Tessenei,[64] and on 21 January occupied Aicota without opposition. Meanwhile, the advance seemed to be going like clockwork as the composite unit, Gazelle Force[65] reached the strongly defended position at the Keru Gorge held by five Italian battalions. Amadeo, on his white Arabian stallion, Sandor, was determined to delay the allied advance from the North-West and he decided to lead a potentially suicidal cavalry charge against the tanks and 25-pounder artillery guns of "Gazelle Force".

The 4th Battalion of the 11th Sikhs Regiment[66] were in the vanguard and had been advancing for four days when at daybreak on 21 January 1941 Guillet and Sandor led more than 500 of his troopers in a wild charge along the exposed flanks of the British and Indian soldiers,[67] throwing red Italian grenades, 'like cricket balls', which exploded among the defenders, several of whom were cut down by swords. Erupting through the morning mist, they cut through the 4/11th Sikhs, flanked the armoured cars of Skinner's Horse and then galloped straight towards British brigade headquarters and the 25-pounder artillery of the 25th Field Regiment and of 390 Battery of the Surrey and Sussex Yeomanry.[68] They fired at anything that moved at point blank range and literally ran through the entire Indian formation, only narrowly missed capturing an English Brigadier. The British gunners turned their 25-pounders that had been pointing towards the Italian fortifications at Keru, and swiveled them a full 180 degrees to face the enemy charge, now only 200 yards away.[69] Shells fired at two to three feet from the ground cut into the horses legs and chests but also fell on the British troops behind them including Captain Douglas Gray[70] of Skinner's Horse who had ridden in the 1938 Grand National. The British gunners barely had time to notice

63   Cherù.
64   The 9th Indian Infantry Brigade, had remained to cover the Gallabat position.
65   O'Kelly, *Amadeo*, p.148. On 16 October, Gazelle Force, commanded by Colonel Frank Messervy, was created in the Sudan as a mobile reconnaissance and fighting force. It comprised three motor machine-gun companies from the Sudan Defence Force, the 1st Duke of York's Own Skinner's Horse, the reconnaissance regiment from the 5th Indian Infantry Division, who had traded their horses for armoured cars 14 months earlier.
66   Of 5th Indian Division.
67   O'Kelly, *Amadeo*, p.151.
68   O'Kelly, *Amadeo*, p.151.
69   O'Kelly, *Amadeo*, pp.153-156.
70   31 December 1909–October 2004.

they were Eritrean cavalry, led by a young Italian officer, magnificently uniformed astride a beautiful grey charger, as they caused mayhem as the shells exploded amid the Sikhs and Skinner's Horse.

Lasting only seconds, the charge then swerved to the left and the horsemen disappeared into the network of wadis, two to three kilometers from where they started of the charge. Amadeo re-grouped in a dry river bed and Lieutenant Togni got his Yemini infantry into position to defend Amadeo's right flank. Gazelle Force broke off preparations for attack on Keru and sent three tanks forward along with the armoured cars of the Sudanese Defence Force and their Vickers machine-guns. Togni charged and was machine gunned down from the top of the Wadi and of his 31 men,[71] only two returned to Amadeo.[72] However, Togni had saved them from being outflanked but at midday the British advanced with Skinners Horse, the 4th/11th Sikhs, and the Armoured Cars of the Sudaneese. Amadeo spurred Sandor up out of the Wadi and they charged again, now with only 250 horsemen, towards the infantry in the centre who ran for the cover of the armoured cars on either flank.[73] They galloped on through the middle, machine guns thinning their ranks and wheeled from the Indian artillery towards the woods where they had started. There were 200 dead horses and men but the retreating Italian infantry were now through Keru and out of the lowlands on their way towards Agrodat as Amadeo's Gruppe headed back to Ashwari. The charge was one of the most dashing and extraordinary episodes of the Second World War and although not quite the last cavalry charge in history of warfare,[74] it was the last one faced by the British Army who had wasted a day. Although now all but forgotten in the sands of the desert sideshow, Guillet's and Sandor's actions at Keru get a fleeting mention in most histories of the Second World War.

The Italian position at Keru was undone on 22 January and while some Italians managed to escape across country in the night, General Fongoli with his staff and guns and 800 men were taken prisoner.[75] Within nine days, the British forces had advanced 100 miles and broken through the Italian positions in the foothills to capture Agordat on 1 February 1941,[76] after which the Italians consolidated their remaining forces at Keren, 60 miles further east of Agordat towards the Red Sea. There they blew the cliff into the gorge which provided the only road access to the Keren plateau from the west. Meanwhile 5th Indian Division had attacked Barentu and despite facing 8,000 defenders and 32 guns settled in prepared defences,[77] they occupied the town on 2

---

71   O'Kelly, *Amadeo*, pp.153-156.
72   O'Kelly, *Amadeo*, p.157.
73   O'Kelly, *Amadeo*, p.158.
74   Another cavalry charge took place little more than a year later when a friend of Guillet, Colonel Bettoni, launched the un-mechanised men of the "Savoia Cavalry" against Soviet troops in Russia at Isbuchenskij (Izbushensky) on the Don in August 1942.
75   Stewart, *The First Victory*, p.157.
76   In total 6,000 prisoners had been taken and 80 guns, 26 tanks and 400 trucks captured.
77   Stewart, Andrew, *The First Victory*, p.160.

February 1941. That same day Amedeo and his men arrived at Keren having ridden along the railway line from Agrodat, closely followed by Gazelle Force[78].

On 5 February 1941, the battle for Keren started and initially the resolute Italian defenders prevailed with heavy casualties on both sides. Further heavy attacks took place over the next 10 days, but there was no break through. By 14 March 1941, Platt's force of about 13,000 men faced a re-enforced Italian defence of about 23,000 men. Both sides fought with determination and both suffered heavy losses and it took until 27 March 1941 for Keren to fall.[79] Wartime British propaganda and un-fair post-war stereotypes have represented the Italians as almost comic warriors but no enemy put up a finer or more stubborn fight than those Savoia battalions at Keren, who in the first five days suffered nearly 5,000 casualties, 1,135 of them killed.[80] While hard fighting still lay ahead, the fall of Keren broke Italian resistance and led to the almost immediate capture of Massawa on the coast. The British were hoping to use the harbour facilities for ships bringing munitions and supplies to the North African theatre via the Red Sea but Massawa harbour was wrecked by Italian sabotage of machinery, the sinking of two large floating dry docks, and the scuttling of 16 large ships, blocking access in and out. The harbour was rendered useless for 13 months and the remaining seven Italian destroyers and single motor torpedo boat put to sea on "do or die" missions.

The Indian 5th Infantry Division pursued the demoralised Italians towards the Eritrean capital of Asmara, some 50 miles away, which was declared an open town on 1 April 1941. After Asmara fell, Amedeo and the remnants of his Gruppe made for the village of Azzega in the hills.[81] Now stranded outside the Italian lines, Amadeo wanted to tie down as many British troops as possible since the more he could tie down the fewer there would be to fight Rommel in the Western Desert. His force crippled, Guillet led his remaining men deep into the desert and he decided to fight in Eritrea, understanding that the Eritreans did not want to be unified with Ethiopia and come under the influence of the dominant Amhara. He started to dress as an Arab and shared out his horses, saddles and ammunition to local friendly tribesmen, keeping 30 camels and 15 mules for his men.[82] However, he couldn't bear to part with Sandor. The remnants of Amadeo's force, known simply as the *"Amhara"* (Band) fought under a banner with the Cross of Savoy superimposed with an Islamic Crescent and Guillet became known as *'Comandante Diavolo'* (The Devil Commander) to the natives and as "Italy's Lawrence of Arabia" to the British. They were well armed but

---

78   O'Kelly, *Amadeo*, p.166.
79   The British Commonwealth forces had a little under 4,000 men killed, wounded or missing. The Italians suffered about 3,000 men killed and several 1,000 men wounded, injured, or sick.
80   Compton MacKenzie,, *Eastern Epic: September 1939-March 1943: Defence* (London: Chatto & Windus, 1951), p.60.
81   O'Kelly, *Amadeo*, p.180.
82   O'Kelly, *Amadeo*, p.183.

lacked ammunition, but it was the absence of support from outside the occupied area that effectively ended his almost one-man war.

Meanwhile in the south, on 24 January 1941, Cunningham's main force had invaded Italian Somaliland from Kenya. The Italians had already withdrawn to the defensive terrain of the mountains of Ethiopia and the motorised Nigerian Brigade of the 11th African Division advanced 200 miles up the coast and occupied the major seaport and Somali capital of Mogadishu. Meanwhile, the 12th African Division pushed up the Juba River towards the Ethiopian border town of Dolo. By early March Cunningham's forces had captured most of Italian Somaliland and were advancing through Ethiopia towards the ultimate objective, Addis Ababa. The British were also having success in the east where on 16 March 1941, two Sikh battalions and one Somali commando sailed from Aden and landed on both sides of the port of Berbera.[83] They met a few hungry men, suffering from malaria, stood in formation on the beach waiting to surrender to the arriving British force. This was the first successful Allied landing on an enemy beach during World War II and re-captured British Somaliland from its Italian occupiers and in late March, they linked up with advancing forces from the Southern Front enabling Cunningham to be re-supplied through the port of Berbera. On 6 April 1941 he liberated Addis Ababa, having advanced 1,725 miles from Kenya in 53 days. Emperor Haile Selassie made a formal entry to the city on 5 May 1941,[84] five years to the day after being forced to flee his capital in 1936.

On 13 April 1941, Cunningham's northward advance linked up with Platt's forces, but some 200 miles north, Platt's forces were gathering at Amba Alagi, a 12,000-foot mountain between Asmara and Addis Ababa which the Italians had decided to defend in force, driving galleries into the solid rock to protect their troops and hold ample ammunition and stores. In this mountain fortress, the 7,000 defenders,[85] under command of the Duke of Aosta, thought themselves to be impregnable, but by 14 May 1941 Amba Alagi was surrounded and fortunately, before the final assault, an artillery shell hit an Italian fuel dump, causing oil to flow into the remaining drinking water. This forced the Duke of Aosta to surrender on 18 May 1941.[86] The campaign in Italian East Africa was all but over, although minor pockets of resistance persisted until the final surrender of the Italian forces in East Africa in November 1941. Despite the surrender, scattered Italian units fought a guerrilla war from the deserts of Eritrea and Somalia to the forests and mountains of Ethiopia until September 1943. However, with the Red Sea and Gulf of Aden coastlines cleared of Axis forces, United States ships could proceed to the Suez Canal, relieving the enormous strain on the shipping

---

83   By British naval "Force D" consisting of cruisers HMS *Glasgow* and *Caledon*; destroyers HMS *Kandahar* and *Kipling*; auxiliary cruisers *Chakdina* and *Chantala*, Indian trawlers; *Netavati* and *Parvati*, two transports and ML 109.

84   A day which has since been observed as the national holiday of Liberation Day.

85   Glover, *An Improvised War*, p.156.

86   He had endured the last months of fighting while suffering a severe attack of malaria and died of malaria and Tuberculosis a few months later.

resources of the United Kingdom. In January 1942 Ethiopia became an independent nation again, with Haile Selassie restored as its leader.[87]

Guillet, faithful to the oath to the House of Savoy, continued his private war against the British, while in the Western Desert, Rommel,[88] sought to reverse the earlier Italian disasters. He launched a series of commando raids, plundering convoys and shooting up guard posts, and for nine months he was one of the most famous Italian "guerrilla officers" in Eritrea and northern Ethiopia. Amedeo Guillet could boast at never being betrayed, despite the fact that the Eritreans knew perfectly well who he was and where he lived. Guillet's Eritrean troops paid a high price, losing approximately 800 men in little more than two years. Two British intelligence officers, the urbane Major Max Harrari[89] of the Irish Hussars and the driven intellectual Captain Sigismund Reich of the Jewish Brigade, who was eager to get on with the task of killing Germans, were responsible for hunting down the tiresome Italian officer. One day one of Reich's patrol of 100 Sudanese troops advanced in a thin line from the road towards the hills where Amadeo and his troops were hiding. Amadeo handed Sandor's reigns to one of his men and gave the order to charge on foot.[90] His men broke through the line to safety but in the melee the man holding Sandor was shot and killed. Sandor galloped away, lost forever to Amadeo but soon to be the property of Major Max Harrari who rode him in the ménage at Asmara. [91]

The British never got the man himself and when finally cornered, Amadeo disbanded his force and decided to escape. After numerous adventures, including disguising himself as a water seller, Guillet escaped across the Red Sea to neutral Yemen, where for a year he trained soldiers and cavalrymen for the Imam's army. Despite the opposition of the Yemenite royal house, he eventually succeeded in embarking incognito on a Red Cross ship repatriating sick and injured Italians and finally returned to Italy a few days before the armistice. In reward for his services Amadeo was promoted to Major and, against his wishes, spent the rest of the war as an intelligence officer, befriending many of his former British enemies from East Africa, including the promoted Colonel Harari, finishing the war on missions in occupied German territory. Harari caught up with Amedeo in newly liberated Rome in 1945 and later became his close friend and biographer until Max's death in 1987. After the war, Guillet entered the Italian diplomatic corps and served throughout the Middle East and North Africa until retiring

87   He reigned until 1974 when the monarchy was abolished by the Derg. The Italian colony of Eritrea was placed under British military administration for the remainder of the Second World War. In 1950, Eritrea was made part of Ethiopia, but the unification proved to be unpopular and led to the Eritrean War of Independence. Eritrea became independent in 1993. Following 1945, Britain regained control of British Somaliland and conquered Italian Somaliland, administering both militarily as protectorates, until, on 1 July 1960, the two territories united to form the Somali Republic.
88   15 November 1891–14 October 1944.
89   18 February 1927–21 September 2014.
90   O'Kelly, *Amadeo*, p.200.
91   O'Kelly, *Amadeo*, pp.201-202.

from public service to County Meath in Ireland in 1975 for the peace and quiet and to enjoy the foxhunting as a member of the Tara Harriers and the Meath Hounds. His prize possession in his retirement study was a pale horse's hoof, shod in the Italian style and mounted on silver with the inscription "Sandro. Barbary grey. 12 years old Max Harari, Asmara. June 1942" along with a photograph of Sandor looking out of his stable with the words "To Amadeo in memory of the wonderful animal that was the cause of our friendship".[92]

It might be tempting to think that Sandor and the Second World War was the last battlefield success of the horse. But an equine hero of the cold war era can claim that accolade. Sergeant Reckless is the forgotten hero from "The Forgotten War" between United Nations (UN) forces and the Chinese communist People's Volunteer Army. She was a little chestnut Mongolian mare whose heroism during fierce combat in Korea was such that the US Marine Corps were to make her an honorary staff sergeant.

In the first year of the Korean War there were sweeping movements up and down the peninsula.[93] Combat raged from the 38th Parallel south to the Pusan Perimeter then, with the landing at Inchon and the Perimeter breakout, up to the Yalu, and finally a retreat south again in the face of the massive Chinese intervention. After the United Nations resumed the offensive in January 1951 and stopped the Communist counter-attacks, the front stabilized north of Seoul. With the start of armistice negotiations in July 1951, the war settled into a static phase with action characterized by limited regimental, battalion, company or platoon attacks to seize or recover key tactical terrain. The "Battles of the Outposts" was the period of fighting that took place in the final two years of the war, with fixed defences, trench lines, bunkers, patrols, wiring parties and minefields reminiscent of the Western Front in 1915–1917. The war was to go on in this manner until the signing of the armistice on 27 July 1953, and nearly half of the United States casualties in the war occurred during this" static" phase of combat. Since both sides intended to create a demilitarized zone by pulling the opposing forces back two kilometres from the line of contact, they both focused on the seizure of a line of strong outposts, known as the Jamestown Line, in order to hold defensible terrain when the armistice came into effect. Soldiers knew that an armistice could be signed at any time and no one wanted to be the last casualty of the war. This presented a massive leadership challenge at every level as they sought to minimize casualties while accomplishing the mission. Americans have appropriately called the Korean War "The Forgotten War" and the "static" phase has become the forgotten part of the forgotten war. Our hero's story was played out on this Jamestown Line, which extended 250 kilometres (160 mi) across central Korea.

The story of *Sergent Recklass* began in October 1952 when a Marine raiding force was nearly cut off by Chinese troops as it fought its way back into Allied lines. To cover the retreat, the battalion created a 'fire curtain' using recoilless rifles, which had

92   O'Kelly, *Amadeo*, p.288.
93   25 June 1950–27 July 1953.

been developed prior to WWII, and by the time of the Korean Conflict, perfected into a deadly tank-killer, projecting a 75-mm shell with precision. It could be carried by three or four men but the rounds were heavy, each weighing 24 pounds. Hence, too much time was wasted and too many troops exposed to fire to maintain the rate of fire necessary to sustain such a curtain. It required ammunition runs over hills and across paddies to the firing positions in an exhausting race against time and space. On this occasion the fire was slowing to an intermittent cough when the last of the raiders got back to the main body.

This incident convinced 2nd Lieutenant Eric Pedersen, who was the commanding officer of the Recoilless Rifle Platoon, Antitank Company, 5th Marine Regiment, that a horse could prove invaluable in helping to carry ammunition for his platoon's weapons. The next day, though suffering from leg, hip and face wounds, Pedersen hooked a trailer to his jeep and took the rough road south to the Seoul Race Track. All racing had been cancelled for the duration of the war but he met breeders eager to sell their horses and spotted a small young Mongolian chestnut mare named, Ah-Chim-Hai meaning "Flame of the Morning". Pedersen paid $250 from his own pocket to a young Korean boy, Kim Huk Moon, who sold his beloved horse so that he could buy an artificial leg for his sister, Chung Soon, who had stepped on a land mine. Kim's loss was the Marines' gain and the little horse was transported to base camp where, and even though it was dark when they arrived, members of the platoon welcomed the new recruit. The troops renamed her "Reckless" after the nickname the Marines had gave the recoilless rifle and that night in October of 1952, "Reckless" was recruited into the Marine Corps to carry ammunition to the front lines.

Without adequate provisions for a horse, *Reckless'* first meal consisted of a loaf of bread and uncooked oatmeal but soon, the Quartermaster arranged proper fodder, bringing a trailer full of barley, sorghum, hay and rice straw to camp. Not only did she like apples and carrots, but would eat and drink everything, including scrambled eggs, coffee, Hershey bars, candy from the rations, Coca Cola, and even blankets and hats when she was being ignored. Reckless was lucky that there were Marines who had prior experience with horses and over the next few days the platoon built a bunker and fenced in a small area for a pasture to make their new charge as comfortable as possible. During her first few nights at camp, she was tied in her bunker, but soon she was given free rein to roam about, sometimes visiting the Marines in their tents, and some even allowed her to spend the very cold nights with them and sleep standing up next to the stove.

Reckless' training was the responsibility of two experienced horsemen, Private First Class Monroe Coleman and Platoon Sergeant Joseph Latham. Soon the long hours of serious training began as Latham put the recruit through" hoof" camp, teaching her how to become accustomed to friendly fire and not to bolt when the recoilless rifles back-blasted as they fired. When she first heard the sound of the terrific blast, *Reckless* went straight up into the air and came down trembling with fright. Coleman tried to sooth her, but Reckless only snorted until finally after a series of blasts, she settled down and no longer showed fear when the weapons was fired. Latham taught her how to cross over communication lines and barbed wire and also trained her to head toward a bunker when rounds hit behind the lines, so that on yelling "Incoming!" she would go straight to a bunker. Pedersen had asked his wife to send a much-needed pack saddle so that *Reckless* could learn to carry loads of up to six rounds, although he made it clear that she was not to carry heavier load unless absolutely necessary.

Soon the time came for her to carry her first load in combat when in January 1953 a platoon from "Dog" Company conducted a raid north of Outpost Berlin, supported by a gun section from the Recoilless Rifle Platoon and on that day Reckless hauled ammunition all day long. *Reckless* also carried grenades, small-arms ammunition, rations, sleeping bags, and barbed wire in addition to her primary duty of packing ammunition for the recoilless rifle. She proved herself to be invaluable when the 5th Marines were tasked to string communications wire, since she could string more telephone wire in a day than almost a dozen Marines. In February Reckless was again used in "Raid Charlie," when it is estimated that she made 24 trips from the ammunition supply point to the firing sites, travelling over 20 miles and carrying a total of 3,500 pounds during the day.[94] They would strap the six feet long gun, which usually took two men to handle, on one side and strap ammunition on the other to balance the load on the 14.1-hand pony. Not only did this little Mongolian mare who weighed only 900 pounds transport ammunition for the company, but she also transported injured soldiers back to base camp, and even provided cover for some of them during the battle. And what is amazing is that she did this all on her own. It was no wonder that she returned to her pasture and bunker after dark with head hanging. She was met by Lieutenant Pederson at the bunker and fed a bucket of warm bran mash as two Marines on each side of her gave her a thorough rubdown and covered her with a blanket. Before her friends left she was sound asleep. Thankfully, not all her days were so tough, and she spent many of them resting in her pasture between missions.

Reckless' finest hour came during the Battle of Outpost Vegas when the Chinese attempted to regain the initiative following the winter. The night of 25 March 1953 was clear. In the darkness the men manning three outposts had no ides it would erupt into one of the most tenacious battles the Marines would ever fight. The outposts were about 1,500 yards forward to the 5th Marines' front line, with Vegas, on the right being the highest of the three, Reno on the left and a small hill called Reno Block, a defensive position manned every night by a reinforced squad in-between. Suddenly, at 7:00 p.m. the quiet was shattered when all three outposts were barraged by enemy artillery, mortar and small arms fire as two battalions of Reds attacked. For the next five days, screaming Chinese and stubborn Marines clashed for this particular piece of real estate. Reno was lost with all its defenders and Vegas was lost with heavy casualties. The second battalion, 5th Marines, was ordered in for the counter-attack to recapture Vegas, with *Reckless* and her rifles in close support. Enemy in-coming artillery and mortar shells were producing staggering losses and D Company of the

94   See < http://www.sgtreckless.com/Reckless/Welcome.html > (Accessed 13 May 16).

second battalion was reduced from a full complement to just 16 men in less than two hours whilst E Company suffered nearly as badly.

It was under these brutal conditions that the Marine's war horse showed her indomitable spirit, following her orders without supervision or guidance. To supply the guns, the little chestnut had to carry her load of 75-mm shells across a paddy field and into the hills. The distance to the firing positions was over 1,800 yards and the final climb to the firing positions was at a nearly 45-degree angle. On the first few trips Latham or Coleman, led her to the front lines but after the fourth or fifth trip, with some of the gun crew wounded, they were no longer spare to lead her. So, knowing exactly what her job was, she started making the trip by herself, returning from the forward position to the dump alone. Upon being loaded, she took off across the paddy without order or direction, and thereafter marched the fiery gauntlet alone. Eye witnesses reported that amid artillery in the flare light,[95] they could see the little Mongolian mare heading up that slope to the gun pit alone. They would tie a wounded Marine on her and turn her around and she would head down the ridge with all the artillery and mortar fire coming in. She also provided a shield for several Marines who were trapped trying to make their way down. The marines would unload the wounded off her back and again tie gun ammo on her before she would turn around and, on her own, head right back up. Imagine a horse loaded with a wounded soldier, being smacked on the rump at the top of the hill, and heading back to the "safety" of the rear. To then imagine the same horse, loaded with ammunition, and trudging back to the battle where artillery is going off, without anyone leading her is almost unbelievable. How many horses head back to their stable on their own or return to you in the field? Enemy soldiers could see her as she made her way across the deadly "no man's land" and it's difficult to describe the elation and the boost in morale that little white-faced mare gave Marines as she outfoxed the enemy to bring vitally needed ammunition up the mountain.

On that day *Reckless* made 51 trips up that steep hill to the firing sites, usually by herself. All three weapons were kept in action and one fired so fast the barrel crystallized. In all she trudged more than 35 miles across no man's land, through rice paddies, and up steep mountain trails. With steady nerves, bravery, and a sense of duty beyond imagination, she carried 386 rounds of ammunition weighing over 9,000 pounds (almost five tons) and carried many wounded soldiers down the mountain to safety.

Vegas was retaken and held against murderous counterattacks until the violence ebbed and Vegas was secured. Survivors of this campaign are primarily those who were injured early and carried out of harms way by *Reckless* for medical treatment, as well as those who were called into the battle from the rear to replace the dead and injured. Only two soldiers left that field uninjured and *Reckless* herself did not escape injury, being wounded once in her left flank, once above an eye and her ears were cut

95   Marine Harold Wadley, one of only two men to leave "Hill Vegas" alive.

by barbed wire. However, she never stopped and she was awarded two purple hearts for those wounds which weren't serious enough to get her a quick ticket home.

She saw more action in the war since the battalion was still on the front line when the Korean cease-fire was signed in July 1953. The entire unit, including its war horse, was assembled for a final parade before returning state-side. At a ceremony as formal as could be arranged on a wind-swept Korean field, *Reckless* was cited for her bravery and Major General Randolph Pate,[96] division commander, pinned sergeant's chevrons to her shiny new red-and-gold silk blanket. It was now *Sergeant Reckless,* and her citation said, "Disregard for her own safety and conduct under fire were an inspiration to the troops and in keeping with the highest traditions of the Naval Service. *Reckless'* attention and devotion to duty make her well qualified for promotion to the rank of sergeant. Her absolute dependability while on missions under fire contributed materially to the success of many battles."

Pate had first seen the mare when the First Marine Division was in reserve for a brief period and noted: "I was surprised at her beauty and intelligence and believe it or not, her esprit de corps. Like any other Marine, she was enjoying a bottle of beer with her comrades. She was constantly the centre of attraction and was fully aware of her importance. If she failed to receive the attention, she felt her due, she would deliberately walk in a group of Marines and in effect, enter the conversation. It was obvious the Marines loved her."

The Marines refused to leave *Reckless* behind in Korea, but Government red tape threatened her trip by ship to the States. However, thanks to considerable string-pulling, favour-cashing, and public support stirred by *Reckless'* story in the *Post*, she was eventually brought across the Pacific to California on a freighter as a guest of Pacific Transport Lines. She first touched American soil on 10 November 1954, in San Francisco. A weather delay caused her to miss an appearance on The Ed Sullivan Show, but Reckless attended a Marine birthday ball instead, travelling up in an elevator to be the guest of honour and indulge her taste for cake.

After the war, *Reckless* retired at Camp Pendleton in California where she spent the rest of her life as the 1st Marine Division's mascot, attending all their change of commands, retirements, birthday ball receptions, civilian parades and other functions. When the 5th Marines held a regimental parade honouring the heroes of the Vegas battle, *Reckless* passed in review with her unit and throughout the rest of her life, the soldiers' love and respect for the horse remained immense. The General issued the order that there was never to be any more weight than a blanket put on her back again, and so, when *Reckless* went on her daily jog, the Marine accompanying her went on foot.

She still loved to eat anything including potato chips, peanut butter and jelly sandwiches and would drink anything out of a can or cup, from coffee to beer. Her last promotion was to Staff Sergeant in 1959, an honour never bestowed on an animal

96   11 February 1898–31 July 1961.

before or since. *Reckless* was decorated with two Purple Hearts, the Good Conduct Medal, Korean Service Medal, a Presidential Unit Citation with a star, a United Nations Service Medal, a Republic of Korea Presidential Unit Citation, National Defense Service Medal, Navy Unit Commendation, and other honours. She wore them proudly on her red and gold blanket, along with a French Fourragere that the 5th Marines earned in WW1 whenever she was paraded around at official functions. She had become a celebrated marine. Generals and colonels came to call on her; newspapermen interviewed her, and she appeared on television.

She later gave birth to three colts and a filly, although one died a month after birth, but Fearless, Dauntless, and Chesty grew up with her and saw her through her golden years, until her death at a comparatively young age of 20 on 13 May 1968. She is buried at Camp Pendleton, where there's a monument to her at the stables. In the 1990s, she was featured in the LIFE magazine collector's edition "Celebrating Our Heroes" as one of America's 100 greatest heroes of all time, alongside George Washington, Abraham Lincoln, and Mother Teresa. As one of the US forces heroes perhaps she should have a bronze statue on the Potomac in Washington DC to help America remember its forgotten war.

Sergent Reckless has been appropriately recognised but not all of our equine heroes have received the praise they are due. Those that have received honours have tended to be those associated with a rider of status. *Copenhagen*, *Sir Briggs*, *Ronald*, *Vonolel*, *Comanche*, Jack Seeley's *Warrior* and *Old Baldy* have all received official recognition. By contrast, every attempt was made to eliminate the Appaloosa from the face of the earth and their lasting tribute remains the survival and popularity of their breed. Trooper Mossop's *Warrior*, *Maidan*, *Tartar*, *Monty*, *Dandy* and *Sandor* all deserve greater official recognition and to have their stories told.

So what can we say about our equine heroes at the end of their stories? Firstly they are all genuine heroes, worthy of some decoration. As mentioned in the introduction, all the horses in this book were true heroes who lived up to the military virtues of Courage, Commitment, Discipline, Respect, Integrity and Loyalty. The courage of *Ronald* in leading the Charge of the Light Brigade, *Warrior* leaping down the Devils Staircase, *Sgt Reckless* carrying ammunition and casualties alone under fire, and *Monty* and his Waler chums charging the guns at Beersheba, would all be worthy of a VC or other decoration had they been undertaken by a human soldier. Few human warriors have displayed the endurance and commitment displayed by *Warrior* in carrying Trooper Mossop ten miles when injured and dying, or *Volonel* carrying his General and *Maidan* carrying 18 stone of Colonel Brownlow the 300 miles in the heat of the Afghan plains to Kandahar. The Appaloosa breed's 1,700 miles across America is just outstanding. The steadfastness under fire of *Sergent Reckless* and *Copenhagen* are exemplars of discipline showing respect for the commands of their riders and handlers. The integrity of a horse is hard to assess, as it is for a human, but the long and distinguished service of *Tartar* and *Comanche* despite their wounds could not be described as in any way fake. All these horses displayed loyalty to their riders even if they had no concept of loyalty to any higher organisation or cause.

But what do these equine heroics say about us as humans? I believe they serve two functions. Firstly they provide an exemplar of military virtue without the vices of pride and personal ambition which so often create a more complex moral exemplar when human military biographies are examined. Secondly, the innocence of the horse prompts a compassion for the participants which is often harder to evoke when the human participants of war, with all their faults and foibles, are examined, or when the helplessness of the massed soldiery is lost in the statistics of mass casualty returns. If their stories can prompt compassion for their suffering, and that compassion can be extended to provide a greater empathy with the human condition in war, then telling their story will have been worthwhile.

Bibliography

Printed Publications

Adkin, M., *The Charge: The Real Reason Why the Light Brigade were Lost* (London: Pimlico, 2004)

Anderson, H. Allen, *Canadian River Expedition* cited at Handbook of Texas <http://www.tshaonline.org/handbook/online/articles/qfc01>

Archer, Rosemary, *The Arabian Horse* (London: J. A. Allen, Breed Series, 1992).

Archer, Rosemary, Colin Pearson and Cecil Covey, *The Crabbet Arabian Stud: Its History and Influence* (Northleach. Gloucestershire: Alexander Heriot & Co. Ltd., 1978).

Atwood, Rodney, *The March to Kandahar: Roberts in Afghanistan.* (Barnsley: Pen & Sword publishing, 2008).

Barker, A. J., *Rape of Ethiopia, 1936* (London: Ballantine Books, 1971).

Barnard C.J. General Botha in the Spioenkop Campaign January1900", *Military History Journal Vol 2 No 1 – June 1971.*

Barrie, Douglas M., *The Australian Bloodhorse* (Sydney: Angus & Robertson, 1956).

Barthorp, Michael, *The Zulu War: Isandhlwana to Ulundi* (London: Cassell, 2002).

Bauld, Gibby and Cooke, Victoria and Robert, *21st Light Horse, "Horses in the Boer War* (Wagga Wagga, NSW, Australia.

Bradsher Dr. Greg *The Tale of Tartar the War Horrse* <http://blogs.archives.gov/TextMessage/2013/10/23/the-tale-of-tartar-the-war-horse/>

Brett-James, Antony, *Ball of Fire: The Fifth Indian Division in the Second World War* (Aldershot: Gale & Polden,1951).Brown, Dee, *Bury My Heart at Wounded Knee; An Indian History of the American West*, (London, Vintage Books, 1991).

Brown, Dee, *The Amercian West* (London: Simon and Shuster, 2004)

Brown, Dee, *Bury My Heart at Wounded Knee* (London: Vintage Books, 1991)

Bruce, Anthony, *The Last Crusade: The Palestine Campaign in the First World War* (London: John Murray, 2002).

Chandler, David, *Dictionary of the Napoleonic Wars* (New York: Macmillan, 1979)

David, Saul, *Victoria's Wars* (London: Penguin, 2006).

de Steiguer, J. Edward., *Wild Horses of the West: History and Politics of America's Mustangs* (Tucson: University of Arizona Press, 2011).

DiMarco, Louis, A., *War Horse: A History of the Military Horse and Rider* (Yardley, Pennsylvania: Westholme Publishing, 2008).

Dobie, Frank, *The Mustangs* (Boston: Little, Brown and Company,1952).

Dunkley, Stephen *General de Wet 1854 – 1922* <http://thediariesofavillageidiot. blogspot.co.uk/2009/03/general-de-wet.html>

Ewing, G. *Lord Roberts' famous march from Kabul to Kandahar August 1880* < http:// www.garenewing.co.uk/angloafghanwar/articles/kandahar_march.php>

Fallon, Donal, *The Grave of Vonolel, the Famous and Bemedalled Horse.* <https:// comeheretome.com/2010/06/22/the-grave-of-vonolel-the-famous-and-bemedalled-horse/ on 18 May 16>

Farwell, Byron, *The Great Boer War* (Barnsley: Pen & Sword, 2009).

Fitzpatrick, A., *The Ultimate Guide to Horse Breeds* (London: Hermes House, 2011).

Forczyk, Robert, *Nez Perce 1877: The Last Fight* (Oxford: Osprey, 2011).

Gade, Gene, *Ride of a Lifetime* <http://www.historynet.com/ride-of-a-lifetime.htm>

Geer, Andrew *Reckless, Pride of the Marines*, (New York: Stratford Press, 1955).

Glover, Michael, *The Peninsular War 1807-1814* (London: Penguin Books, 2003).

Glover, Michael, *An Improvised War: The Abyssinian Campaign of 1940-1941* (London: Leo Cooper, 1987).

Greaves, Adrian, "The Battle of Hlobane, 28 March 1879." *Journal of the Anglo Zulu War Society 15* (June 2004).

Greene, Jerome A., *Nez Perce Summer-The U.S. Army and the Nee-Me-Poo Crisis* (Helena, MT: Montana Historical Society Press, 2000).

Gulick, Bill, *Chief Joseph Country: Land of the Nez Perce.* (Caldwell, Id: The Caxton Printers, 1981, reprinted 1985).

Haines, Frances, *Appaloosa: The Spotted Horse in Art and History* (Austin, Texas: University of Texas Press, 1963).

Hamilton, Jill, *Marengo: The Myth of Napoleon's Horse* (London: Fourth Estate, 2000).

Hampton, Bruce, *Children of Grace-The Nez Perce War of 1877* (New York: Henry Holt and Company, 1994).

Harper, Gordon, *The Fights on the Little Horn: Unveiling the Mysteries of Custer's Last Stand*, (Philadelphia & Oxford: Casemate, 2014).

Harris, Tristan, *The Charge of Huj: The Story Behind the Worcestershire and Warwickshire Yeomanry's Role in the 1917 Palestine Battle* <https://malvernobserver.co.uk/news/the-charge-of-huj-the-story-behind-the-worcestershire-and-warwickshire-yeomanrys-role-in-the-1917-palestine-battle-3375/>

Hermes, Walter, *Truce Tent and Fighting Front: United States Army in the Korean War: July 1951 – July 1953.* Washington, DC: Center of Military History, 1966 <http://www.history.army.mil/books/korea/truce/fm.htm>

Hibbert, C., *Wellington, A Personal History* (London: Harper Collins, 1997).

Hoffman, Nancy Lee White, (1992) *Sgt. Reckless; Combat Veteran* cited at <https://www.mca-marines.org/leatherneck/sgt-reckless-combat-veteran>, (accessed on 16 May 16).

Hoig, Stan, *A Travel Guide to the Plains Indian Wars* (Albuquerque: University of New Mexico Press, 2006).

Holmes, Richard, *The Little Field Marshal: A Life of Sir John French* (London: Weidenfeld & Nicolson, 2004).

James, Philip and Wilson, Richard, *The Charge at El Mughar* <http://www.dorsetlife. co.uk/2007/11/the-charge-at-el-mughar/>

Josephy, Alvin M, Jr., *The Nez Perce Indians and the Opening of the Pacific Northwest* (Lincoln: University of Nebraska Press, 1978).

Jowett, Philip, *The Italian Army 1940–45: Africa 1940–43* (Oxford: Osprey, 2001).

Kane, Kathryn, *From Denmark to Belgium: Copenhagen – Wellington's Great Warhorse* <https://regencyredingote.wordpress.com/2011/01/14/from-denmark-to-belgium-copenhagen-wellingtons-great-warhorse/>

Kane, Kathryn, *Bloody Sunday: Copenhagen and the Waterloo* <https://regencyredingote.wordpress.com/2011/01/21/bloody-sunday-copenhagen-and-the-waterloo-campaign/>

Kane, Kathryn, *From Paris to Stratfield Saye: Copenhagen as a Civilian* <https://regencyredingote.wordpress.com/2011/01/28/from-paris-to-strathfield-saye-copenhagen-as-a-civilian/>

Keegan, J, *War Path: Travels of a Military Historian in North America* (London: Pimlico, 1995).

Kelly, Darryl. *Trooper Sloan 'Scotty' Bolton, DCM The Beersheba Charger* <www.anzacday.org.au>

Knight, Ian & Castle, Ian, *Zulu War 1879; Twilight of a Warrior Nation* (Wellinborough: Osprey, 1992).

Knight, Ian, *The Zulu War* (Oxford: Osprey, 2003)

Laband, John & Knight, Ian, *The Anglo-Zulu War* (Stroud: Sutton, 1996).

Laffin, J., *Brassey's Battles; 3,500 Years of Conflict, Campaigns and War A-Z* (London: Brassey, 1986).

Lawrence, Elizabeth Atwood,   *His Very Silence Speaks – Comanche, the Horse who Survived Custer's Last Stand* (Wayne State University Press, 1989).

Lawrence, James, *Raj: The Making and Unmaking of British India* (London: Little, Brown & Company, 1997).

Lee, Chester Anders, *Chief Joseph: The Biography of a Great Indian* (USA: Literary Licensing, 1936, reprinted 2011).

Livesey, Anthony, *Great Commanders and their Battles* (London: Marshall Editions Ltd, 1987).

Livesey, Anthony *Great Battles of World War I* (London: Marshall Editions Ltd, 1989)

Lock, Ron, "Blood on the Painted Mountain: Zulu Victory and Defeat, Hlobane and Kambula 1879", originally published in the June 1996 issue of *Military History* magazine.

MacDonald, Callum A., *Korea: The War Before Vietnam* (New York: Free Press, 1986).

Mather, Jill, *Forgotten Heroes – The Australian Waler Horse* (Ourimbah, NSW: Bookbound Publishing, 2012).

Mather, Jill *War Horses; Hoof Prints in Time: Amazing true stories of heroic Australian Walers and New Zealand horses 1914-1918* (Ourimbah, NSW: Bookbound Publishing, 2012).

McAdam, John, "Hlobane Plateau on horseback – Retracing the route of Lieutenant Colonel Redvers Buller VC." *Journal of the Anglo Zulu War Society 20* (December 2006).

MacKenzie, Compton Eastern Epic: September 1939-March 1943: Defenc (London: Chatto & Windus, 1951).

Mileham, Patrick, *The Yeomanry Regiments; Over 200 Years of Tradition.* (Staplehurst: Spellmount, 2003).

Mockler, Anthony, *Haile Selassie's War: The Italian–Ethiopian Campaign, 1935–1941.* (New York: Random House, 1984).

Morris, Donald R., *The Washing of the Spears* (London: Da Capo Press,1998).

Morris, Suzi (08/12/2012) *Arieana Notebook: Article on Maidan* <http://www.arieana.com/nbmaidan.html>(accessed on 2 January 2018).

Mossop G. *Running the Gauntlet* (Natal: G.C. Button, 1990, first published by Thomas Nelson & Son, 1937).

Murray,Robert A., 'The John "Portuguese" Phillips Legends, A Study in Wyoming Folklore', *Annals of Wyoming 40* (April, 1968) reprinted in *The Army on the Powder River* (Belvue: Nebraska Old Army Press, 1969).

Nel, Chris *SA Boerperd Breed History* <http://www.saboerperd.com/p2/history/sa-boerperd-breed-history.html>

Nilsson, Jeff (posted 14 January 2012) *A War Horse Earns Her Sergeant's Stripes: 1953* <http://www.saturdayeveningpost.com/2012/01/14/archives/post-perspective/marines-find-real-war-horse-1953.html>

O'Kelly, Sebastian, *Amadeo: The True Story of an Italian's War in Abyssinia* (London: Harper Collins, 2002).

Pakenham, Thomas, *The Boer War* (New York: Random House, 1979).

Philbrick, Nathaniel, *The Last Stand: Custer, Sitting Bull and the Battle of the Little Big Horn* (London: Vintage Books, 2010).

Philbrick, Nathaniel, *The Last Stand* (London: Vintage, 2011).

Pickeral, Tamsin, *The Encyclopedia of Horses and Ponies* (Bath: Paragon, 1999).

Preston, Lt. Col. Richard Martin Peter, *The Desert Mounted Corps An Account of the Cavalry Operations in Palestine and Syria 1917-1918* (Boston and New York; Houghton & Miffin Co., 1921).

Race, William Watson and Guttman, Jon, *Zulu Mountain Trap Sprung* <http://www.historynet.com/anglo-zulu-war-battle-of-hlobane.htm>

Race, William Watson and Guttman, Jon, 'Anglo-Zulu War: Battle of Hlobane', <http://www.historynet.com/anglo-zulu-war-battle-of-hlobane.htm>

Rattray, David and Greaves, Adrian, *Guidebook to the Anglo-Zulu War Battlefields* (Johannesberg & Capetown: Jonathan Ball Publishing, 2003).

Robson, Brian, *The Road to Kabul: The Second Afghan War, 1878-1881.* (Stroud: Spellmount, 2007).

Scott, Brough *Galloper Jack* (Newbury: Racing Post, 2012).

Seely, General Jack, *Warrior: The Amazing Story of a Real War Horse* (Newbury: Racing Post Books, 2001), originally published as, *My Horse Warrior* (Hodder & Stoughton, 1934).

Schindler, Hal, *The Salt Lake Tribune: Tartar the War Horse* <www.sltrib.com>

Shirreff, David, *Bare Feet and Bandoliers: Wingate, Sandford, the Patriots and the Liberation of Ethiopia* (Barnsley: Pen & Sword Military, 2009 [1995]).

Smith, Neil (posted 14 April 2013), *The Beersheba Chargers* <http://www.insidehistory.com.au/2013/04/the-beersheba-chargers-by-neil-smith/>

Sprague, Roderick. 'The Meaning of "Palouse"', *Idaho Yesterdays, Summer Issue, 1968: Volume 12, Number 2.*

Stewart, Andrew, *The First Victory: The Second World War in the East African Campaign* (London: Yale University Press, 2016).

Strang, G. Bruce (Ed) *Collisions of Empire: Italy's Invasion of Ethiopia and its International Impact* (London: Ashgate, 2013).

Thompson, Major-General C W, *Records of the Dorset Yeomanry (Queen's Own) 1914-1919*, (Sherbourne: F. Bennett & Co. Ltd., 1921).

Thornton (1936) Addendum: Fitzsimmons 1973 *The Origin and History of the Basuto Pony* <http://www.malealea.com/basuto-pony.html>

Von Der Heyde, N., *Field Guide to the Battlefields of South Africa* (Cape Town: Struick, 2013).

Watt, Steve, *The Imperial Yeomanry* published in Military History Journal Vol 13 No 6 – December 2006 *Pietermaritzburg* <http://samilitaryhistory.org/vol136sw.html>

West, Elliott, *The Last Indian War: The Nez Perce Story* (Oxford: Oxford University Press, 2009).

Whetstone, A. and Welch, C. *The Little Book of Horse Racing* (UK: Green Umbrella Publishing, 2008).

White, Linda, *The Arabian Horse In History: Maidan Gallant Heart, Iron Will* <https://issuu.com/arabian-horse-times/docs/ed-maidan>

Wilfong, Cheryl, *Following the Nez Perce Trail* (Corvallis, OR: Oregon State University Press, 1990).

Wilson M, *A History of New Zealand's Military Horse: The Experience of the Horse in the Anglo-Boer War and World War One* <http://ir.canterbury.ac.nz/bitstream/10092/959/1/thesis_fulltext.pdf>

Woodham-Smith, Cecil, *The Reason Why* (New York: McGraw-Hill, 1953).

Young, John. *Horror at the Devil's Pass– The Battle of Hlobane* <http://www.rorkesdriftvc.com/hlobane.htm>

Electronic Sources

http://agreenhorse.blogspot.co.uk/2009/12/horses-of-military-war.html
http://amhistory.si.edu/militaryhistory/collection/object.asp?ID=821

http://www.angloboerwar.com/unit-information/imperial-yeomanry-by-company/
    1946-imperial-yeomanry
https://anzacday.org.au/trooper-sloan-scotty-bolton-dcm
https://www.awm.gov.au/wartime/44/page54_bou
http://www.bwm.org.au/site/Horses.asp
http://www.civilwarhorses.net/links.php?326695
http://www.comandosupremo.com/Guillet.html
http://www.dailykos.com/story/2012/01/27/1058538/-War-Horse-The-Story-of-
    Reckless-U-S-M-C-Today-s-Pootie-diary
www.fs.fed.us/npnht/ Nez Perce National Historic Trail
www.garryowen.com/dandy.htm
http://historion.net/how-jerusalem-was-won-being-record-allenbys-campaign-
    palestine/chapter-xi-two-yeomanry-charges *Chapter XI. Two Yeomanry Charges*
    cited on 13 May 16
www.historyofwar.org/articles/battles_beersheba.html
http://www.jill-hamilton.com/pdf/marengo-the-myth-of-napoleons-horse.pdf
http://www.keepmilitarymuseum.org/middleeast/outline.php
www.lancers.org.au/site/light_horse.asp
https://www.morganhorse.com/about_morgan/history/
http://www.muralmosaic.com/Horse/Panels/132.html
New Zealand Mounted Rifles; The New Zealand Horse and Equipment <http://
    www.nzmr.org/horse.htm>
www.nezperce.org/ Nez Perce Tribe of Idaho
www.nps.gov/nepe/ Nez Perce National Historic Park
What is Endurance Riding <http://www.olddominionrides.org/EndurancePrimer/01.
    html>
http://www.rdgmuseum.org.uk/history-and-research/did-you-know/?n=horses-and-
    horseflesh-losses-in-the-boer-war
http://www.saboerperd.com/a3/general/the-origin-of-the-sa-boerperd.html, *The Origin
    of the SA Boerperd*, (accessed 3 January 2018).
http://www.sahistory.org.za/people/louis-botha
http://www.sgtreckless.com/Reckless/Welcome.html
http://www.stablemade.com/horsecare/horsebreeds/barb.htm
http://studycivilwar.wordpress.com/2014/09/28/sheridans-ride-in-war-and-memory/
http://www.susanhatedliterature.net/2012/02/to-dublins-war-horse-vonolel-
    come-here-to-me/
www.teara.govt.nz/en/horses/6
http://thecoastnews.com/2012/01/sgt-reckless-heroic-warhorse-had-ties-to-north-
    county/
http://thescribblerdotbiz.blogspot.co.uk/2014/02/the-last-charge-on-forgotten-
    front.html
http://www.walerhorse.com/history.html
www.warmemorialsnsw.asn.au/extraimages.cfm?MemNo=350

http://www.warriorwarhorse.com/about-warrior.asp

http://www.westernfrontassociation.com/great-war-people/brothers-arms/2914-the-vc-that-never-was-colonel-souters-gallantry-against-the-senussi-1916.html

John "Portugee" (Famous) PHILIPS <http://wyominggravestones.org/view.php?id=34>.

2018http://www.youtube.com/watch?v=YIo3ZfA9da0 (Video clip of Sgt. Reckless)

Index

2nd Cavalry 59-60, 63, 99-100
4th Light Dragoons 33, 36-39
4th Light Horse Regiment 150-152, 158-159, 168
7th Cavalry 66, 69, 72-74, 79-83, 98-101, 103
8th Hussars 33, 37, 39
11th Hussars 30, 33, 35, 37-39, 43, 45
13th Light Dragoons 33, 35, 38-39, 43
17th Lancers 33, 35, 38-39, 43, 46
24th (2nd Warwickshire) Regiment 113, 116, 121, 128
92nd Highlanders 17, 24, 27, 43, 128-129

abaQulusi 110-117, 119-121
Addis Ababa 177, 180, 185
Afghanistan 126, 129-131, 143, 194
Agagia 153, 156, 160
Aldershot 27, 123, 144, 194
Allenby, General Edmund 157, 163, 165, 168-169
American Civil War iii, 48, 58, 70, 74
Anglo-Boer War 110, 123, 131, 134, 137-142, 145-147, 150-152, 156, 158, 166, 194-195, 197-198
Anglo-Zulu War 108-112, 119, 122-123, 194-197
Antietam, Battle of 51-52, 72
Anzac Mounted Division 156, 158-159
Aosta, Duke of 178, 180-182, 185
Appaloosa iv, 67, 84-85, 89-90, 98, 100, 103-104, 192, 195
Arabs 29, 125, 128-129, 132, 135, 138, 149-150, 157, 172, 174, 180, 184
Arabians iv, 7-9, 13, 18, 29, 67, 105-107, 124-126, 129, 149-150, 182, 194, 198

Arapaho 57-58, 61, 65
Army of Northern Virginia 53, 55
Australian Light Horse 156, 159, 169, 171
Austria 16, 18, 178
Ayub Khan 126, 128-129

Baden-Powell, Colonel Robert 133, 139
Balaclava, the battle of 28, 33-35, 40-44, 46
Barton, Captain Robert 112, 116-118
Basuto ponies iv, 105-108, 117, 120, 123, 132, 137-138, 141, 198
Basutoland 106-108, 141-142
Beersheba 151-152, 157-160, 162-163, 169-170, 192, 196, 198
Belgium 7, 9-10, 13-16, 152, 196
Benteen, Captain Frederick 76-80, 98
Bighorn River 58, 76-78
Black Hills 65, 73, 81
Black Sea 28, 31-32, 34, 45
Blücher, Field Marshall Gebhard Leberecht von 16-17, 23
Boer War, see Anglo-Boer War
Boerperds 106, 123, 132, 148, 197, 199
Boers 107, 110, 112-113, 123, 130-134, 136-147, 150-152, 156, 158, 166, 194-195, 197-199
Bolton, Sloan 'Scotty' 150-152, 158-162, 169-170, 196, 199
Bonaparte, Napoleon 13, 15-16, 18-25, 31, 195
Border Horse 112, 114-115, 117-118
Boston 56, 79, 106, 165, 195, 197
Botha, General Louis 133, 145, 148, 194, 199
Bozeman Trail 57-60, 65

Briggs 34, 44, 46-47, 192
British Army 11, 24, 27, 29, 32, 40-41,
    106, 125, 132, 141-142, 148, 151, 156,
    166, 171, 182-183
British Empire 41, 125-126, 131-132, 137,
    151, 170
British Somaliland 179-180, 185-186
Brownlow, Colonel Francis 128-130, 192
Brussels 11, 16-17, 19, 23-24
Buffalo 49, 58, 62-63, 73, 76, 81, 85, 87,
    103, 108, 115
Buller, Brevet Lieutenant Colonel Redvers
    Henry 110, 112-123, 133, 136, 138,
    141, 146, 197

California 42, 48, 50, 62, 85-86, 191
Canada 81, 91, 98, 100-103
Cape Colony 107-108, 112, 132, 144
Cape Horse 105-107, 132
Cape, The 105-108, 110, 112, 130-133,
    136-137, 144-146, 148, 150, 198
Cardigan, 7th Earl of, Lieutenant General
    James Thomas Brudenell, iv, 28,
    30-31,33, 35-46
Carrington, Colonel Henry B 58-62,
    64-65
Causeway Heights 35-37, 39-40
Cetshwayo, King 108-111, 113
Chasseurs 17, 22, 37
Chauvel, Lieutenant General Sir
    Harry 156, 159, 168-169
Chelmsford, Lord 108-110, 123
Cheyenne 57-58, 60-61, 64-65, 73-74, 77,
    79, 81, 99-102
Cinderella 149, 166
Clearwater River 86, 91-92
Coldstream Guards 20, 112-113, 116
Colenso, Battle of 132-133, 136, 138
Colts 7, 9-10, 71
Comanche iii-iv, 66-67, 69, 71, 73-75, 80,
    82-83, 99, 192, 196
Commando units and operations 113,
    132, 143, 147, 185-186
Commonwealth, The 147, 179-180, 184
Copenhagen iii-iv, 7-10, 13-27, 106, 192,
    196
Crazy Horse 60, 70, 79, 81

Crimean War, the 17, 28, 33-35, 41-43,
    45-46, 112, 129
Crow (tribe) 76, 78, 95, 97-98
Custer, General George
    Armstrong 69-81, 96, 99, 103, 127,
    195-197
Custer's Last Stand 70, 81, 195-196

Dakota Territory 66, 73-74, 103
Dandy iii, 48, 62-64, 77, 80, 192, 199
Dardanelles 32, 35, 152
David, Captain 89, 91, 111
de Wet, Christiaan 138-145, 147-148,
    195
Deene Park 28, 30, 46
Denmark 7, 9-10, 13-16, 196
Desert Mounted Corps 158-159, 165,
    169, 171, 197
Devil's Pass 112, 116, 119-121, 198
Djibouti 177
Dorset Yeomanry 152-153, 155-156, 160,
    164-165, 198
Drakensberg Mountains 106, 141-142
Dutch 16, 22, 105-107, 130-131, 142

East Africa 142, 174, 177-179, 181-182,
    185-186
Eclipse 8-9, 24, 27, 29, 106
Egypt 18, 151-153, 156, 158, 171, 179,
    181
Egyptian Expeditionary Force 156-157,
    162, 168
Eritrea 173-175, 177, 179-181, 184-186
Ethiopia 173-174, 177-178, 180-181,
    184-186, 194, 198
Eton school 11, 33, 110, 125

Fetterman, Captain 59-62, 64-65, 74
First Italo-Abyssinian War 173
First World War 148-152, 162-163, 170,
    194
Flynn, Errol 41, 43, 70, 79
Fort Abraham Lincoln 66, 73-74, 81,
    103
Fort Laramie 57-61, 63-65
Fort Leavenworth 48-49, 51, 57, 69, 103
Fort Phil Kearny 59-65

Fort Reno 58, 63
Fort Riley 69, 72, 74, 82
France and the French 7, 11-23, 26,
    31-32, 36-37, 43-44, 67, 84, 134, 136,
    138, 157, 166, 168-171, 173, 178-179,
    192, 196
Frontier Light Horse 105, 112, 114,
    116-117, 119, 121, 123

Gallipoli 151-152, 159, 162, 171
Gaza 151, 157, 162, 168-169
Geldings 52, 66, 84, 166
General Stud Book 7, 9
Gettysburg, Battle of 54-55, 72
Gibbon, General John 50-51, 74, 76, 81,
    94-95, 103
Godolphin Arabian 8-9, 29, 106
Godolphin Barb 8, 18, 25, 29, 67, 106,
    199
Gold Cup Race 7, 10, 34
Grant, General Ulysses S. 55-56, 65, 135,
    159
Great Plains 57-58, 65, 67-68, 73, 95,
    143
Great Sioux War 65, 73, 81
Grey Eagle 52, 72
Grosvenor, Thomas 7, 10
Guerrilla warfare and activity 15, 58,
    138-139, 141, 143-144, 146, 178,
    185-186
Guillet, Amedeo iv, 174, 176, 178,
    180-184, 186-187, 197, 199

Haile Selassie, Emperor 173, 175,
    177-178, 181, 185-186, 197
Hampshire Yeomanry 136, 139, 148
Heavy Brigade, The 21, 35-37, 39
Henry, Colonel 58, 63, 105
Herod 9, 29, 106
Hlobane Mountain 105, 109-117,
    119-120, 122-123, 133, 195-198
Hooker, Major General Joseph 51-52, 54
Horseshoe Station 61, 63-64
Howard, General Oliver O. 87-88, 91-92,
    94-95, 97-98, 101
Hunter 15, 29, 52, 67, 105, 123, 137, 141,
    155, 165

Idaho 62, 84-88, 90-93, 95, 101-104,
    198-199
Imperial Yeomanry 134-136, 140, 144,
    146-148, 150, 198
Indian Army 152, 169, 171
Indian Mutiny 41, 112, 125, 129
Indian Ocean 109, 179
Iraq 154, 170, 179
Isandlwana, Battle of 108-113, 122-123, 126
Isle of Wight 135, 140-141, 146, 149, 166,
    168
Italian Somaliland 173-174, 177, 179-180,
    185-186

Jerusalem 157, 159, 163, 165, 199
Jockey Club 7-8, 34
Joseph, Chief 87-88, 91-92, 94-95,
    100-104

Kabul 126-128, 130, 195, 197
Kambula 110-111, 113, 115-116, 122-123,
    196
Kandahar 125-130, 185, 192, 194-195
Kansas 48, 68-69, 72-74, 82-83, 103
Kentucky 9, 52, 56, 62, 77
Keogh, Captain Myles Walter 66, 71-74,
    76, 78-80, 82, 99
Keren 181, 183-184
Kimberley 131, 133, 136, 138-139
Kitchener, Lord Herbert 136, 140,
    144-145
Korea i, 187, 191-192, 195-196
Kroonstad 138, 142, 146
Kruger, President Paul 131-132, 142

La Haye Sainte 19, 21, 23
Ladysmith 133, 136, 138
Latham, Platoon Sergeant Joseph iv, 135,
    188, 190
League of Nations 173, 177-178
Lee, General Robert E. 52-56, 72, 162,
    172, 195-196
Libya 153, 174, 179
Light Brigade, the 28, 33, 35-44, 47, 163,
    192, 194
Light Brigade, The Charge of 41-42, 47,
    163, 192

Lincoln, Abraham 53-54, 66, 72-74, 80-82, 103, 192, 196
Lisbon 10, 12-13, 24
Little Big Horn 65, 68-71, 74-75, 82, 96, 99, 197
Lloyd George, David 146, 156, 165-166
Lodge Trail Ridge 60-61
Looking Glass 91-95, 100-101
Lucan, Lord George 33, 35, 37, 41, 43-44

Machine guns 154, 160, 163, 167
Mafeking 133, 139
Magersfontein, Battle of 132-133, 136, 138
Maharajah iii, 124, 135-136, 139-142, 145-146, 148-149, 166
Maidan iii, 124, 127, 129-130, 192, 197-198
Maitland, General Sir Peregrine 22, 136, 139
Maiwand, Battle of 126-127, 129
Marengo 18-19, 25-26, 195, 199
Mares 7, 26, 52, 124, 137, 149, 155, 166, 187-191
Maryland 51, 54, 56
Mascots 81, 191
McClellan, General George Brinton 51, 62, 71-72
Meade, Major General George Gordon 52-56, 82
Mediterranean Sea 18, 31, 152, 156, 165, 168-169, 181
Melbourne 9, 170-171
Mesopotamia 152, 157, 170
Middle East 29, 124, 150-152, 157, 170, 172, 179, 186
Missouri 48, 51, 65, 68-69, 75, 99-100, 103
Modder River 133, 136, 138
Montana 57, 62, 66, 68, 74, 83, 85, 92-95, 97, 103, 195
Monty iii-iv, 150, 158-161, 165, 192
Morgan, Colonel Freddy 33-35, 46, 52
Mossop, George 'Chops' 105, 118-123, 192, 197
Mounted infantry iv, 50, 59, 101, 109, 112, 116, 119, 132, 134, 138, 160, 172

Mughar 163-165, 196
Mussolini, Benito 173-175, 177-180
Mustangs 66-67, 83

Natal 107-109, 112-113, 116, 123, 132, 136, 138, 145, 148, 197
Natal Native Contingent 112, 116
Nebraska 63, 196-197
Netherlands 11, 142
Nevada 42, 66, 83, 127
New Mexico 60, 67-68, 84, 196
New York 35, 72, 131, 165, 194-198
New Zealand 9, 137, 148, 156, 159, 179, 197-199
Ney, Marshal Michel 12, 17, 20-21
Nez Percé 67, 84-104, 195-196, 198-199
Nolan, Captain Louis 33, 36, 39, 42-43
Ntendeka 112-113, 116, 118

O'Kelly, Colonel Dennis 8, 174-177, 180-184, 186-187, 197
Old Baldy iii-iv, 48, 52, 54-56, 192
Ollokot 87-90, 94-95
Orange Free State 106-107, 130-133, 136, 138-140, 142-143, 145, 147-148
Orange River 107, 133, 136, 140, 145, 148
Oregon 50, 62, 65-66, 83, 85-87, 198
Ottoman Empire 31-32, 45, 125, 151, 156-157, 162, 166, 169-170

Paget, Lord George Paget 20, 33, 37-40, 135
Palestine iv, 31, 156-158, 162-163, 165-166, 168-172, 179, 194-195, 197, 199
Paris 15-16, 18, 24-27, 45, 167, 196
Parliament 27, 30, 45-46, 126, 135, 146
Pennsylvania 11, 54-55, 195
Perry, Captain David 89, 91
Philadelphia 55-56, 195
Phillips, John 'Portugee' 61-62, 64, 200
Picton, Lieutenant General Sir Thomas 13, 17, 20
Platt, Major-General William 180-181, 184-185
Ponies 29, 50, 53, 73, 76, 102, 105, 107-108, 119-120, 122-123, 125, 132, 141, 150, 189, 198

Portugal 10-13
Potomac, Army of the 51, 53-54, 72, 192
Powder River 57-58, 65, 74, 197

Quatre Bras, Battle of 16-19, 24, 27

Races and race Meetings 8-10, 33-34, 127
Raglan, Lord Fitzroy 17, 33, 43-44
Red Cloud 57-60, 65
Red Sea 130, 177, 179, 183-186
Reno, Major Marcus 58, 63, 76-80, 189
Richmond 16, 20, 53, 55
Roberts, Lord Frederick Sleigh 125-131,
    136, 138-144, 146
Rome 71-72, 177-178, 186
Ronald iii-iv, 28-29, 33, 35-39, 44, 46-47,
    113, 192
Rorke's Drift 108-109, 123
Rowlands, Colonel Hugh VC 27, 31, 41,
    109
Rundle, Lieutenant-General Sir
    Leslie 139-140, 142-143
Russell, Lieutenant Colonel John
    Cecil 44, 112-116, 118-119, 122

Sandor iii-iv, 173, 175-176, 178, 180-184,
    186-187, 192
Savoy 174, 181, 184, 186
Seeley, Captain 'Galloper' Jack 135-136,
    139-146, 148-149, 166-168, 192, 198
Senussi 153-156, 165, 200
Sergeant Reckless iii, 173, 187, 191
Sherman, General William Tecumseh 72,
    99, 103
Sinai 151, 156-157, 170-171
Sioux 57-59, 60-62, 64-68, 73-74, 78-81,
    98-102
Sitting Bull 66, 73-74, 76, 81, 91, 98-99,
    101-102, 197
Somalia 174, 179, 185
South Africa iv, 105-106, 108, 110,
    130-141, 144-145, 147-148, 151, 198
Stallions 7-8, 13, 17-19, 25-26, 129, 150,
    174, 182
Steeplechase races 33-34, 37, 46, 130,
    137, 174
Stewart, Sir Charles 10, 13

Stewart, 2nd Lieutenant James 48-51,
    53-55, 57
Steyn, President Martinus Theunis 131,
    139, 141-142, 147
Studs 7-9, 25, 29, 106, 125, 194
Sturgis, Colonel Samuel D 82, 97-98
Sudan 123, 136, 153, 179-182
Suez Canal 151, 156, 179, 181, 185
Suffolk 130, 150, 167
Syria 29, 41, 165, 170-171, 179, 197

Tartar iii, 48-57, 59, 192, 194, 198
Terry, Brigadier General Alfred 74, 76,
    79, 81
Texas 66, 68, 194-195
The Reason Why 35, 38-40, 42, 198
The Times 31, 147, 156
They Died with Their Boots On 70-71, 79
Thoroughbreds 7-10, 13, 18, 24, 26, 28-29,
    34-35, 39, 52, 56, 62, 64, 77, 106-108,
    132, 137, 148, 150, 166, 168, 172
Tongue River 57, 60, 99, 103
Toohoolhoolzote 92-93, 101
Transvaal 105, 107, 110-112, 130-133,
    139, 141-142, 144, 147-148
Transvaal Rangers 110, 112
Traveler 52, 56
Tugela River 133, 136
Turkey 27, 32, 43, 150-152, 170

Ulundi 108, 110-111, 113, 116, 123, 194
Union, The (cause) 19-21, 51-56, 72, 135,
    147-148
United Kingdom vi, 9, 152, 173, 179, 186
United Nations 39, 70, 183-184, 187, 192
United States Army 48-50, 65, 68, 72, 75,
    81, 84, 91, 93, 96-97, 102-104, 195
Utah 48-50, 57, 66
Utrecht 106, 111, 145

Victoria, Queen 26, 42, 44, 130, 135
Victoria Cross medal and awards 105,
    109, 119, 121, 125, 133, 136, 147, 168,
    192, 197, 200
Virginia 20, 51, 53, 55
Vonolel iii-iv, 124-125, 127-130, 135-136,
    192, 195, 199

Wagon trains 50, 60, 99, 143
Waler Horse 137-138, 150-151, 171-172, 192, 196
War Office 121, 134-135, 144
Warrior 105, 119-123
Washington D.C. 48, 51, 56-58, 63, 84, 86, 103, 192, 195
Waterloo, Battle of i, iv, 11, 14, 18-20, 23-27, 30, 33, 43, 196
Weatherley, Lieutenant Colonel Frederic Augustus 105, 112, 114-117, 123
Wellesley, Sir Arthur, Duke of Wellington 7, 10-12, 14-16, 27, 43, 152

Western Desert 153, 181, 184, 186
Western Front 156-157, 165-167, 187
White Bird 88-89, 92-94, 101-102
White Bird Canyon 88-89, 91
Wyoming 49-50, 58, 61, 63-67, 74, 83, 97, 197

Yellowstone River 74, 81, 97-98
Yeomanry regiments 30, 46, 134-136, 139-141, 143-144, 146-150, 152-156, 158, 160, 162-165, 169, 182, 195, 197-199